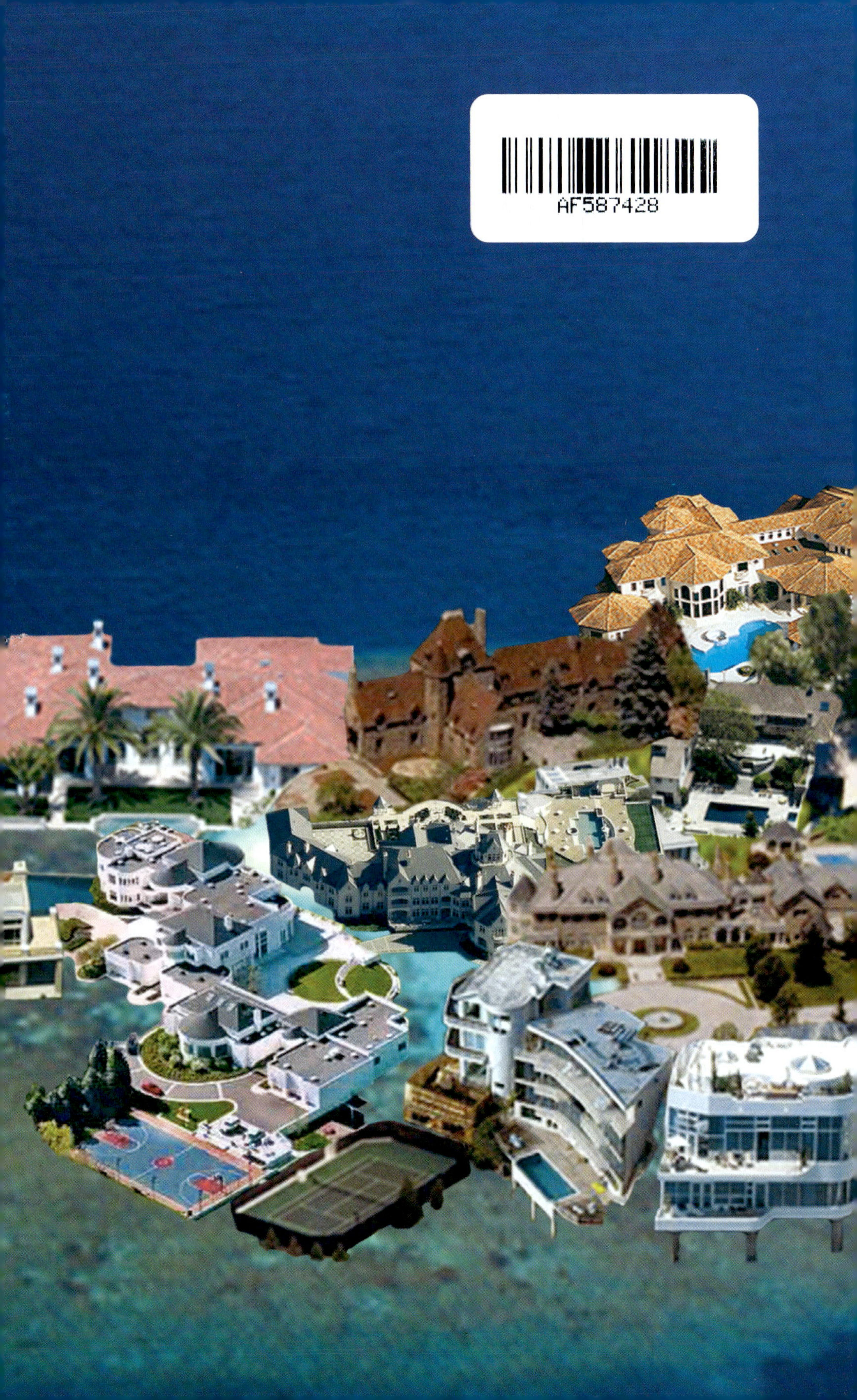

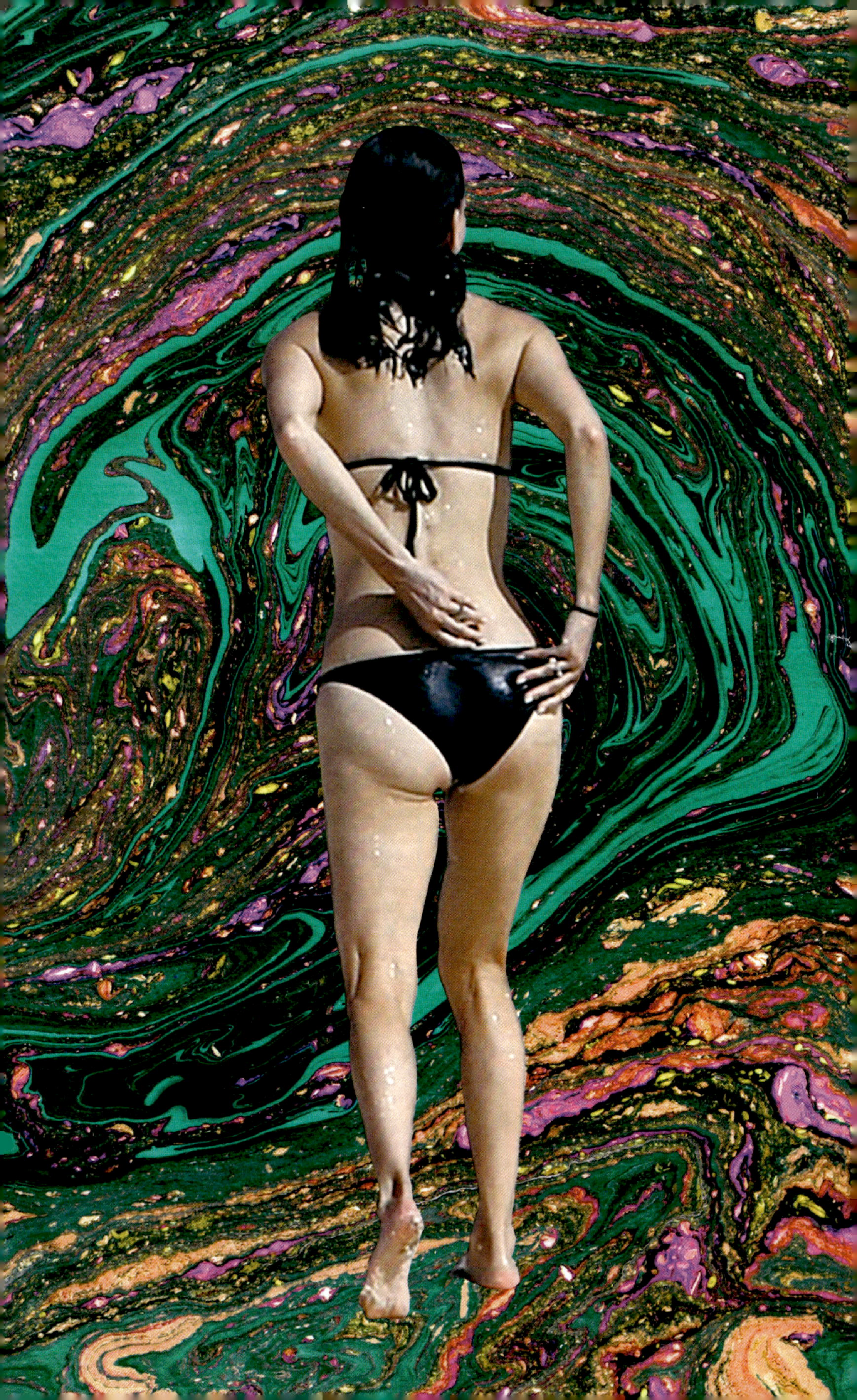

LE GWEN HEA
HAYLEY
ARRY IRINA
HUGH
RY JENNIFE
JAVIER
RY JOEL
JOE
JODIE JULIANNE
JUDE JULIA KEIR
KATIE
KATERINE LAUR
KYLIE
LISA
KRISTEN
LINDSAY
MARCIA
LILY
MAGGIE
SON
MATTHEW
MATT
MICHELLE
NICOL
CHAEL
NICOLE
PATRICK
NAOMI
PARIS
REE
MELA
RACHEL
RO
PHARELL
ROBIN
ROBERT
SANDRA
MUEL
SOFIA

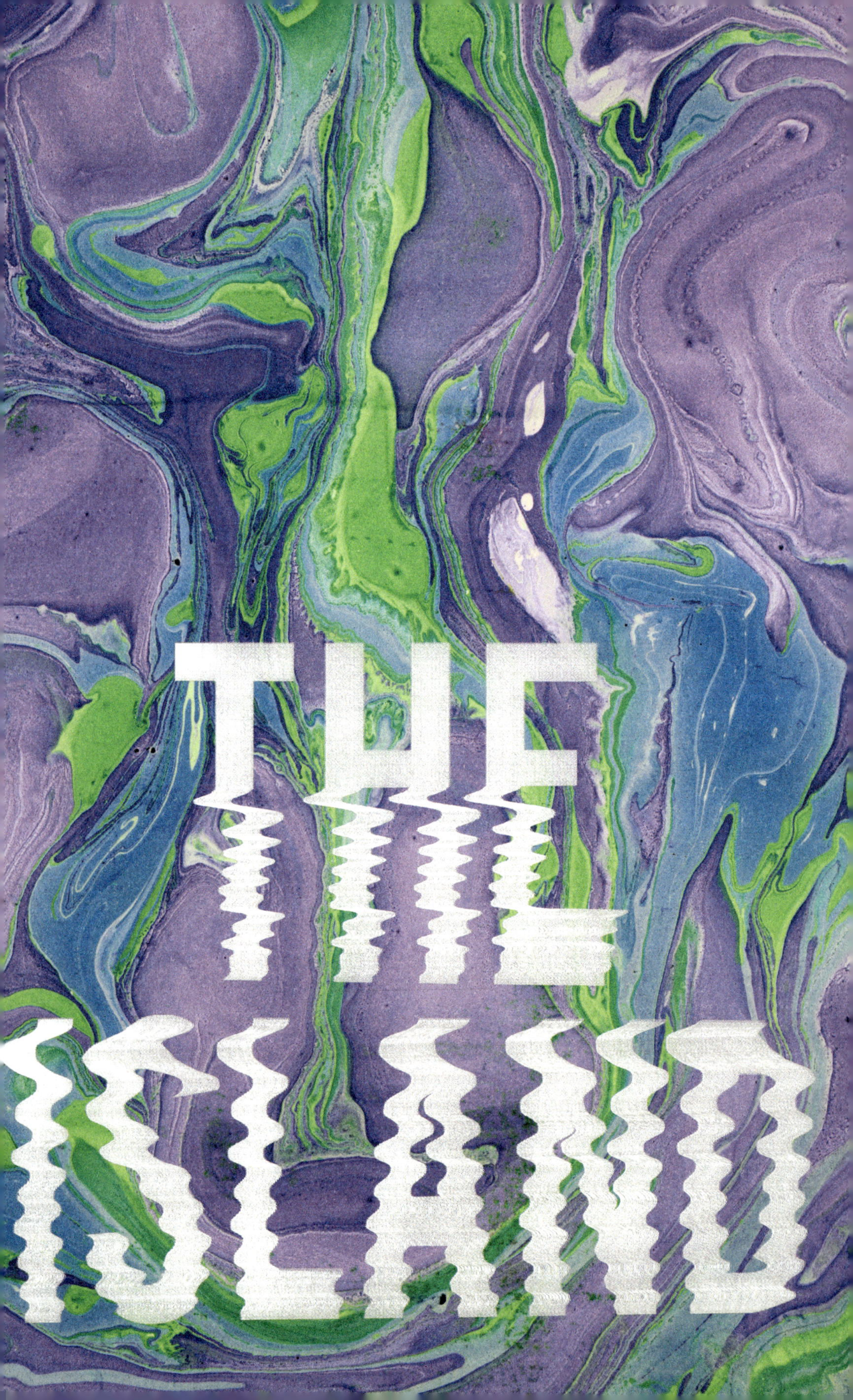
THE
ISLAND

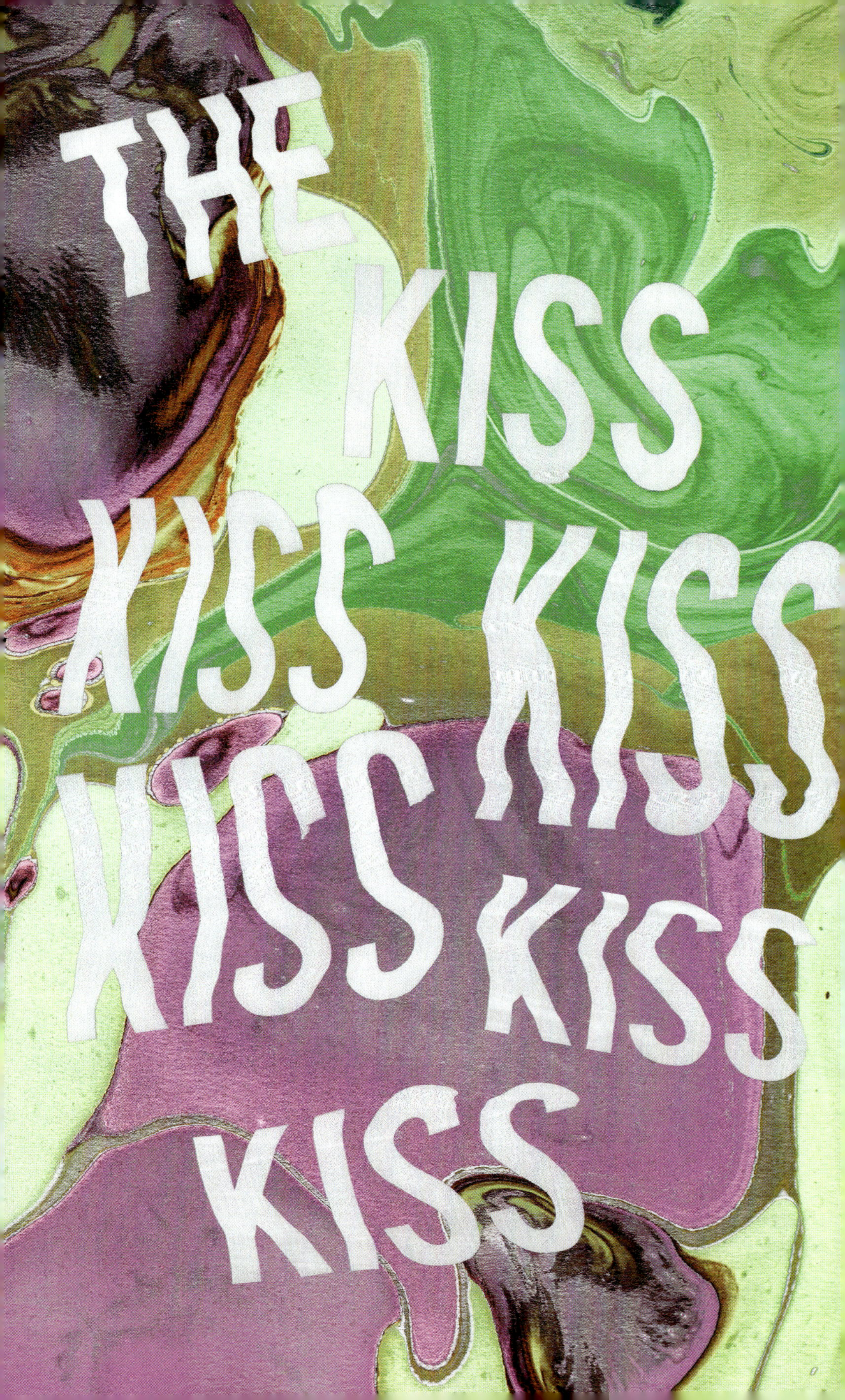
THE KISS
KISS KISS
KISS KISS
KISS KISS
KISS

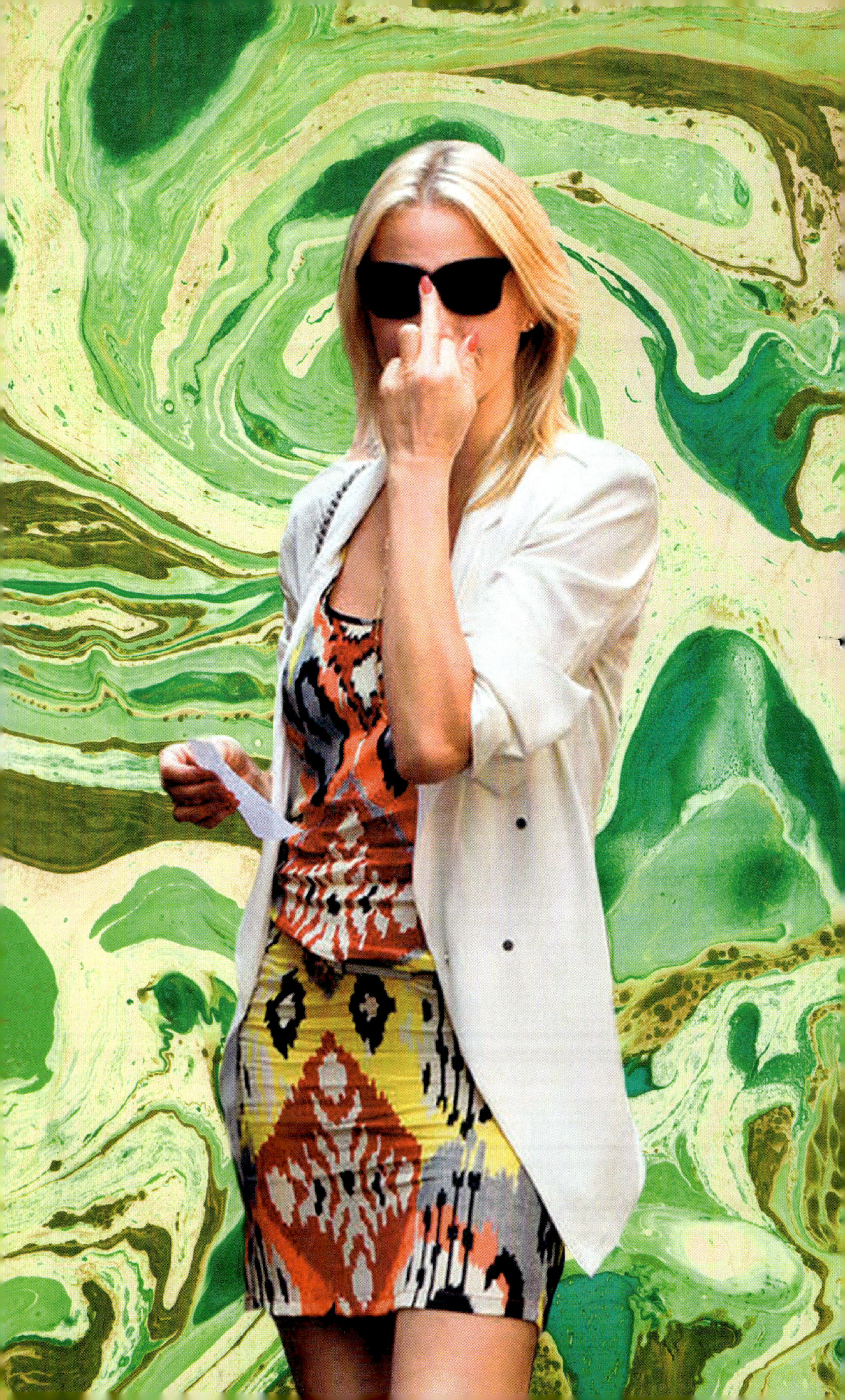

THE
BEACH

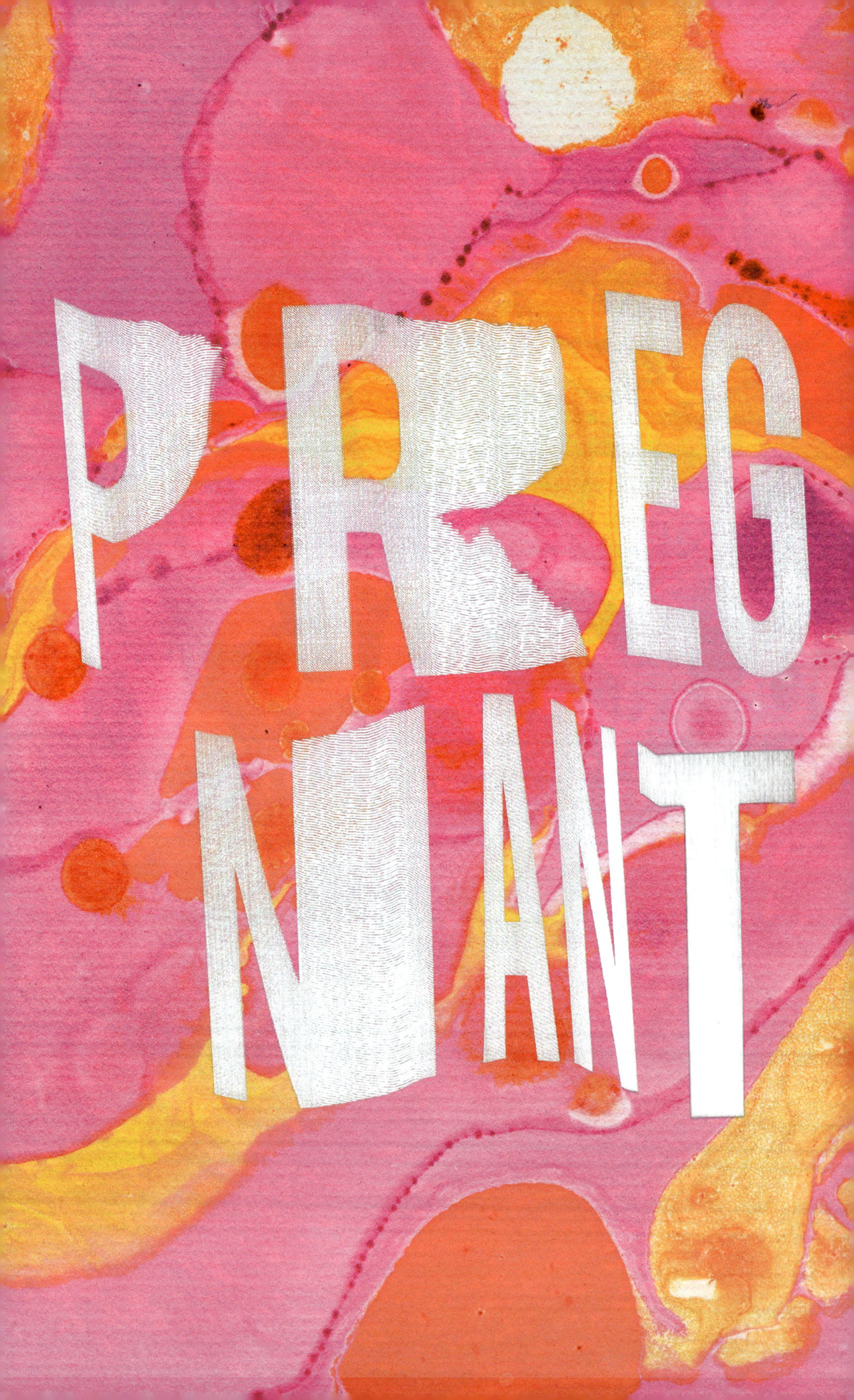
PREG
NANT

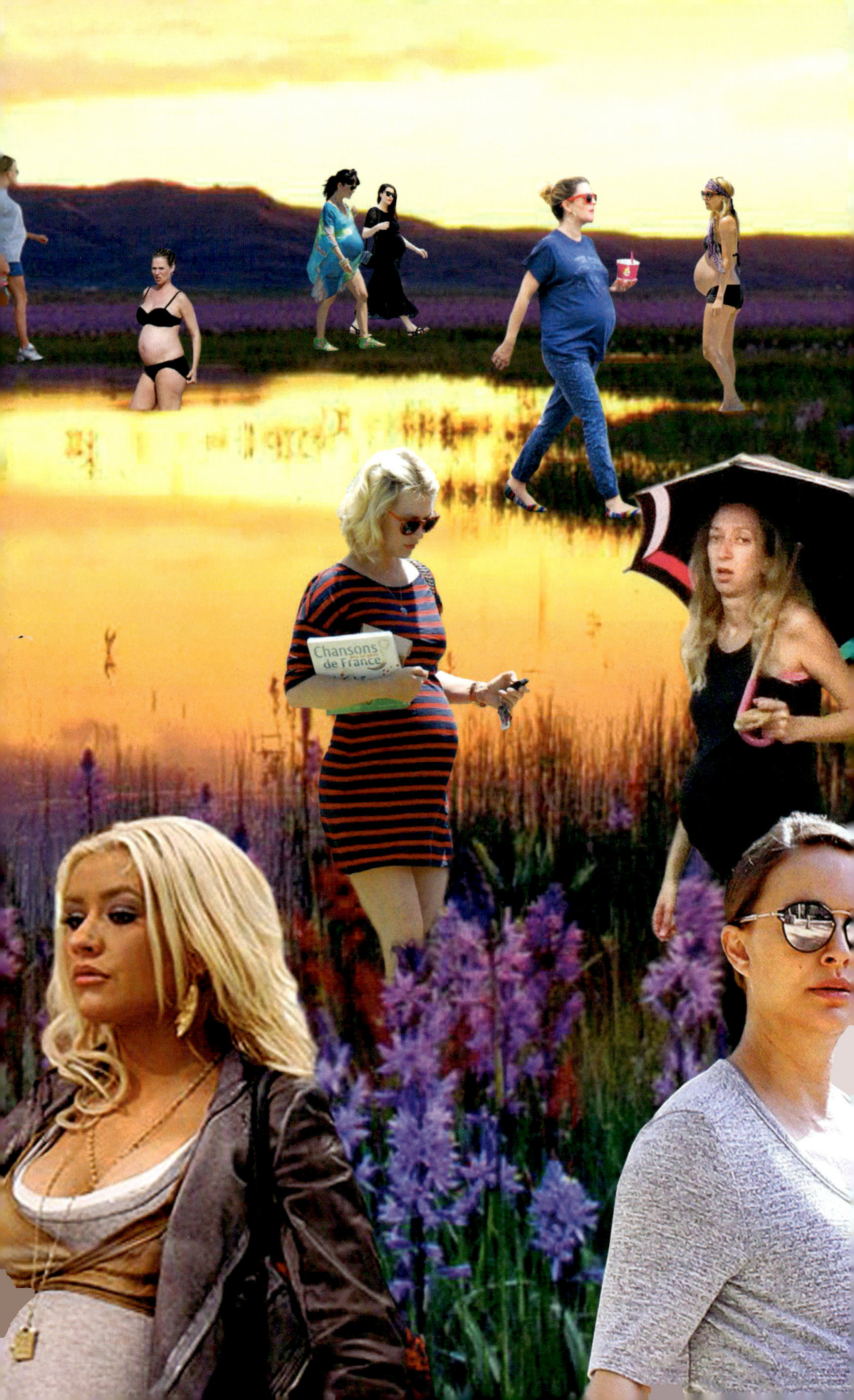
Chansons
de France

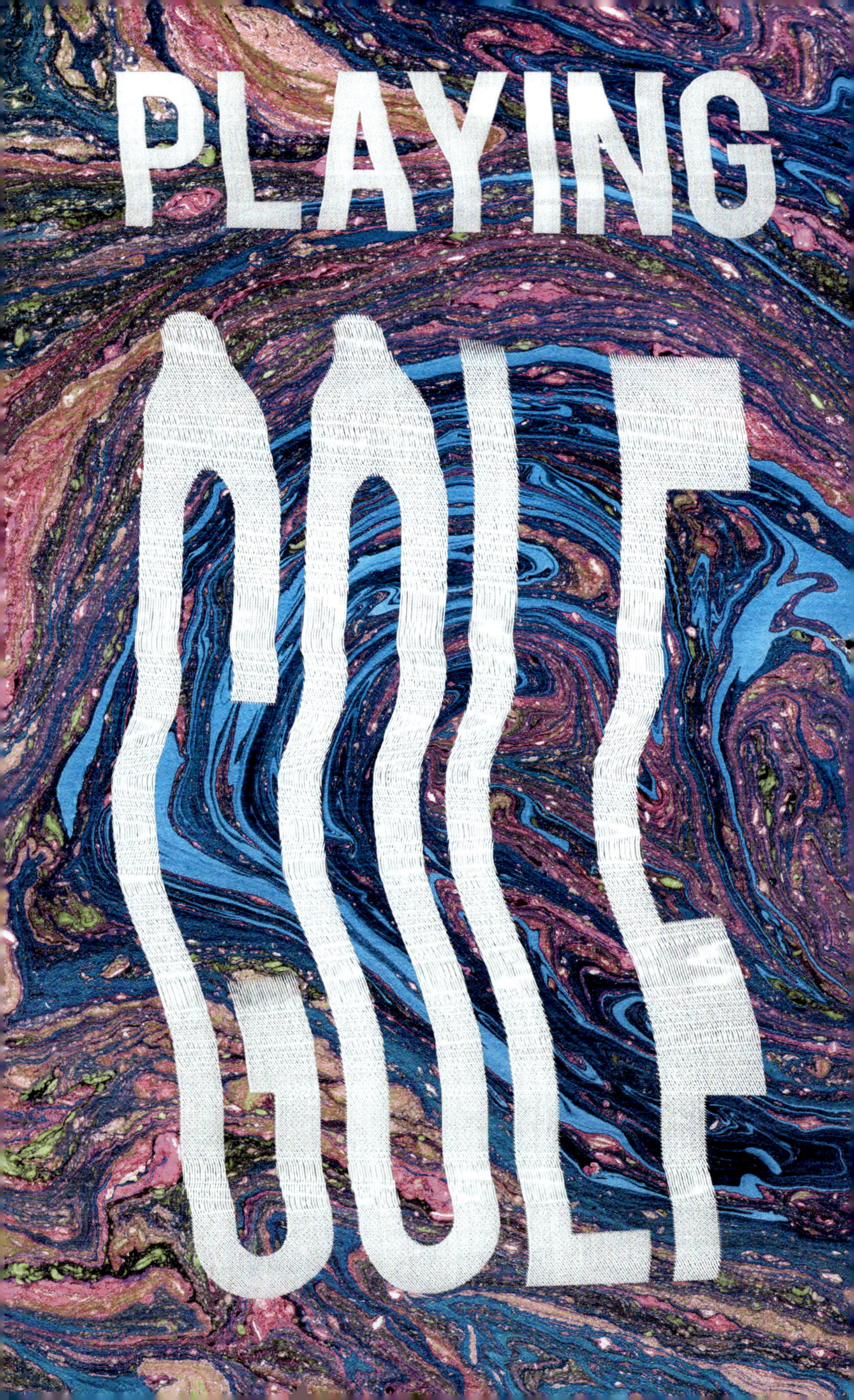
PLAYING
GOLF

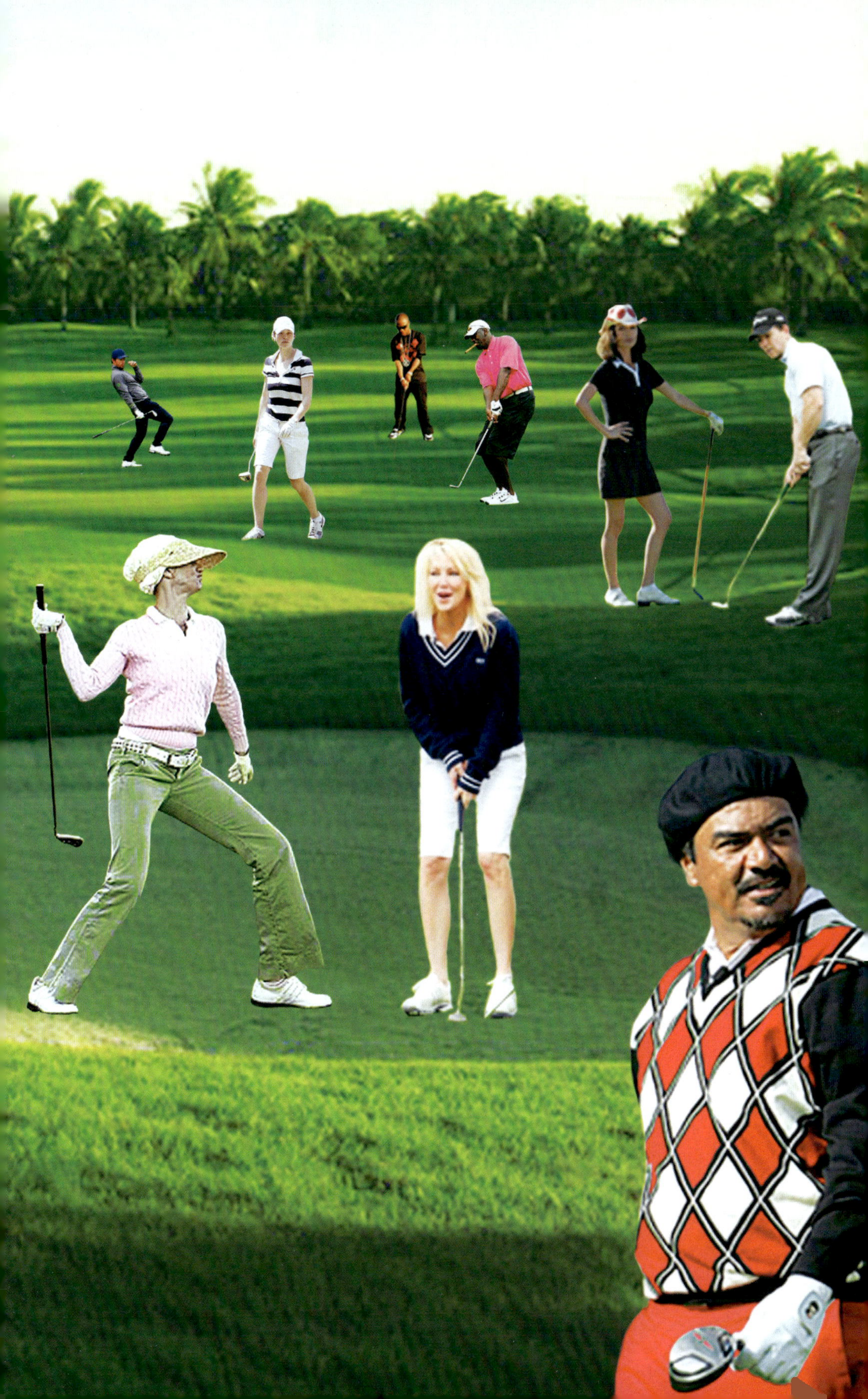

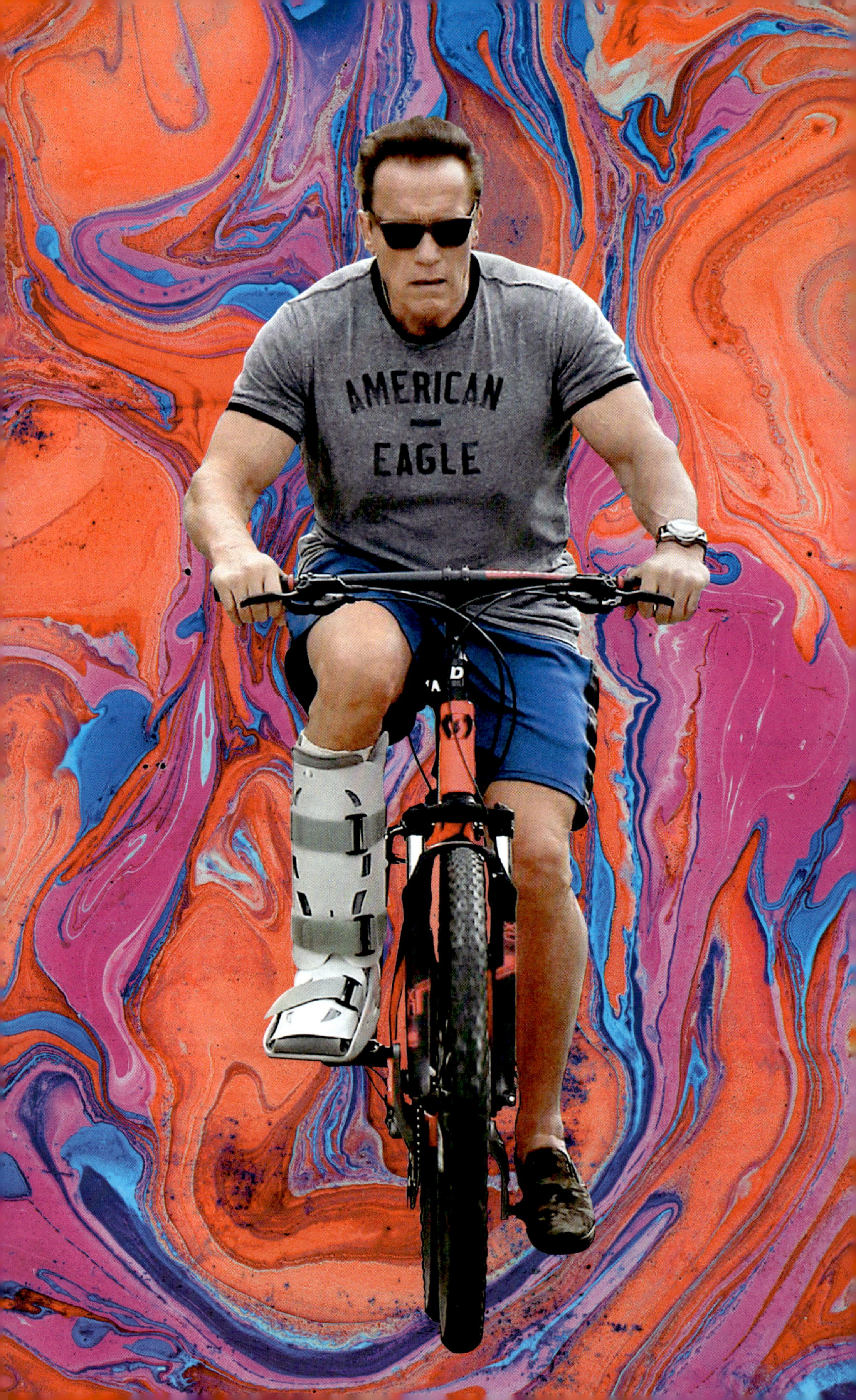
AMERICAN
EAGLE

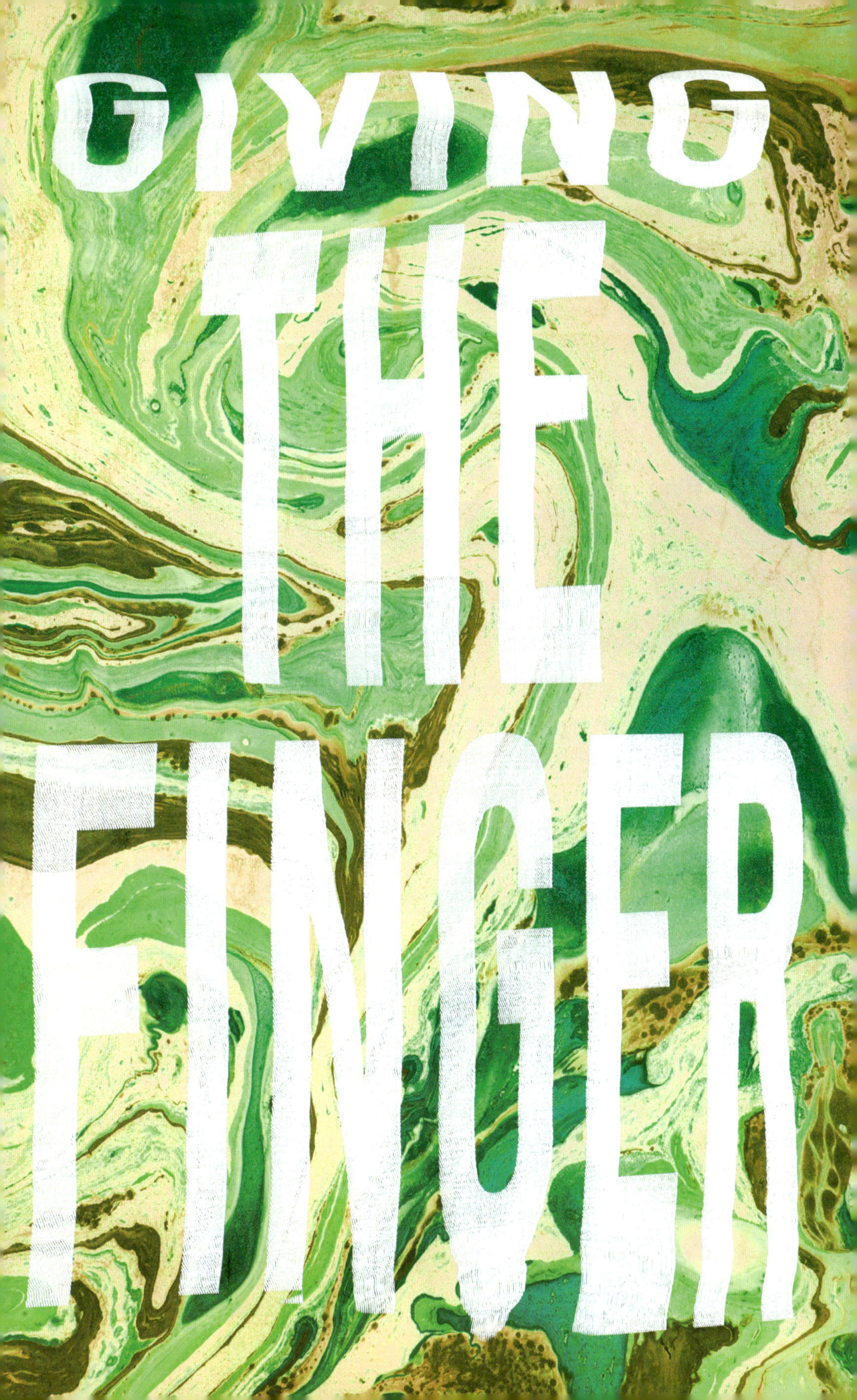
GIVING
THE
FINGER

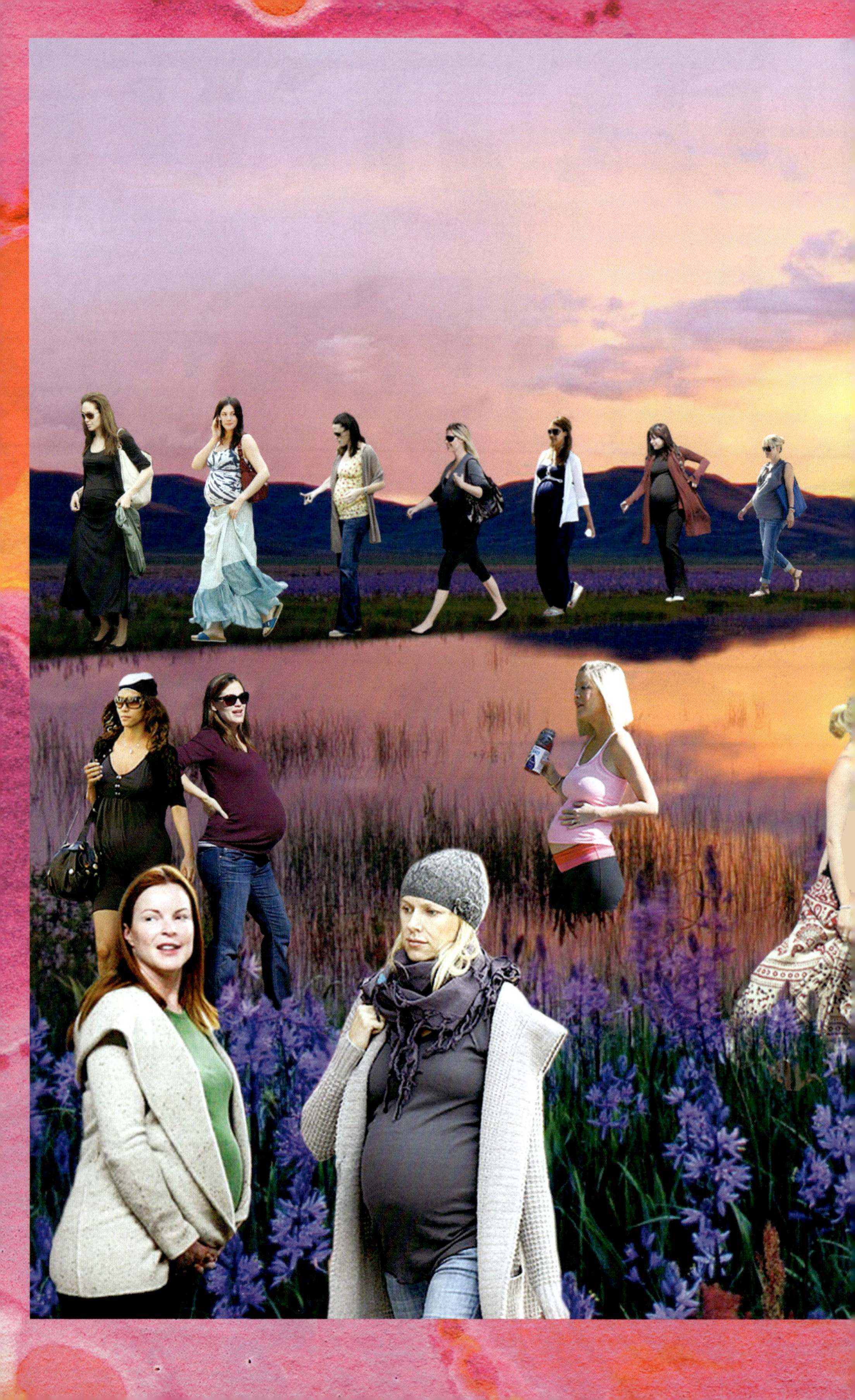

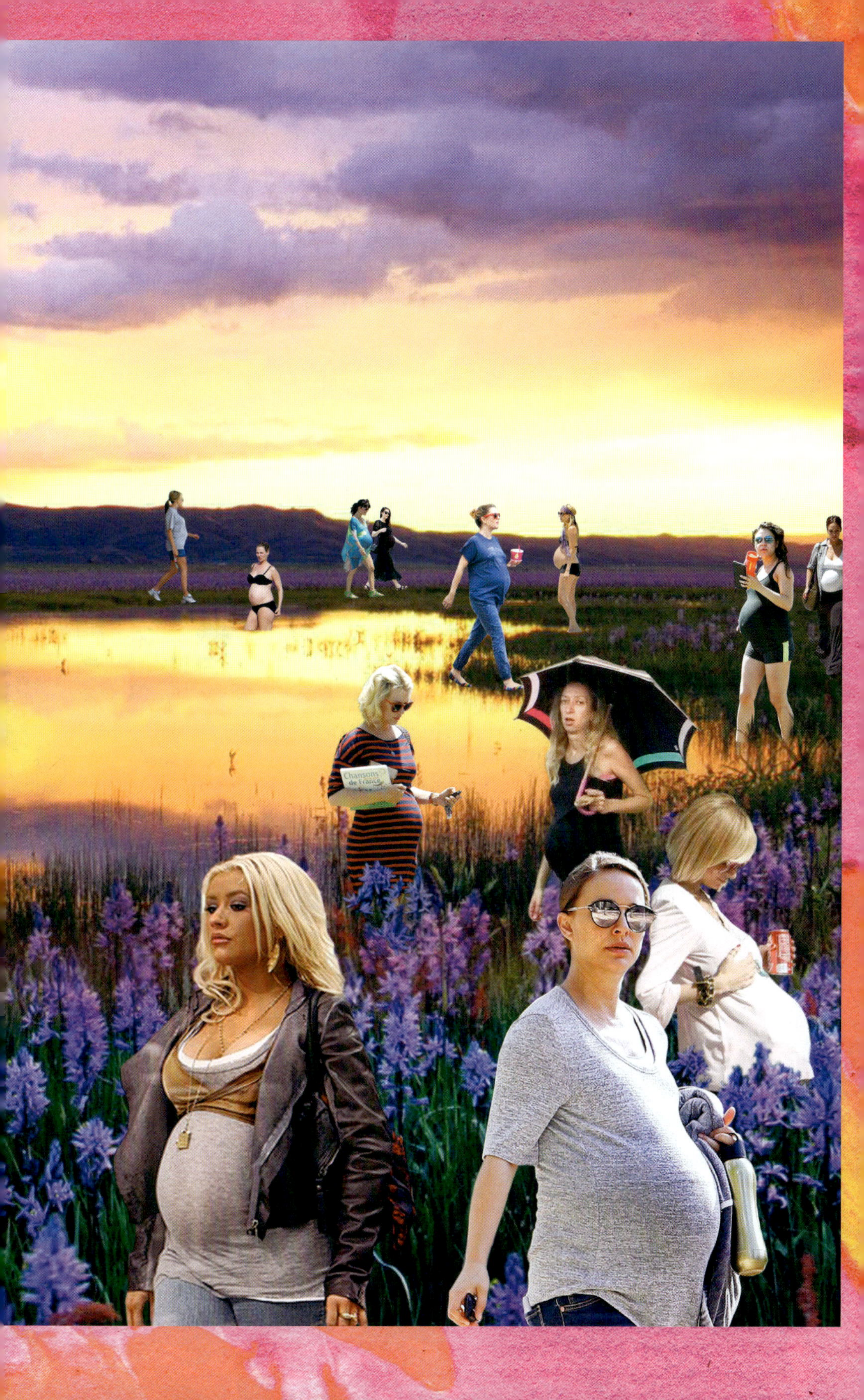
Chansons
de France

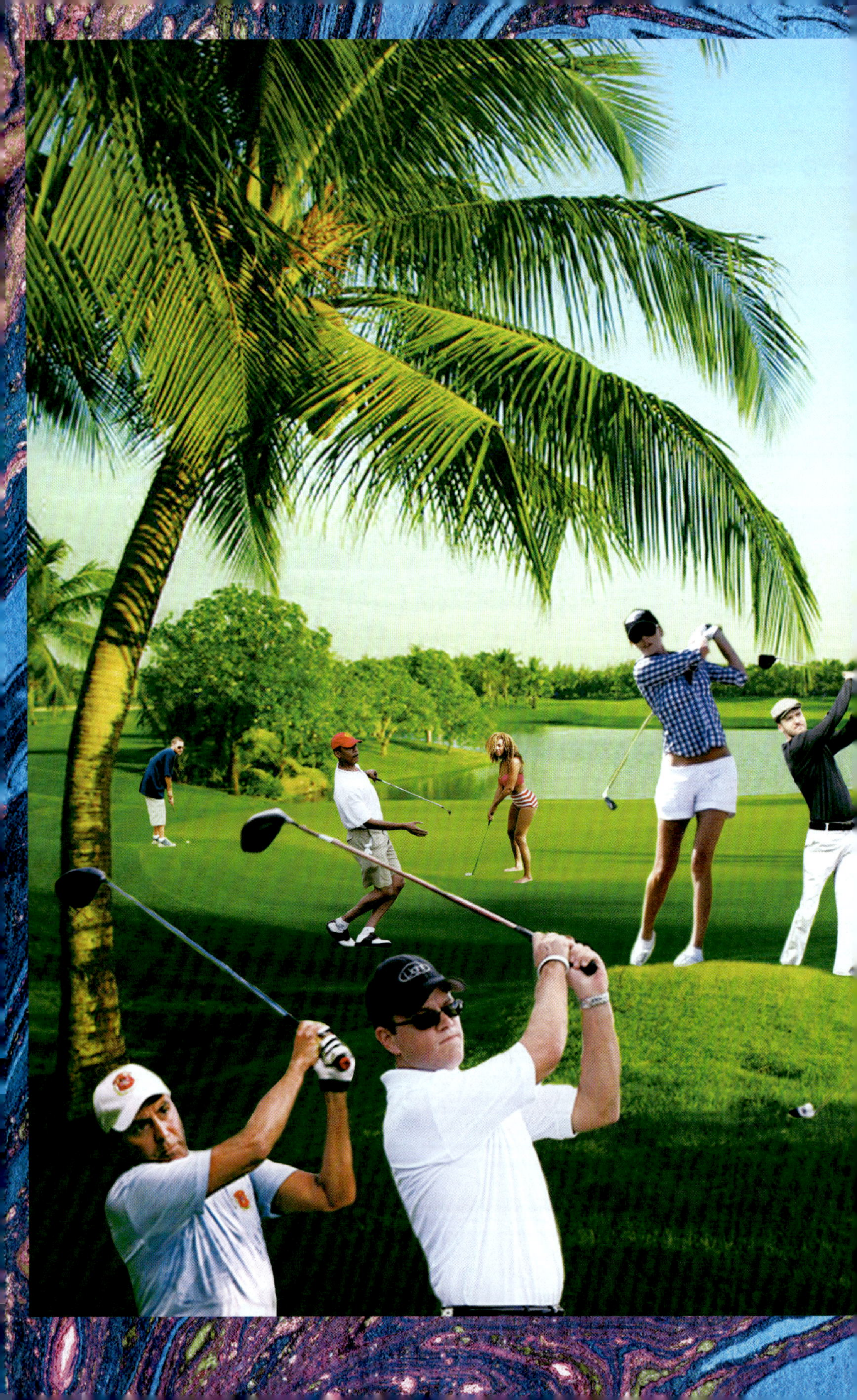

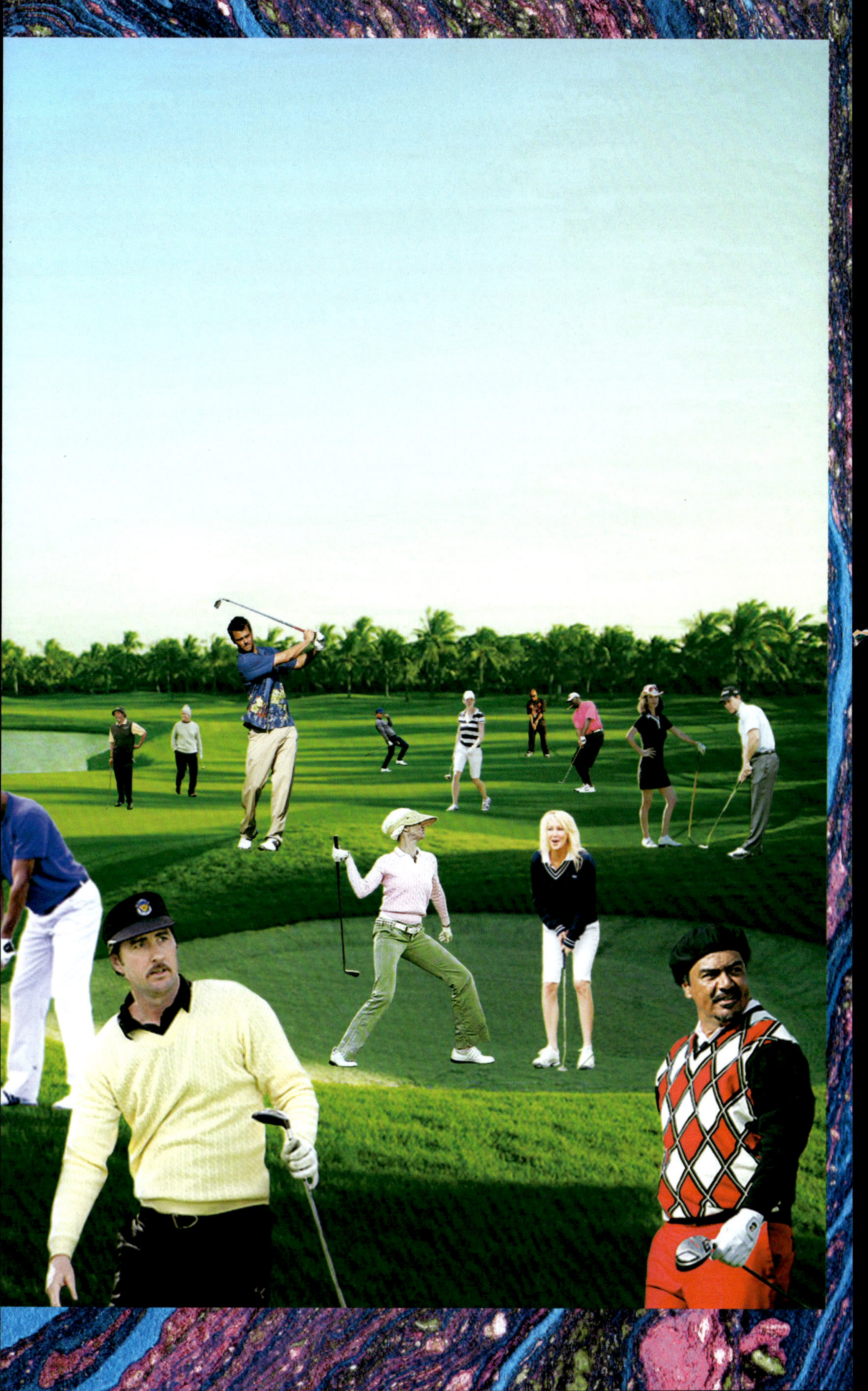

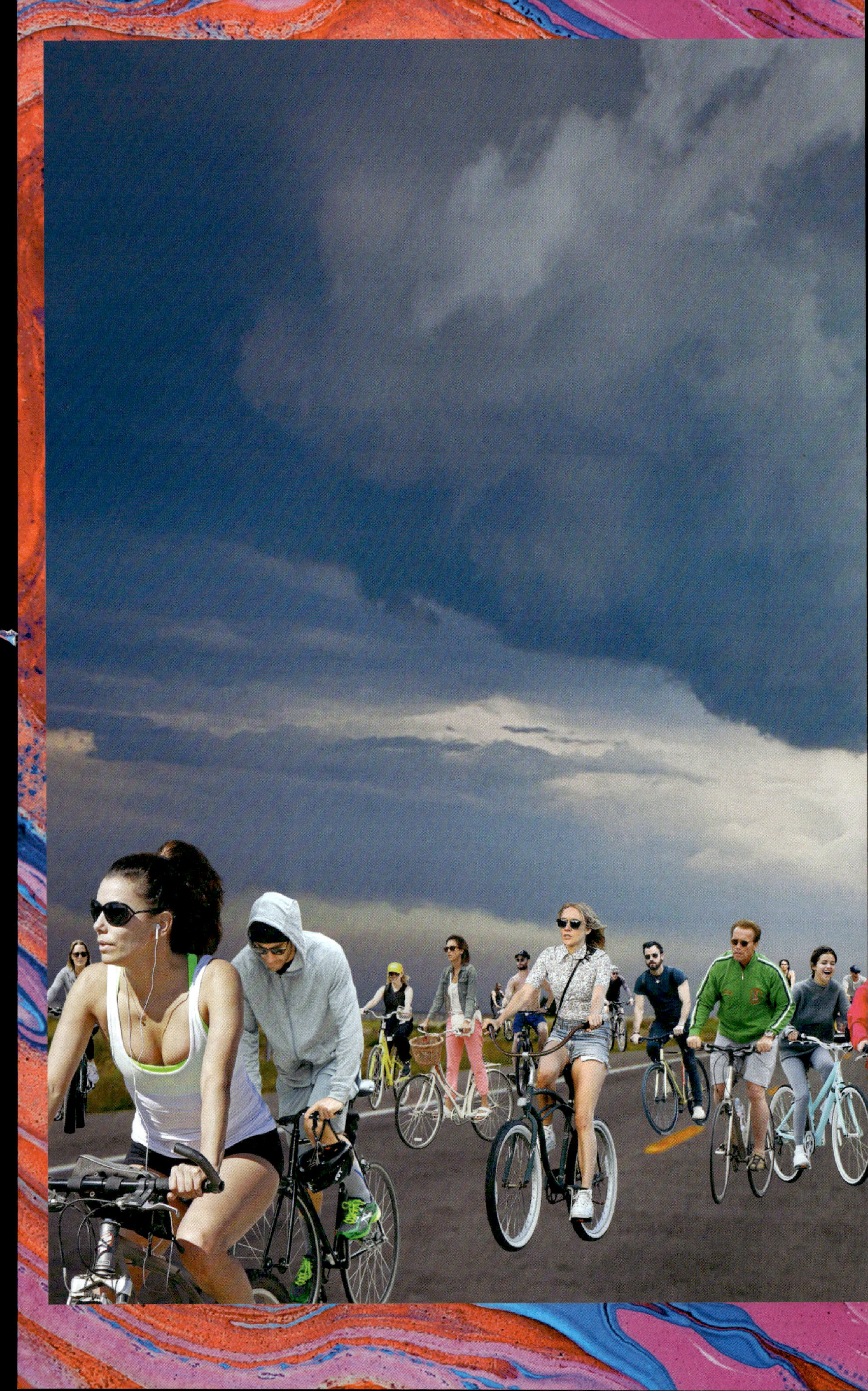

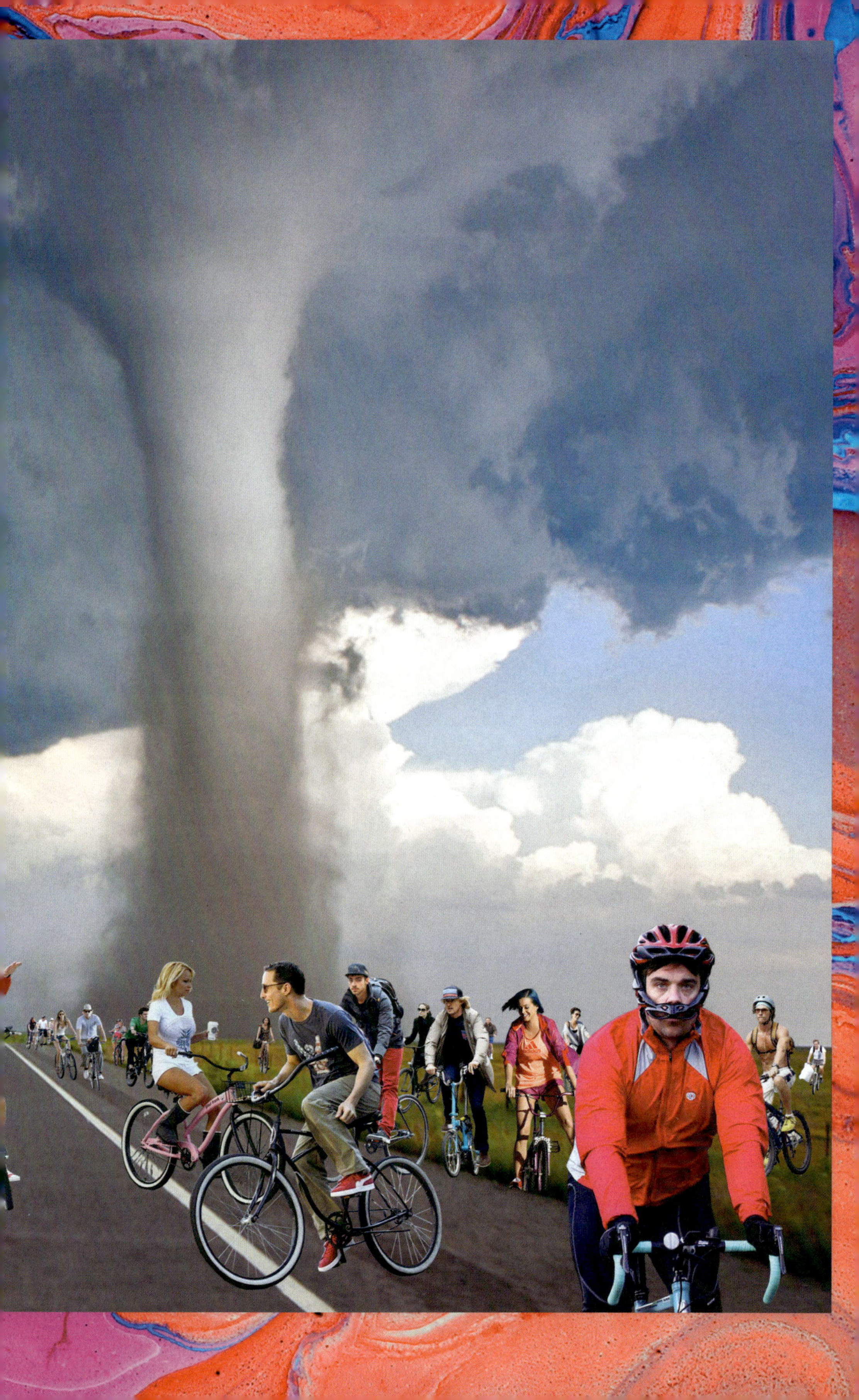

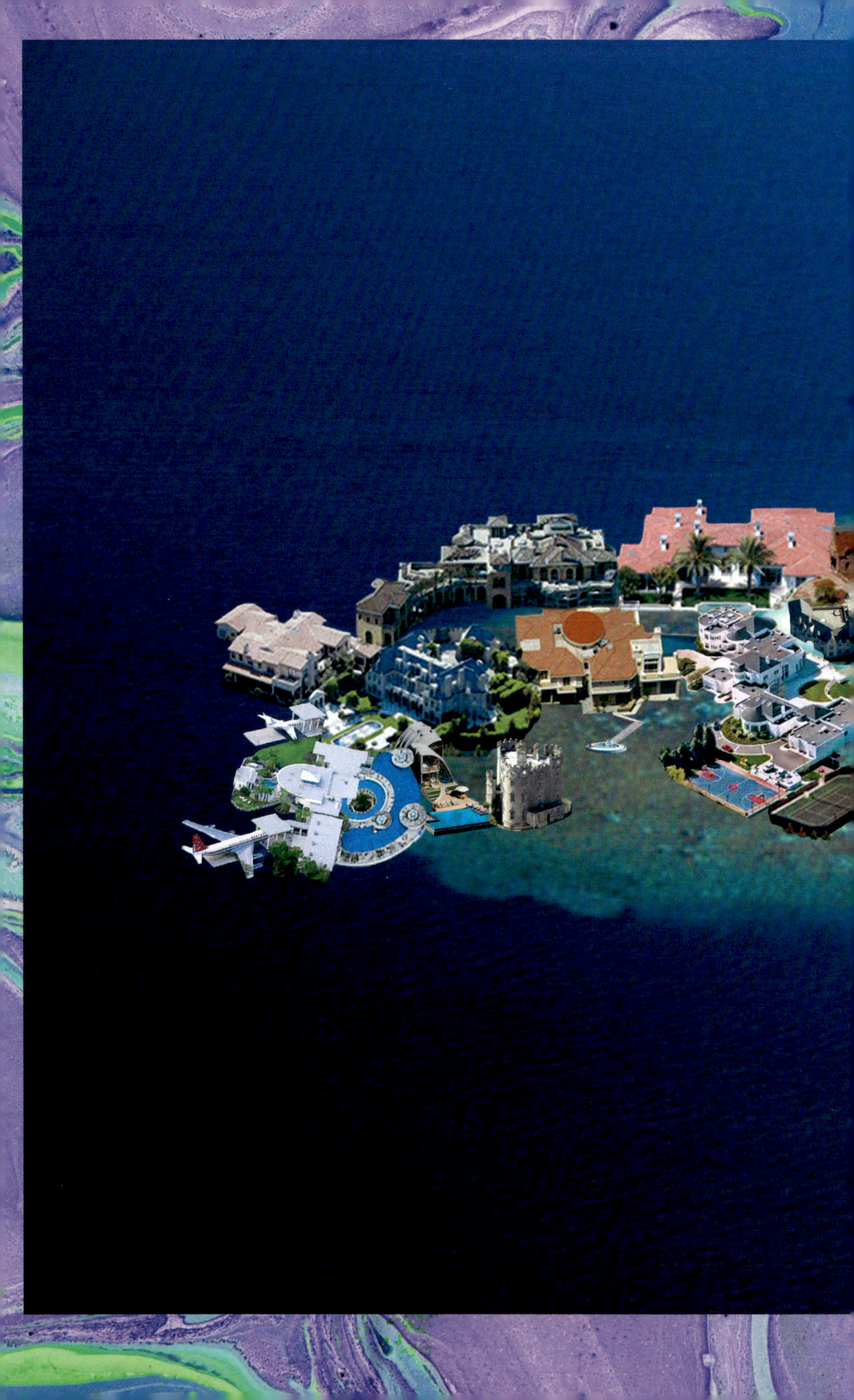

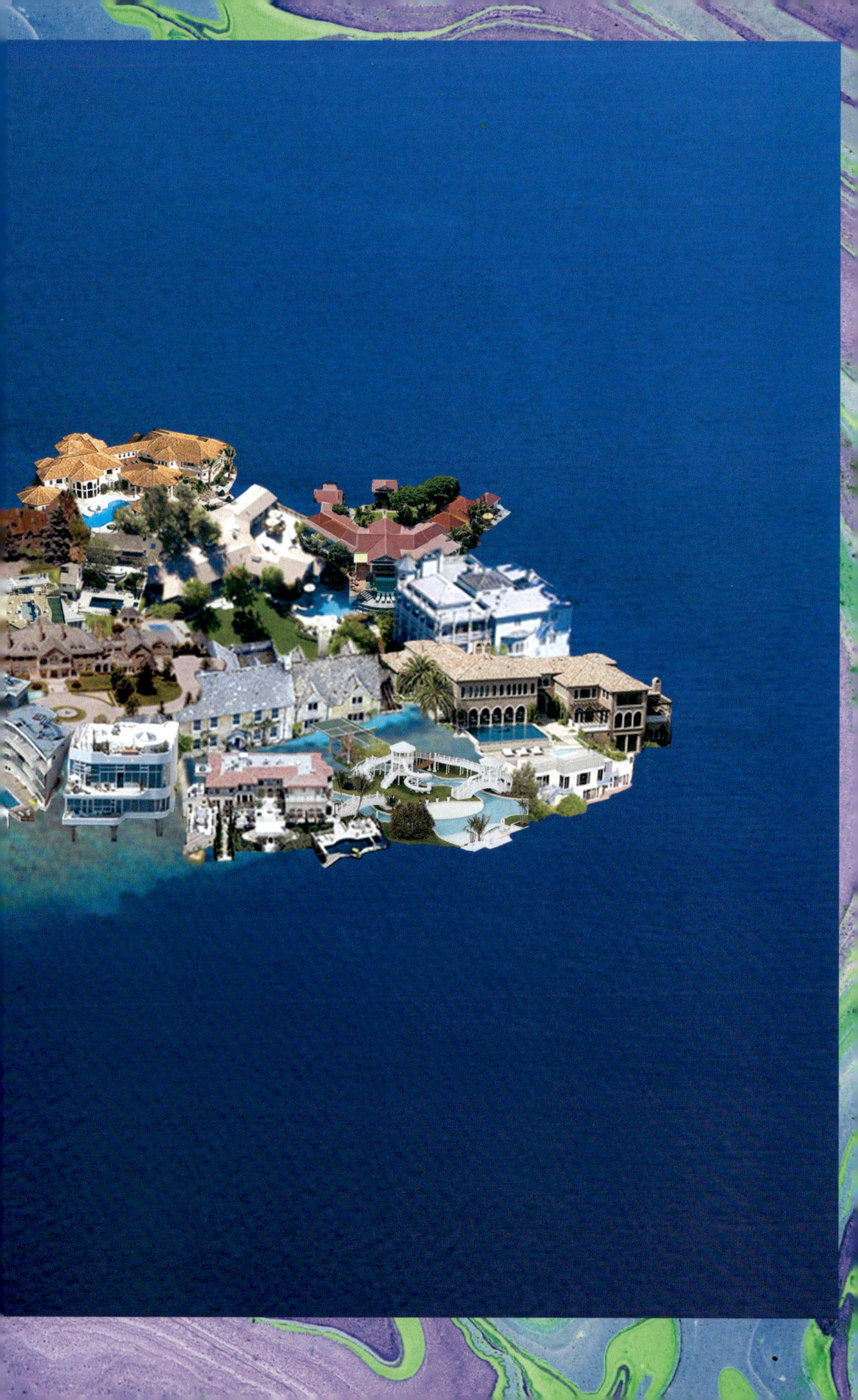

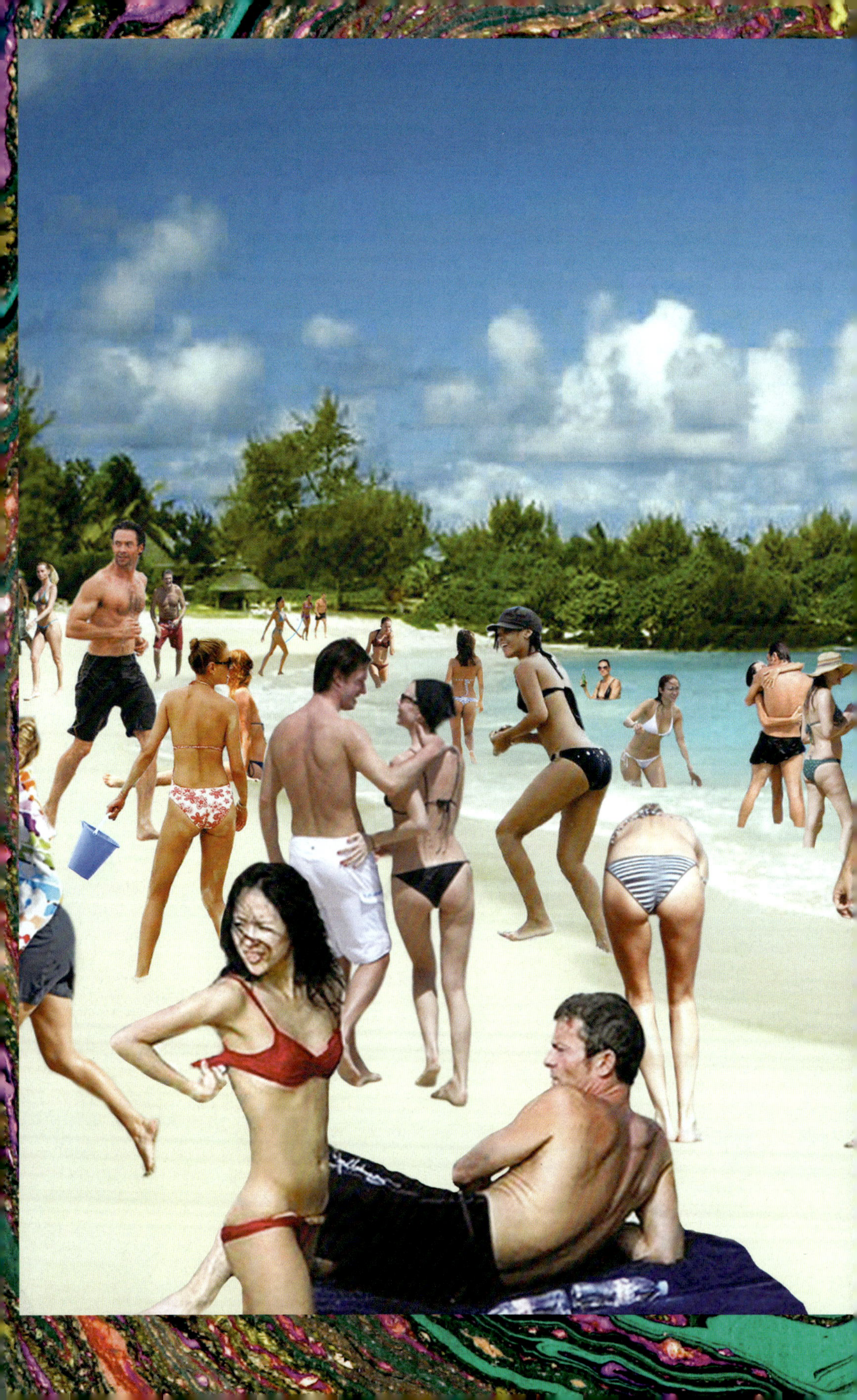

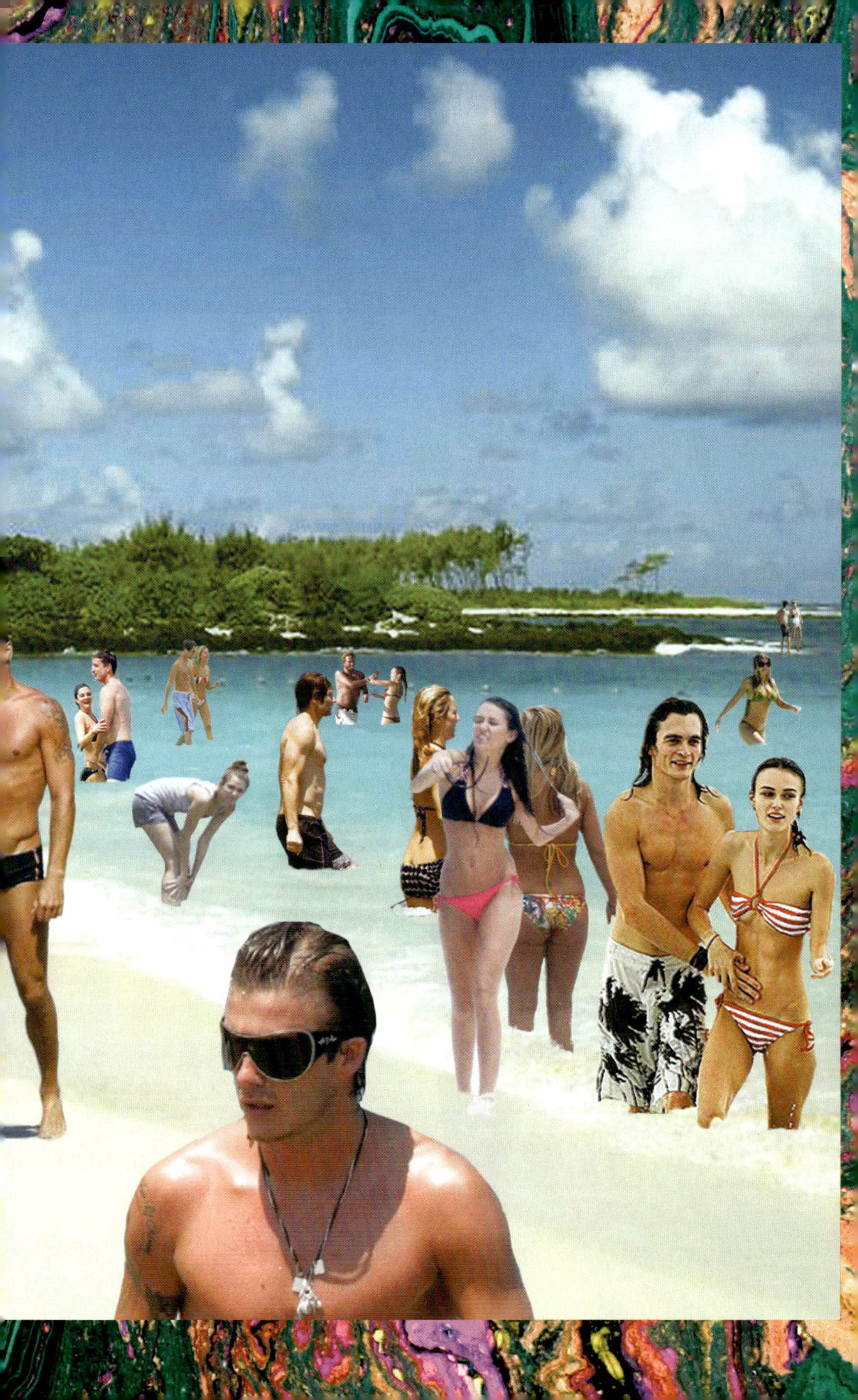

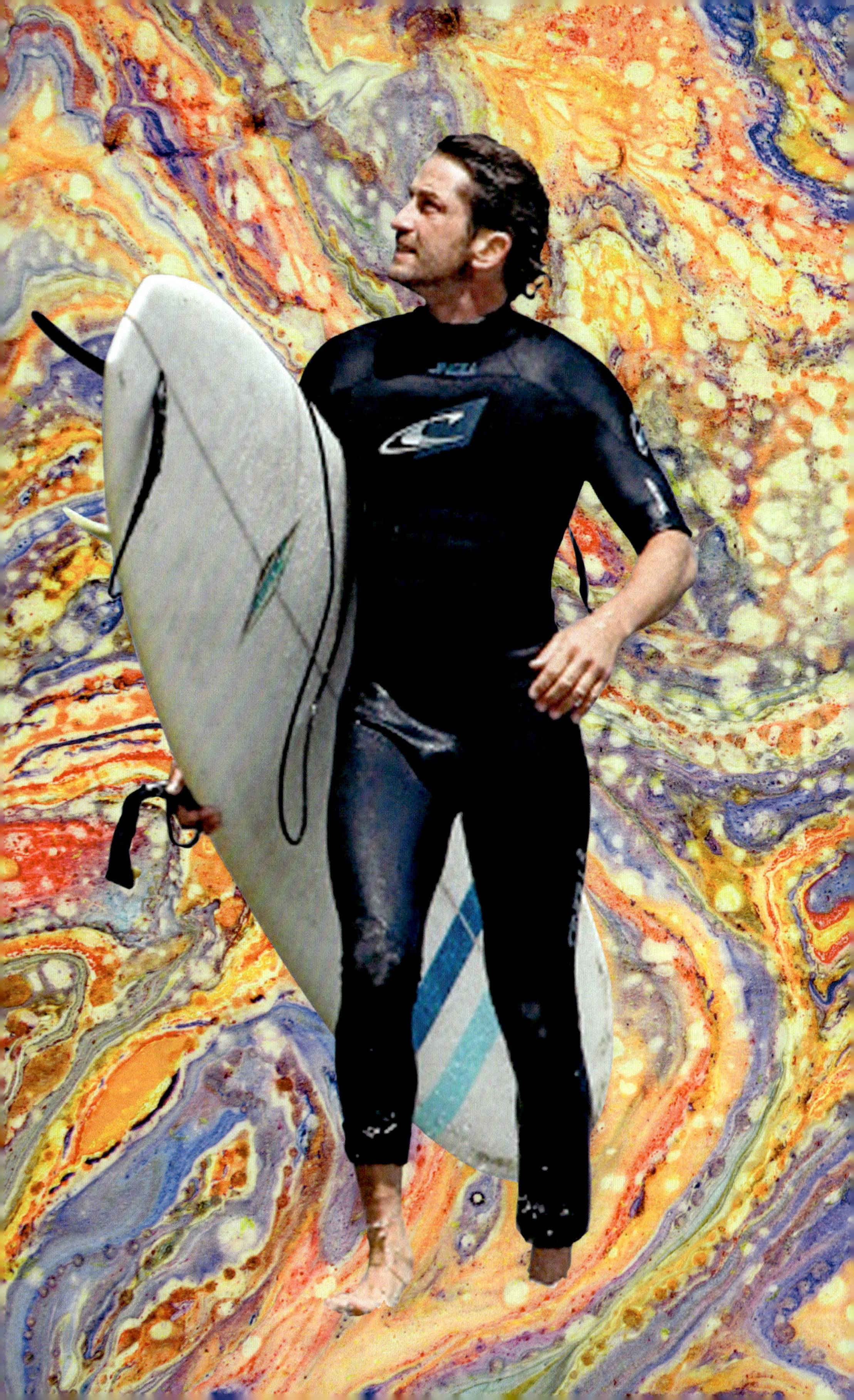

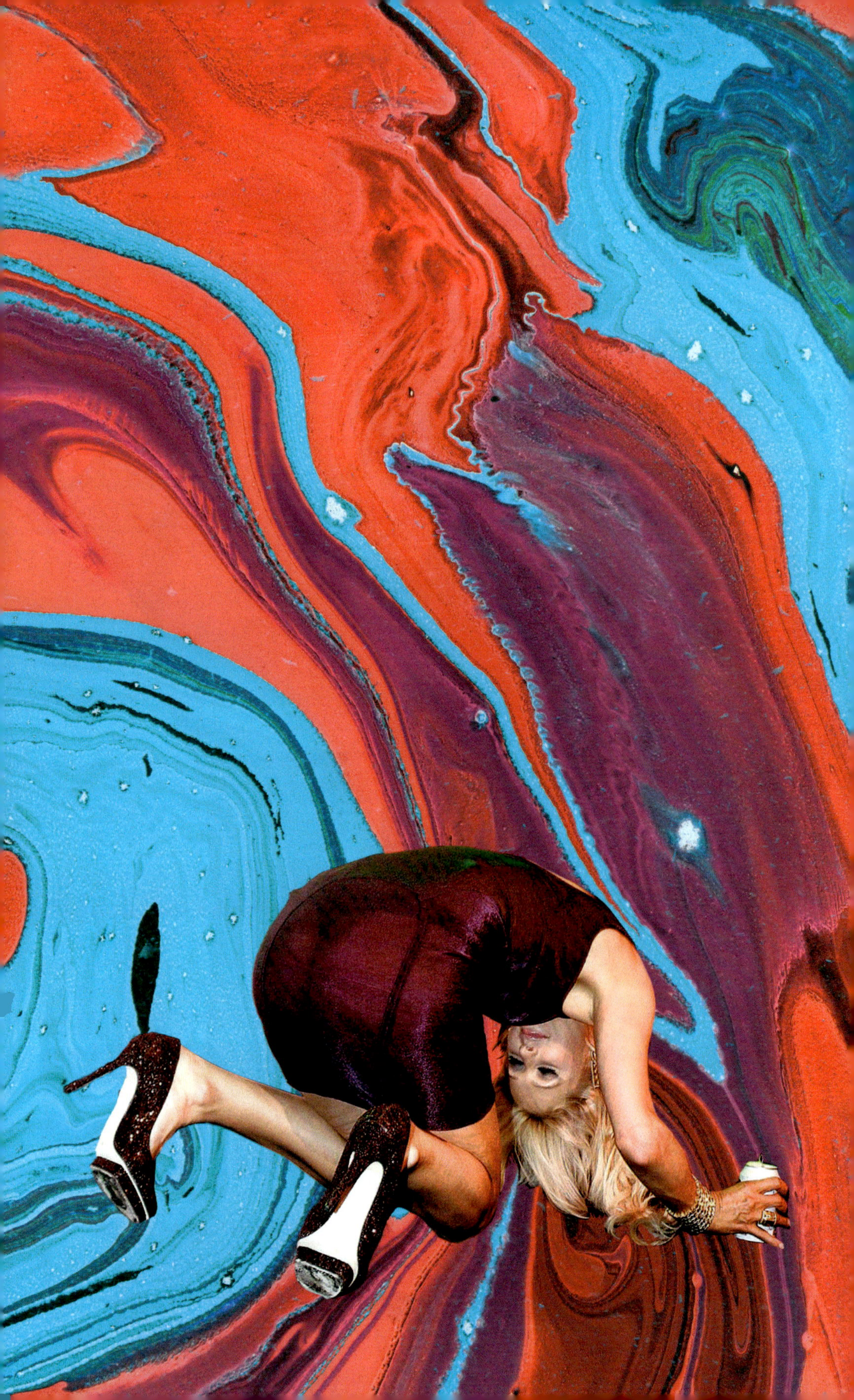

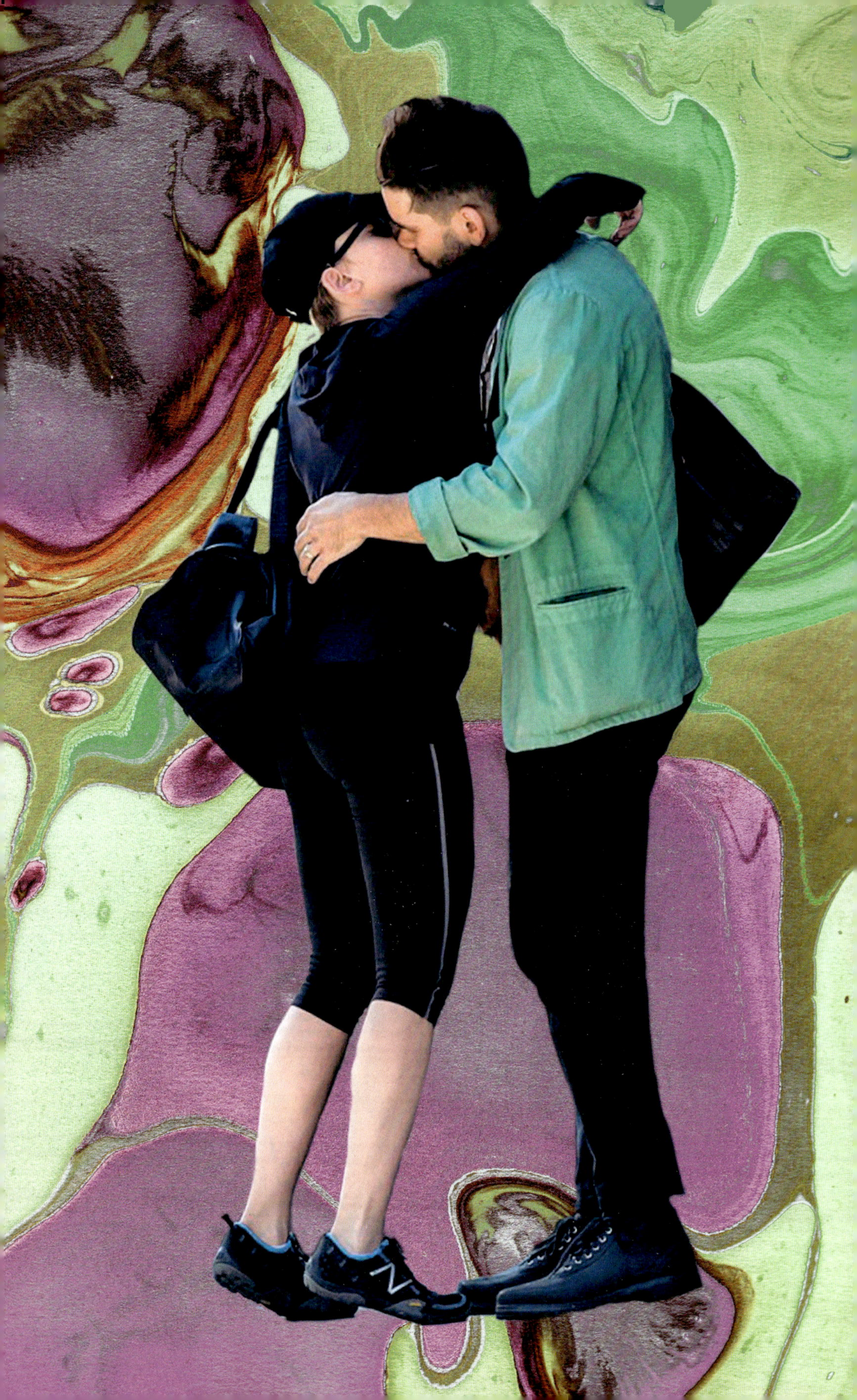

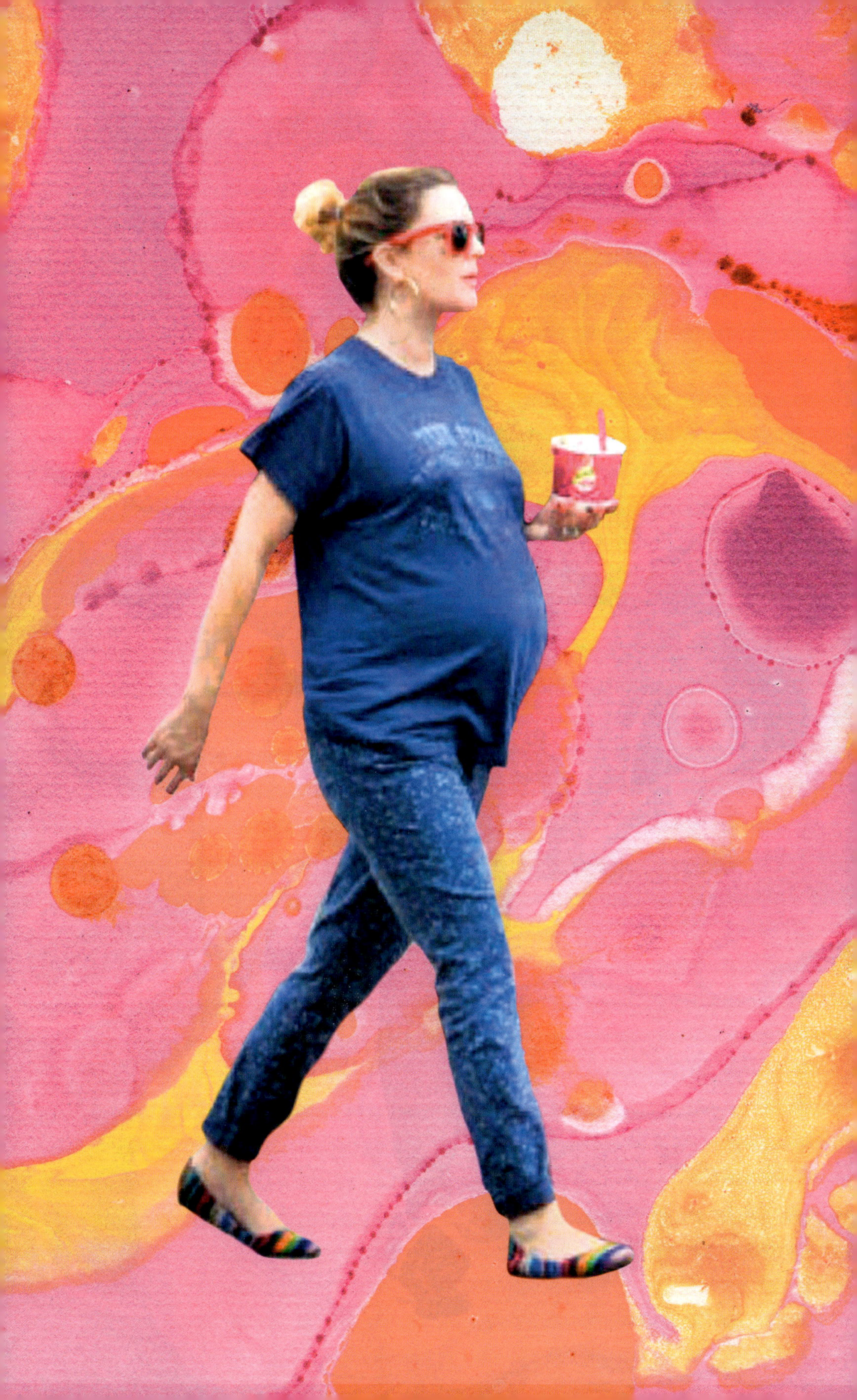

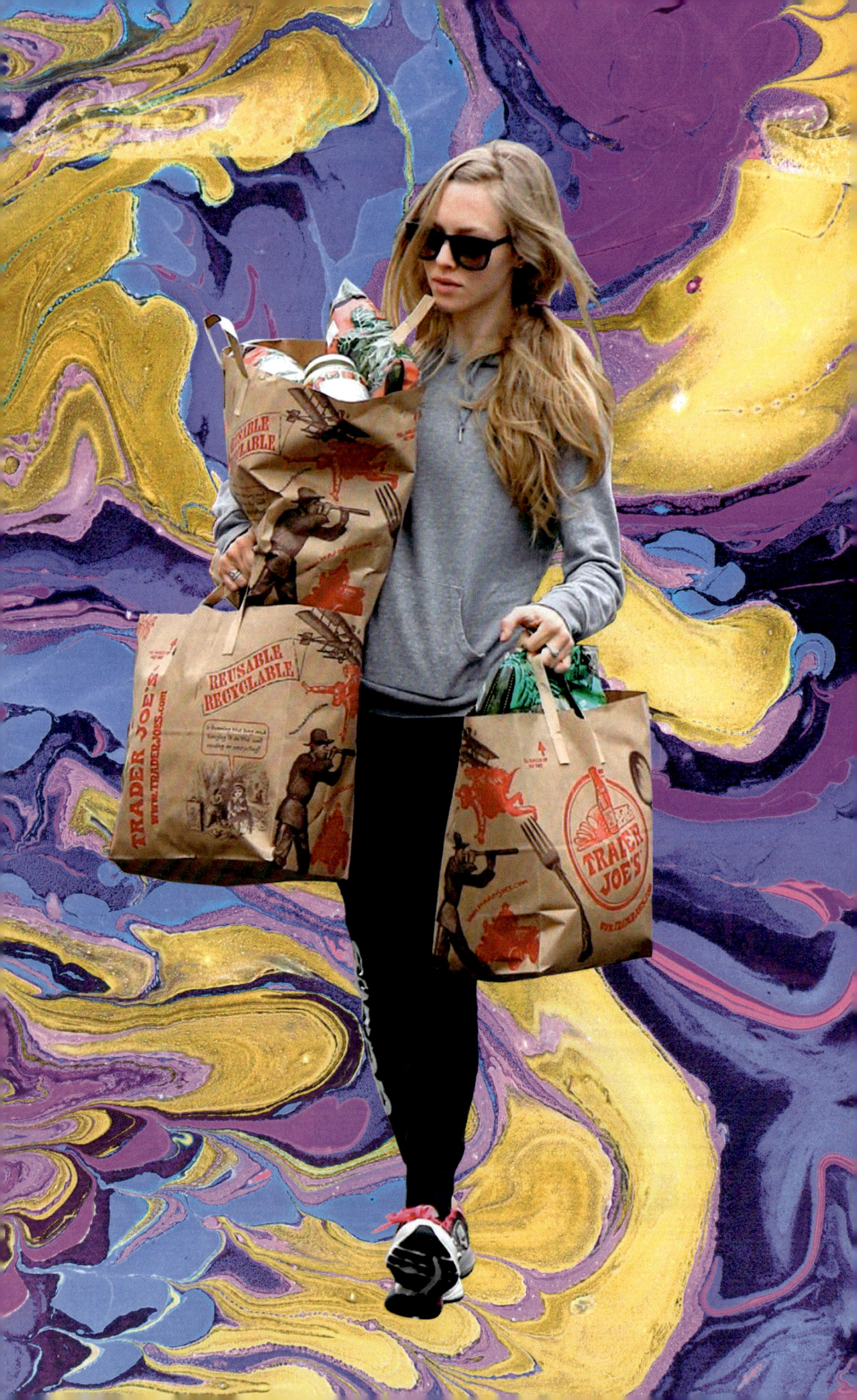
REUSABLE
RECYCLABLE
TRADER JOE'S
WWW.TRADERJOES.COM
REUSABLE
RECYCLABLE
TRADER JOE'S

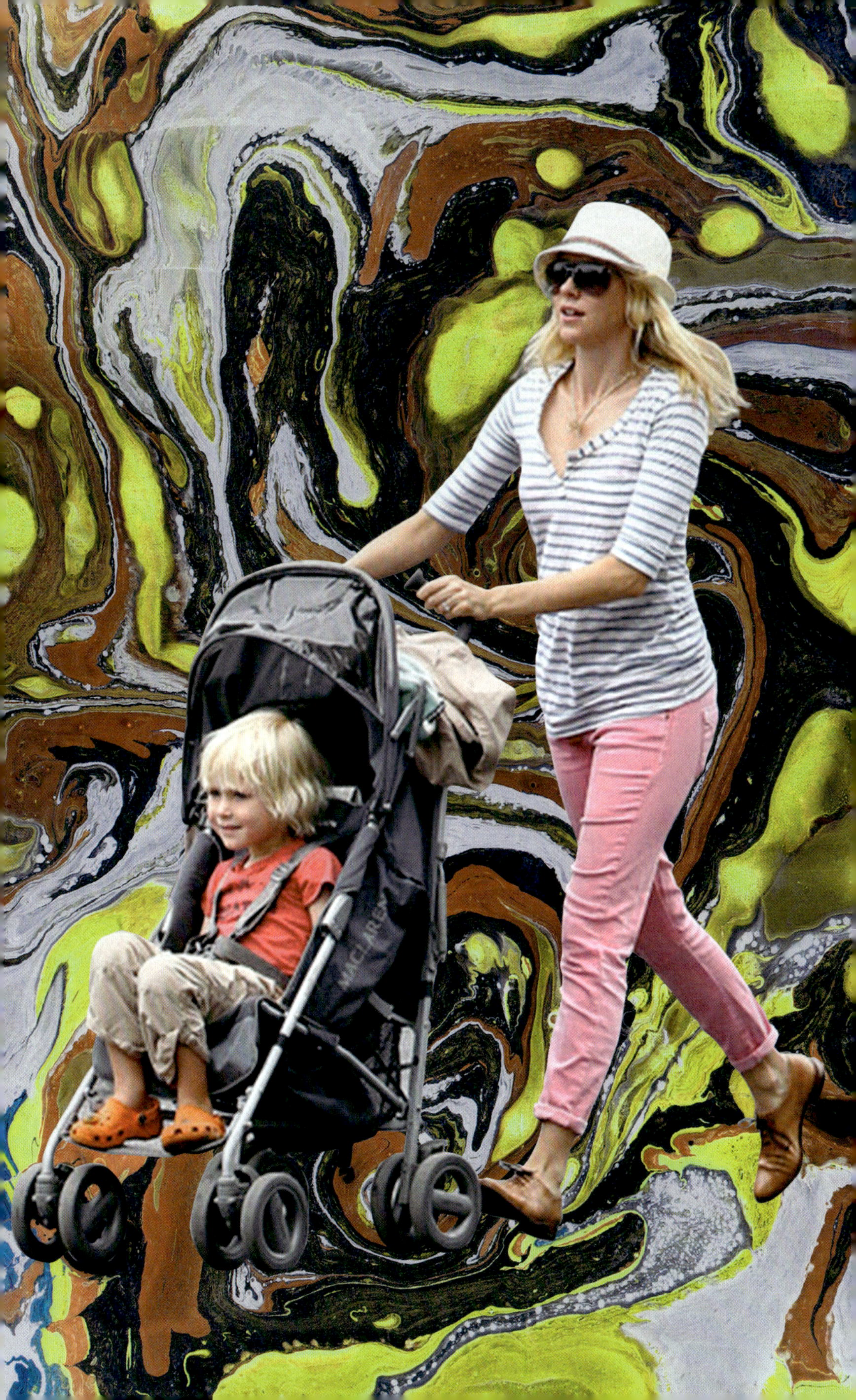

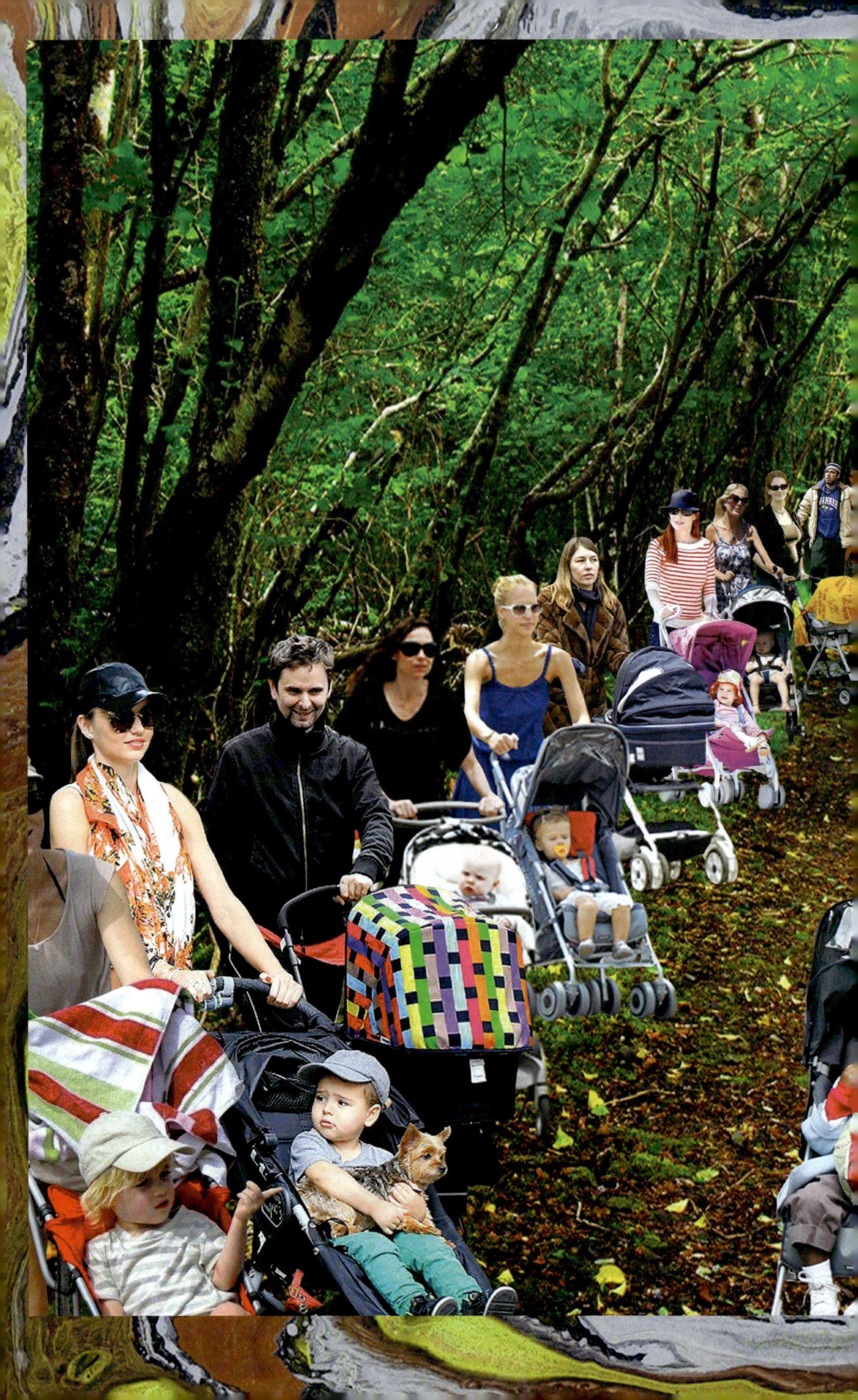

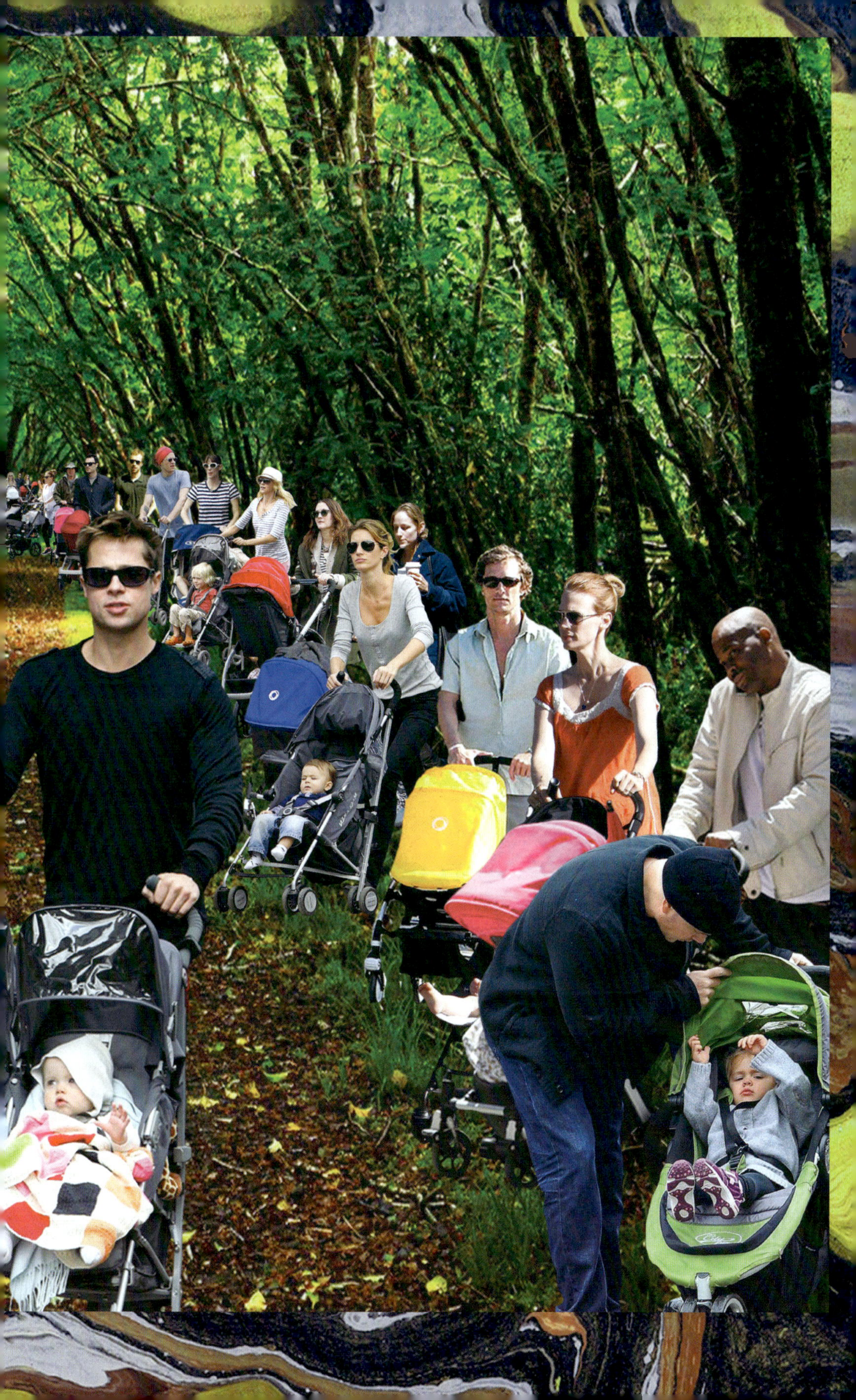

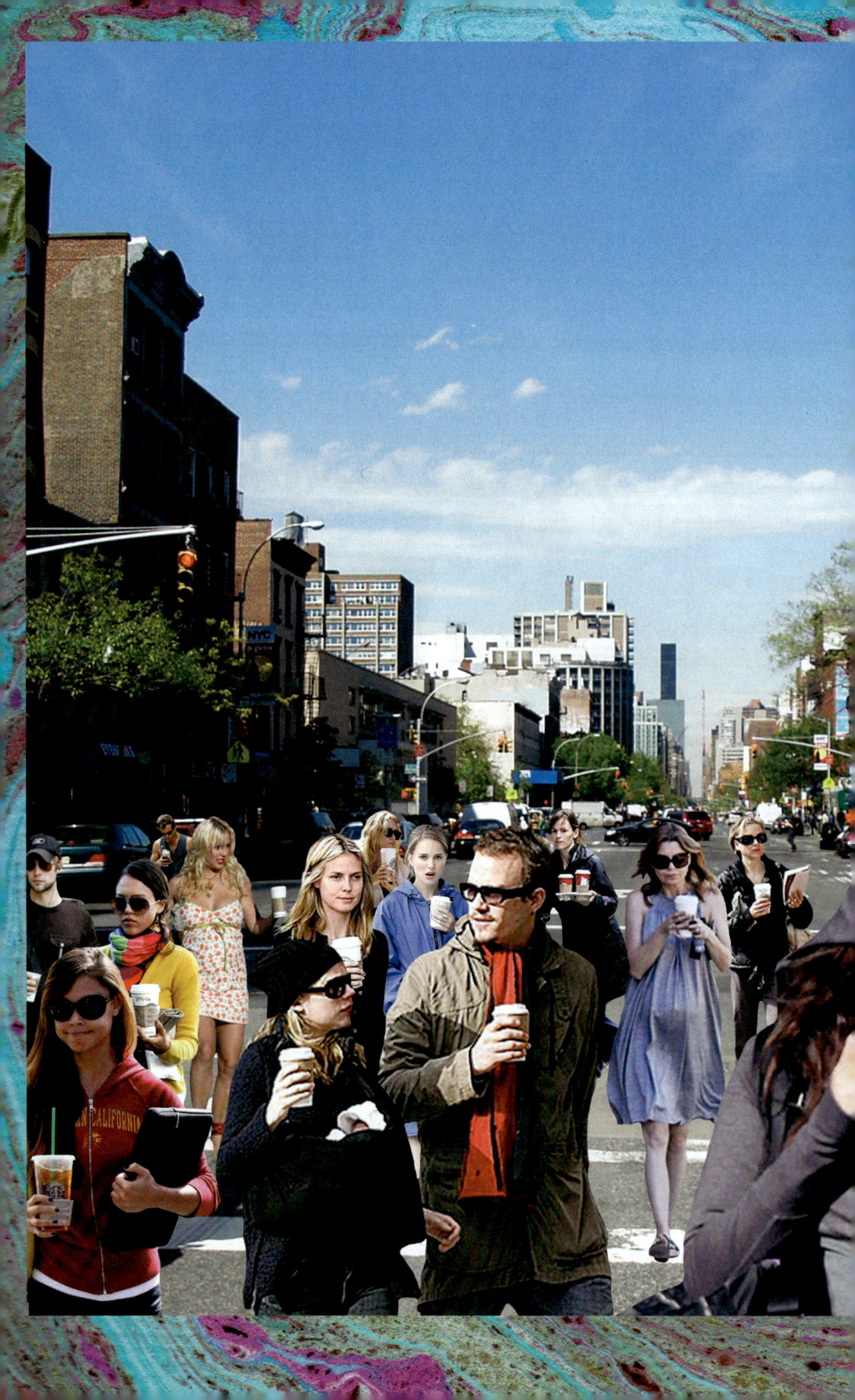
NYC

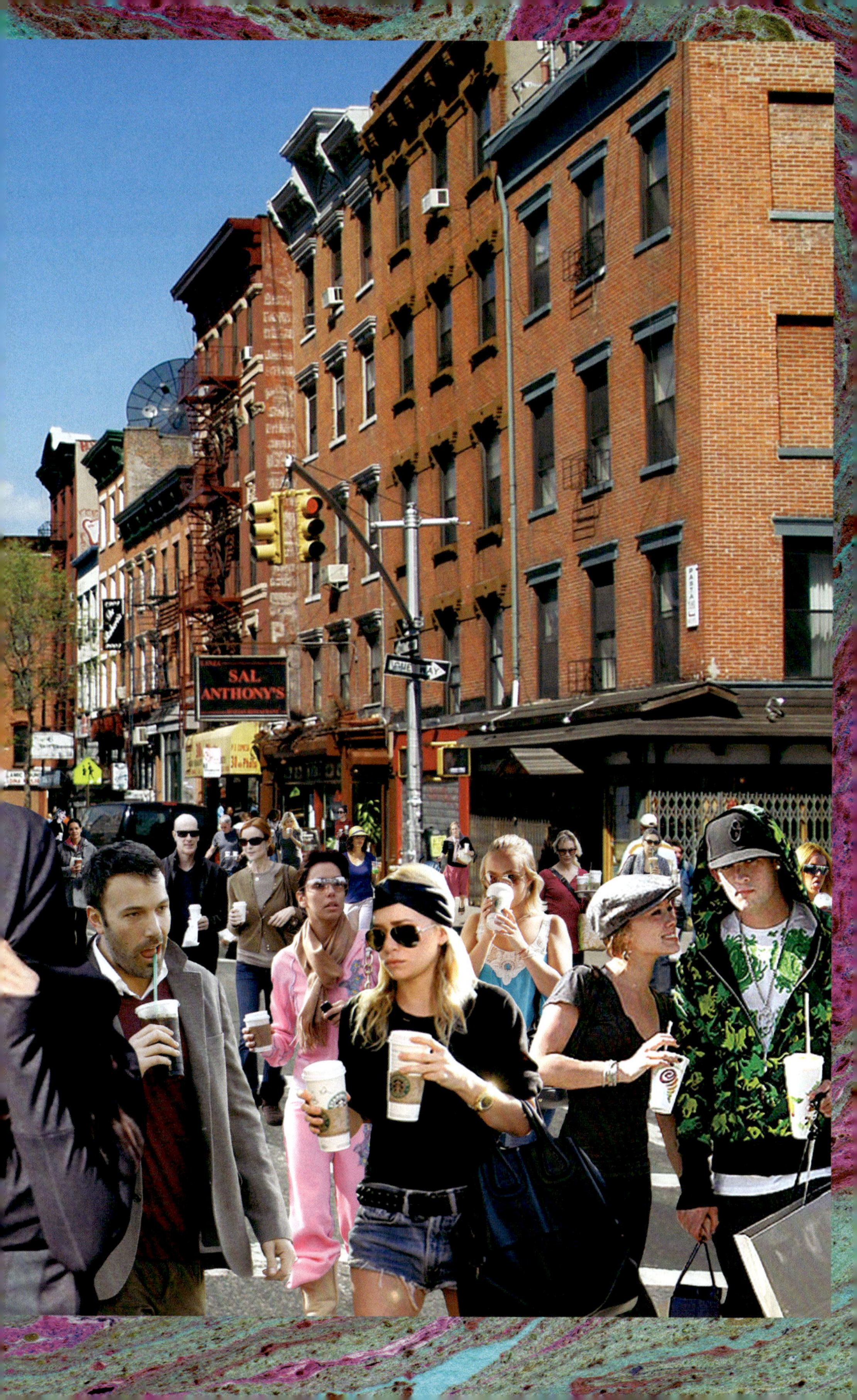
SAL
ANTHONY'S

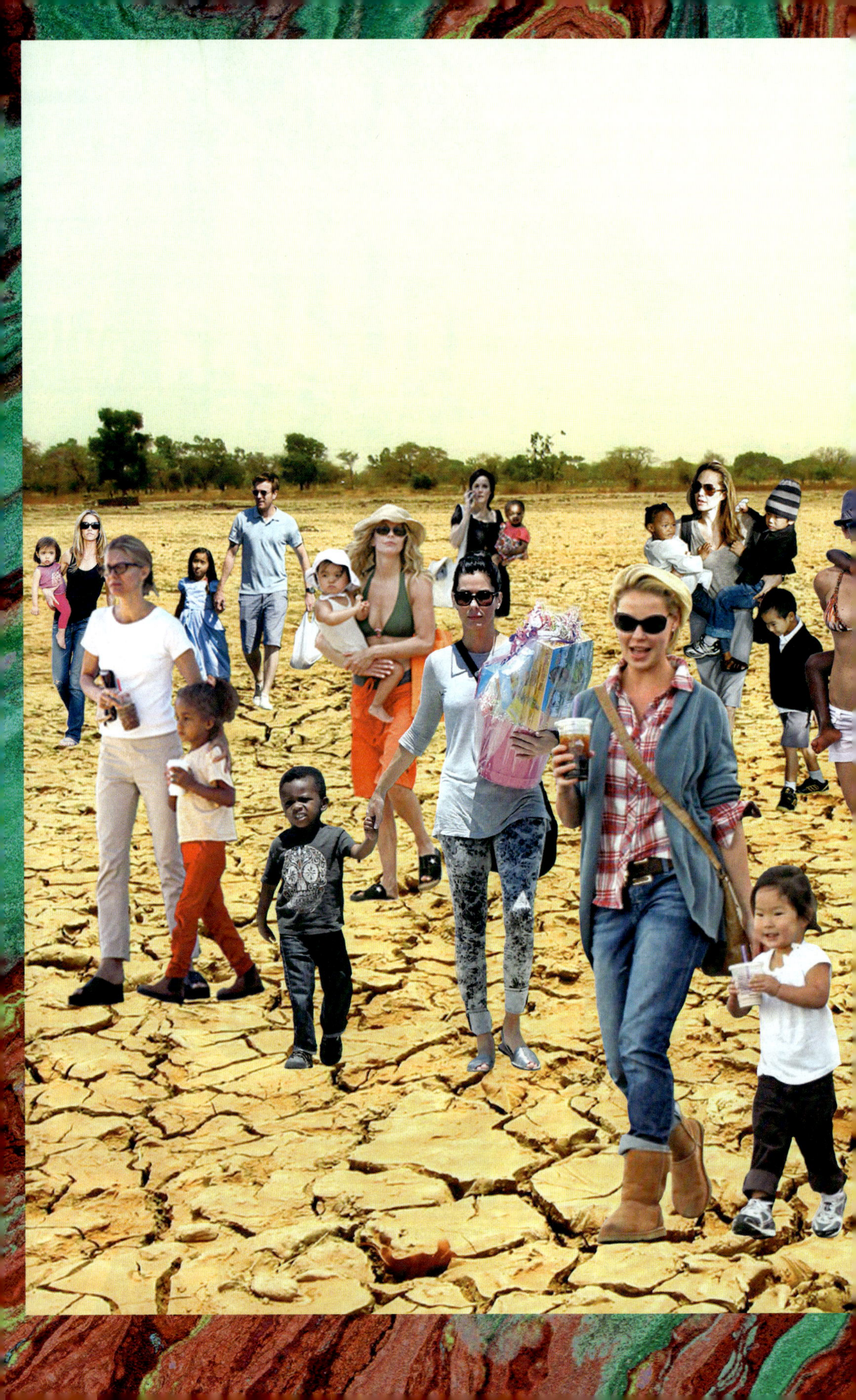

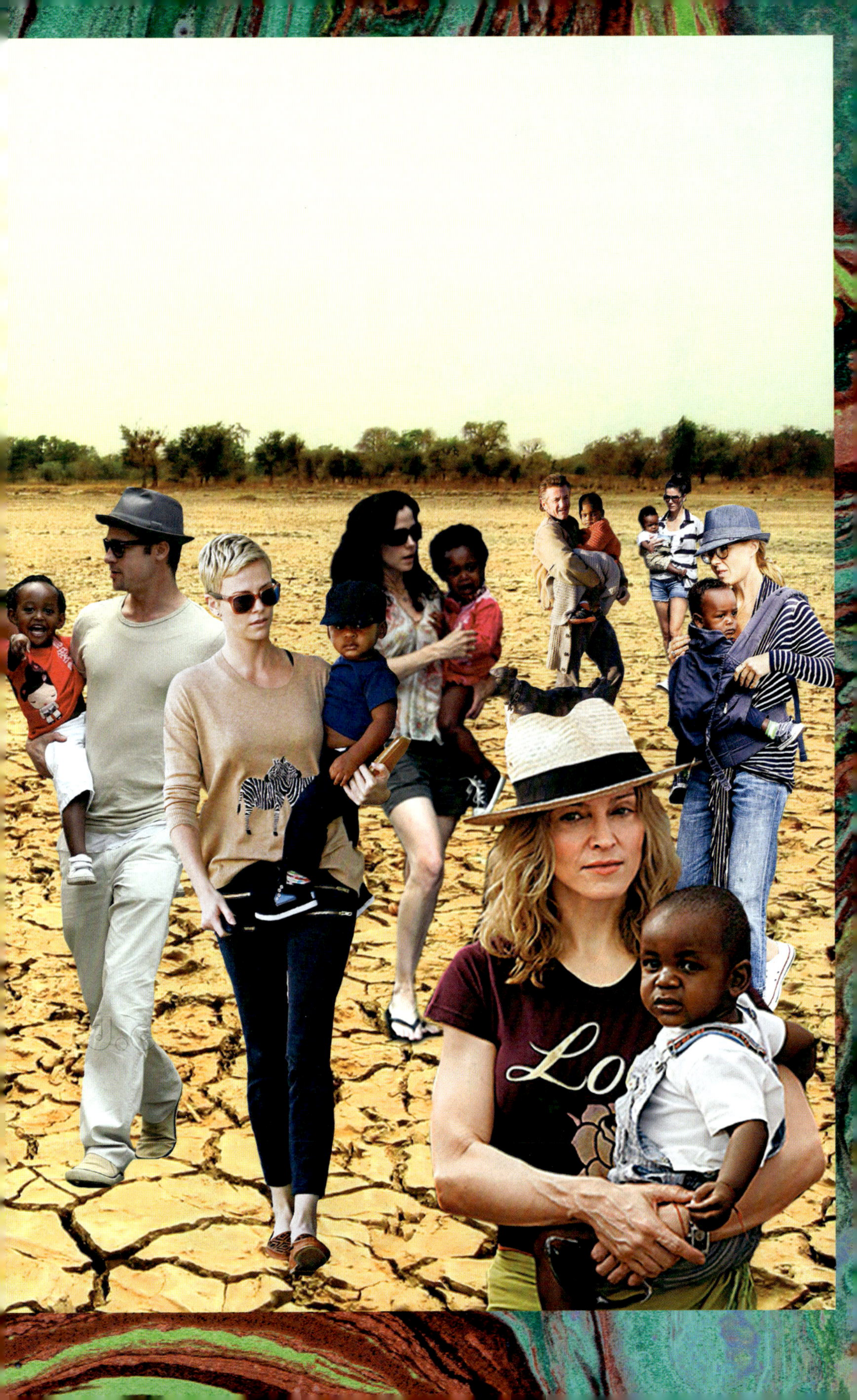

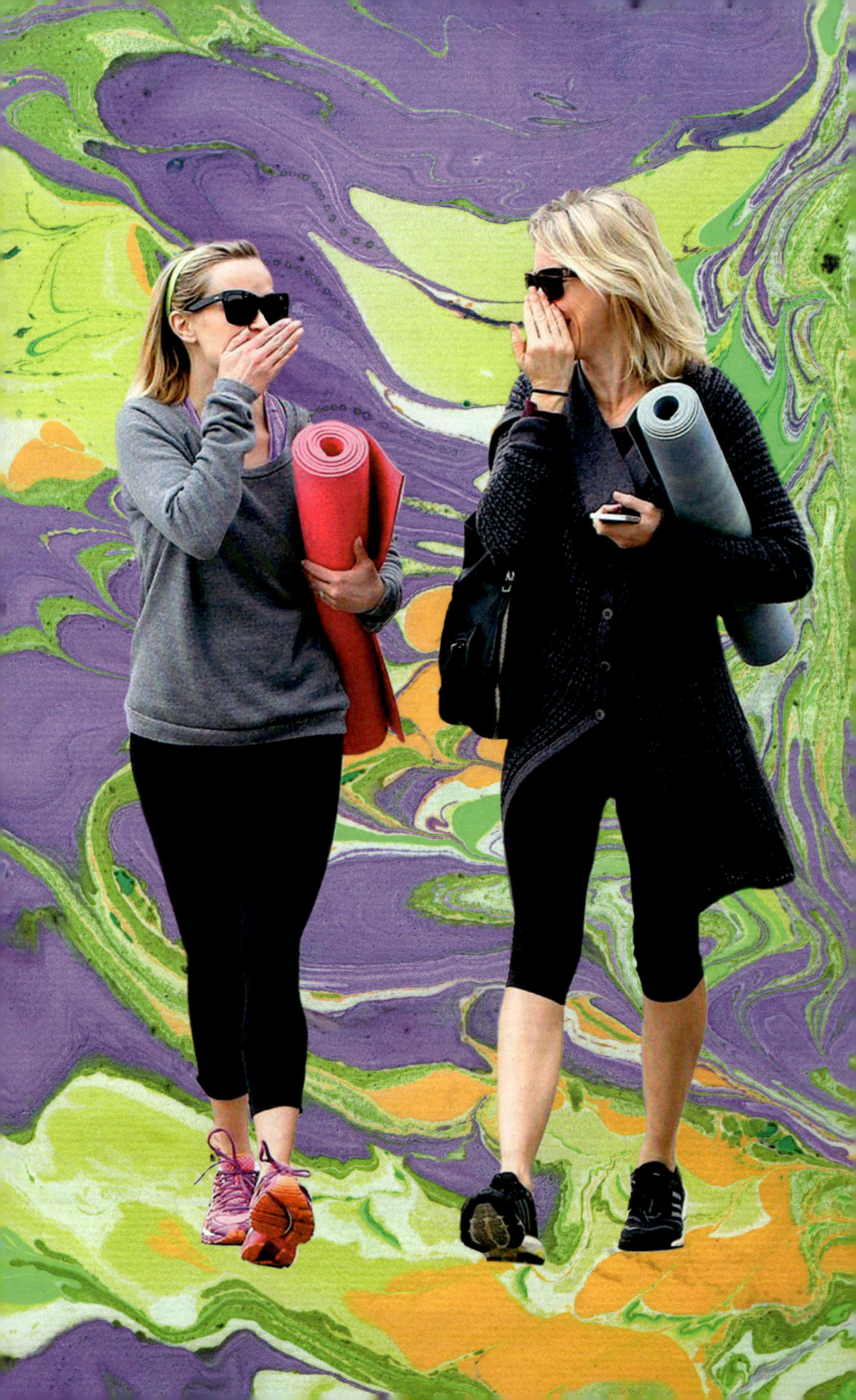

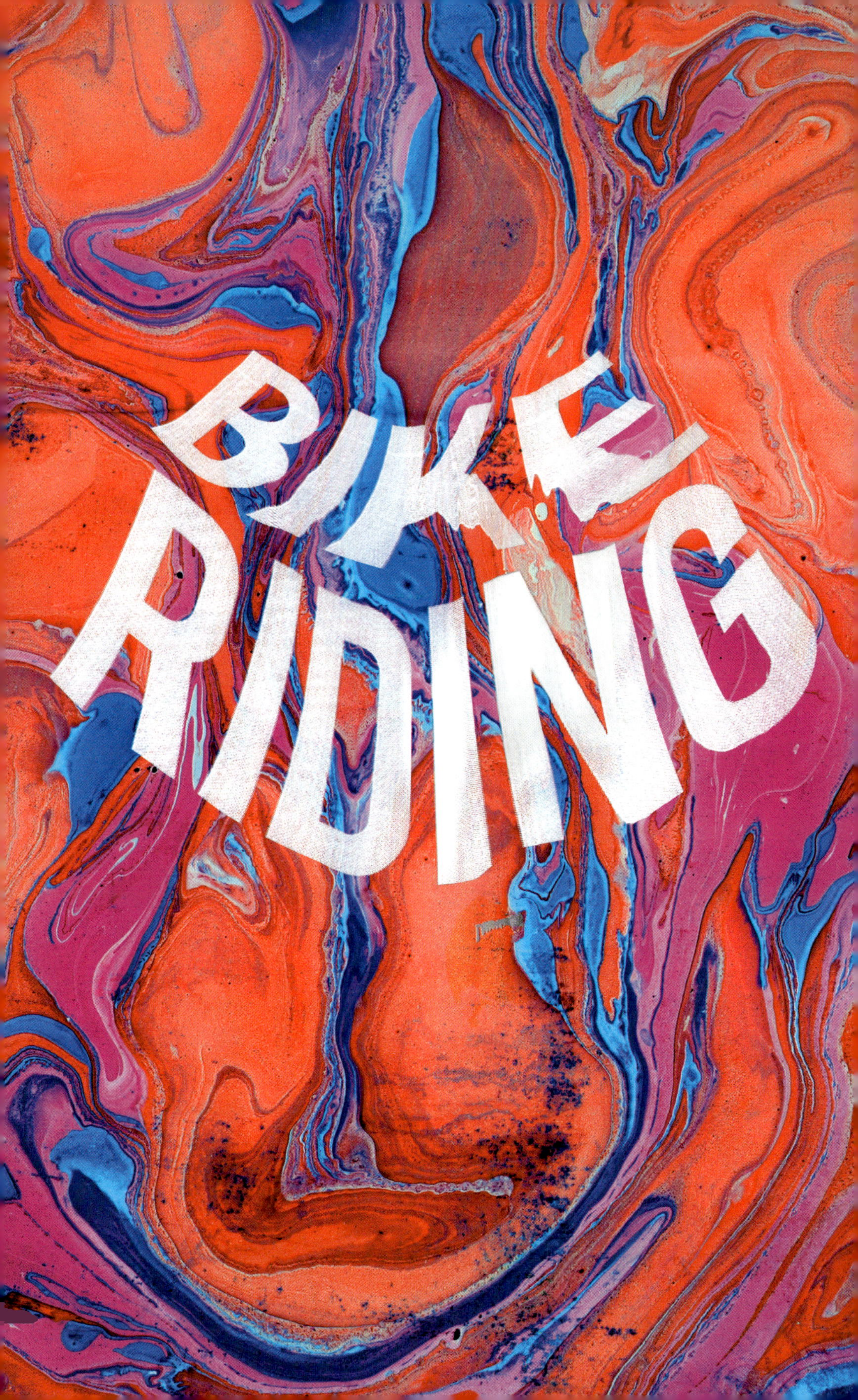
BIKE
RIDING

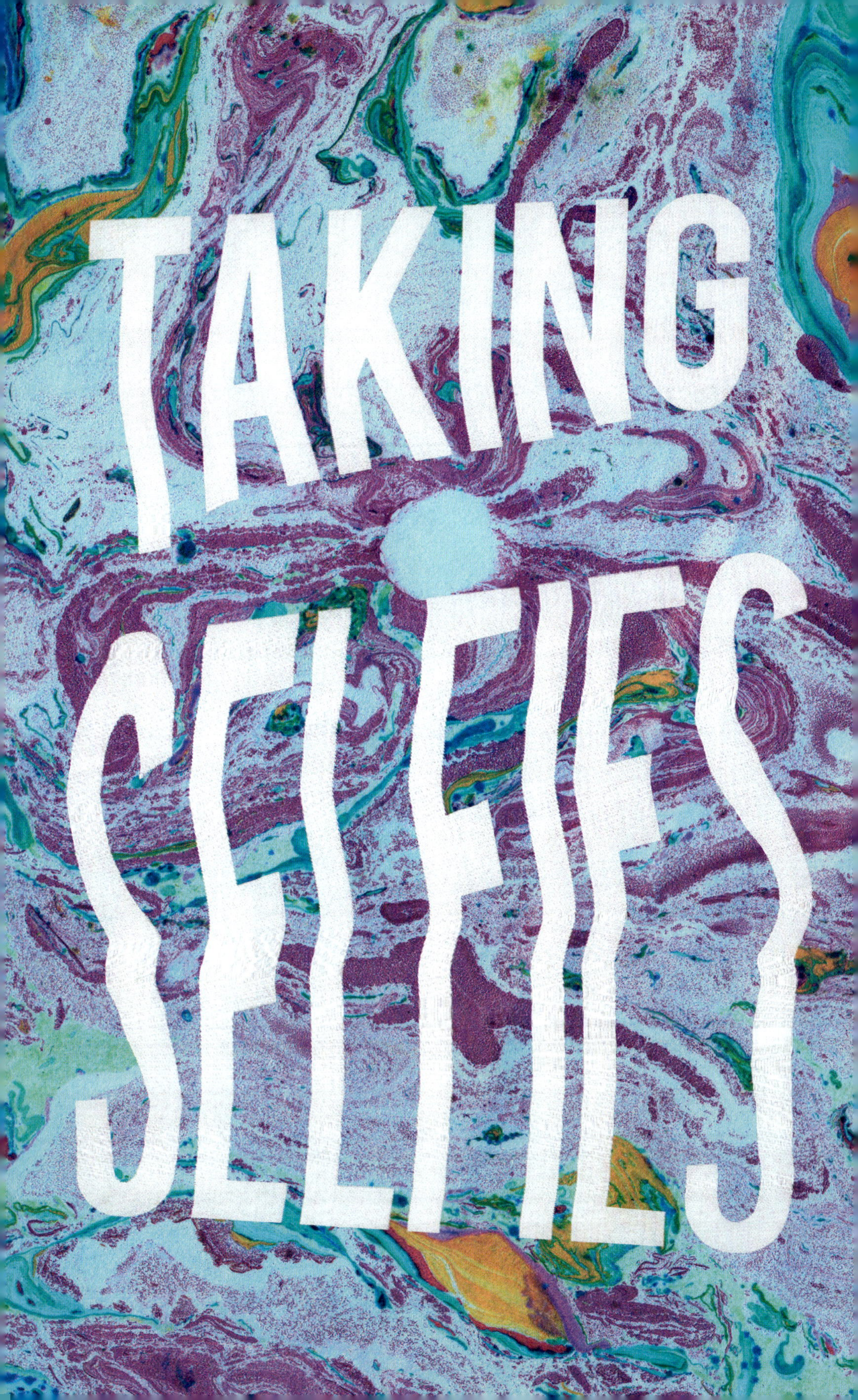
TAKING
SELFIES

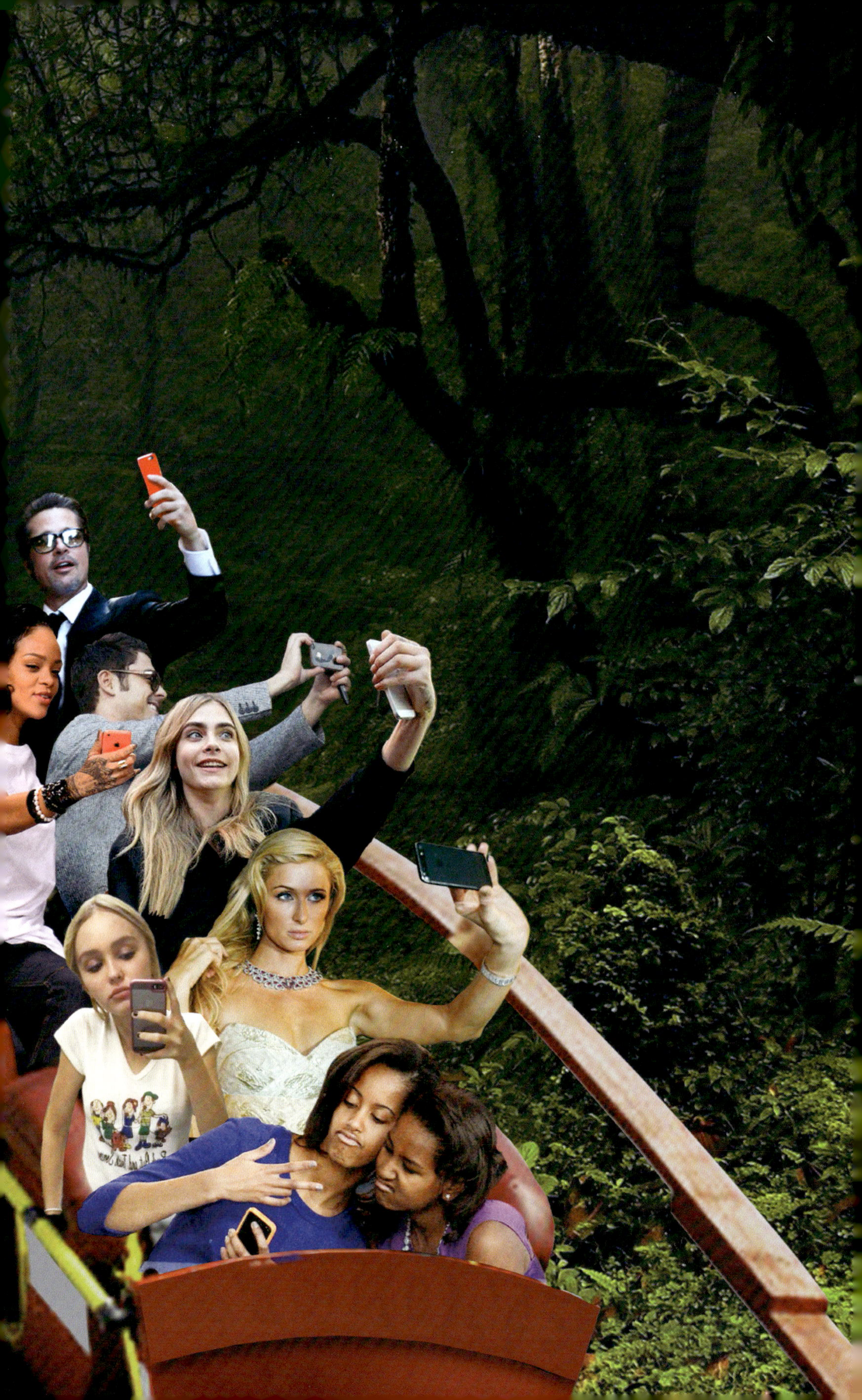

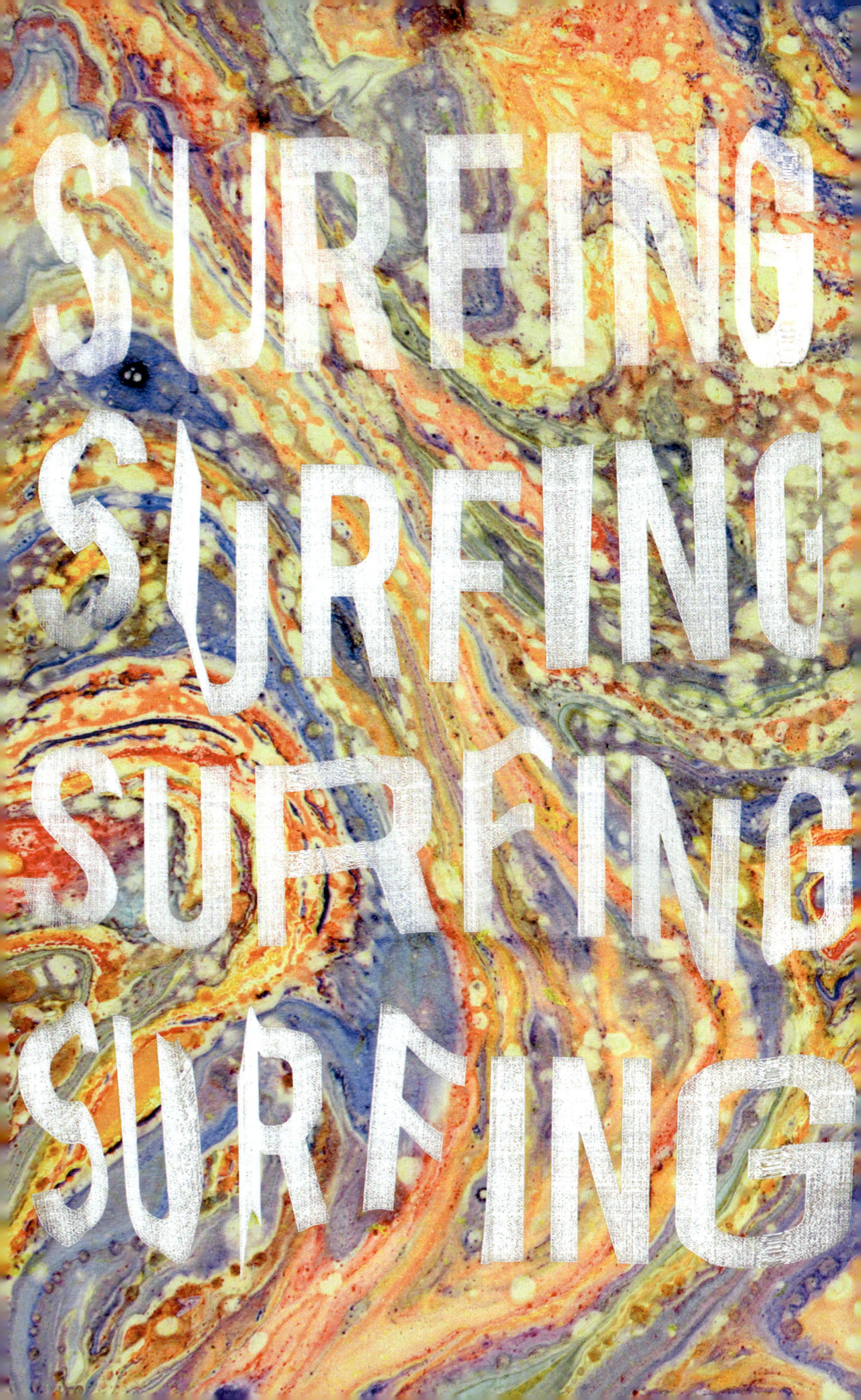
SURFING
SURFING
SURFING
SURFING

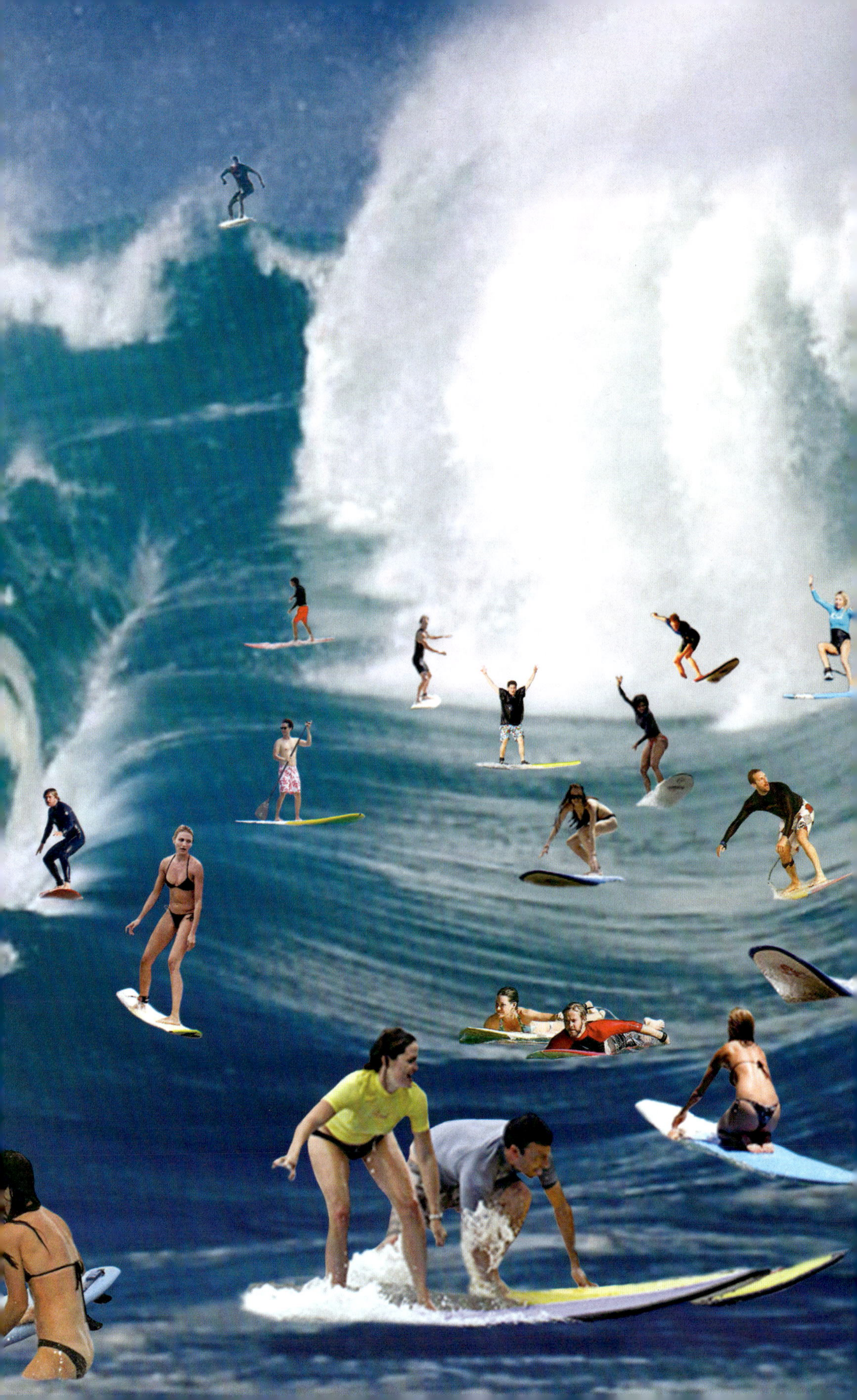

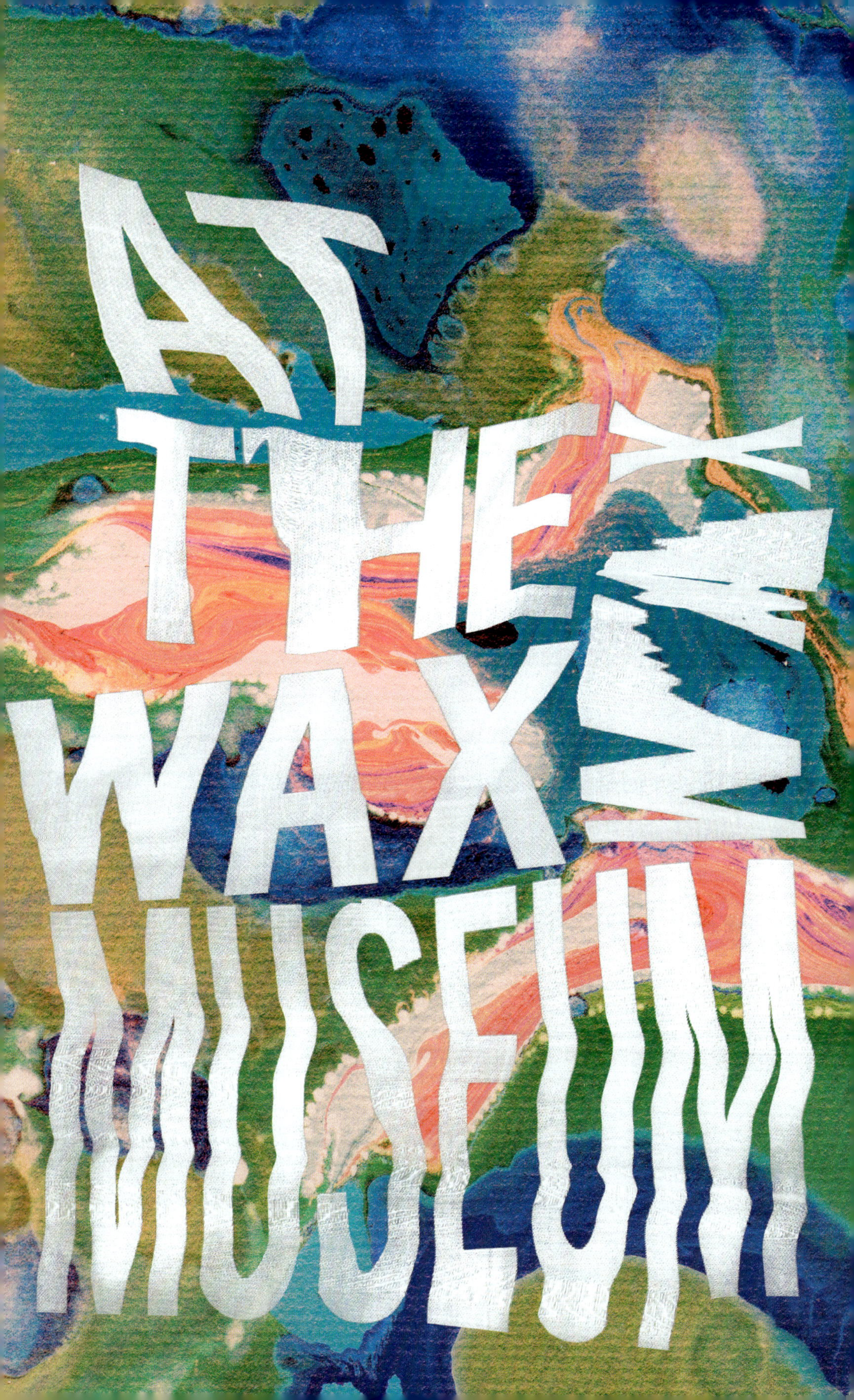
AT THE
WAX
MUSEUM

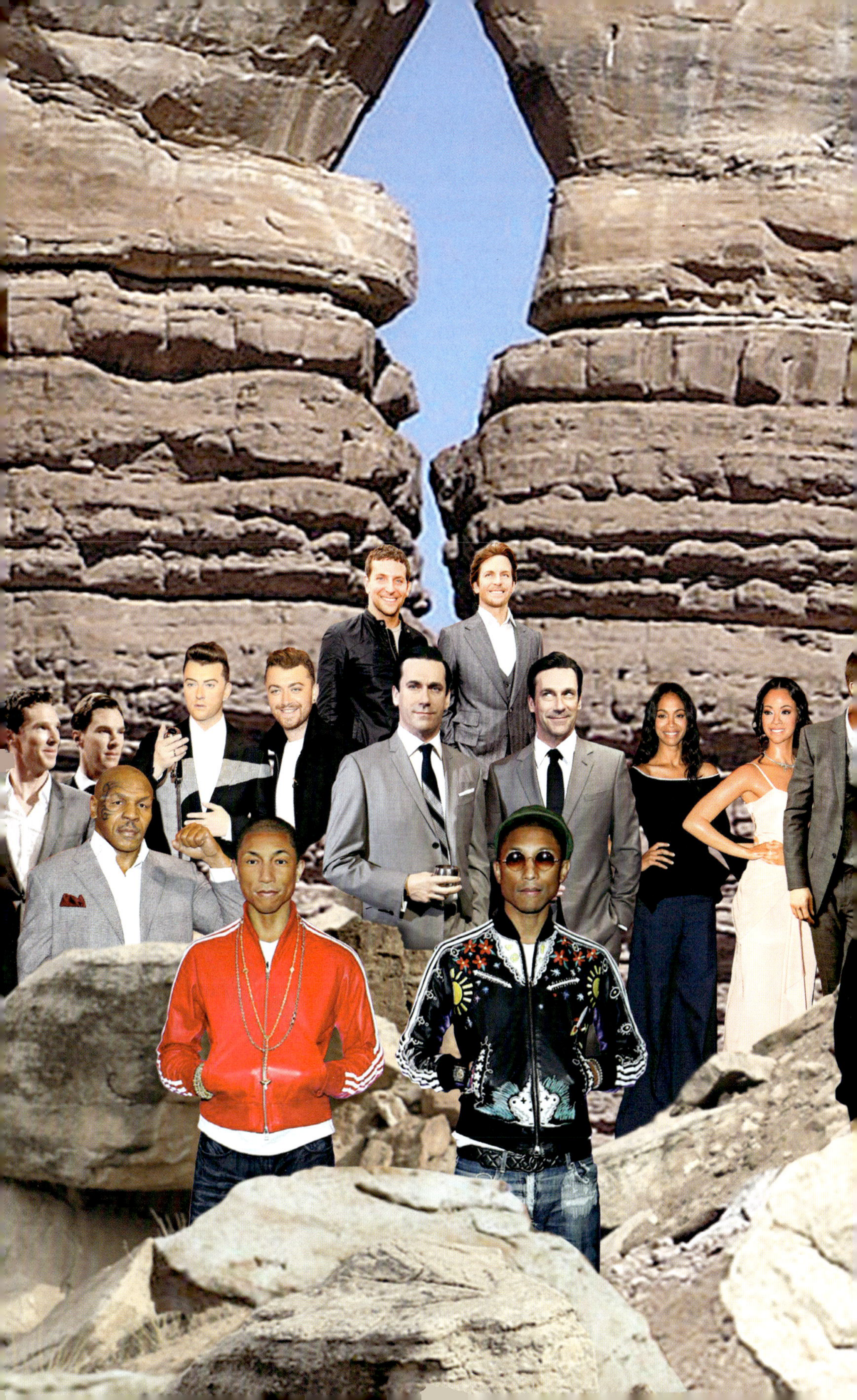

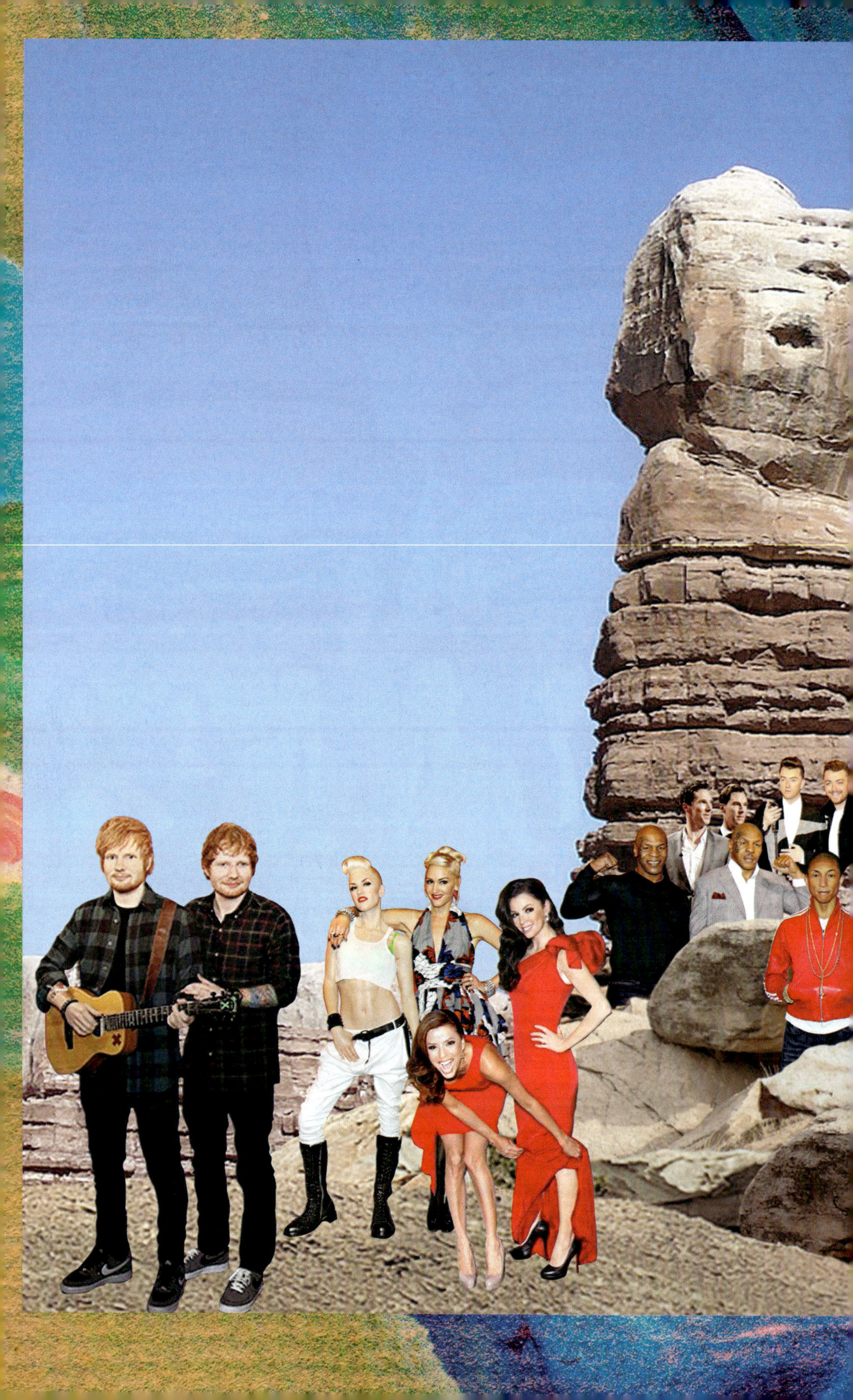

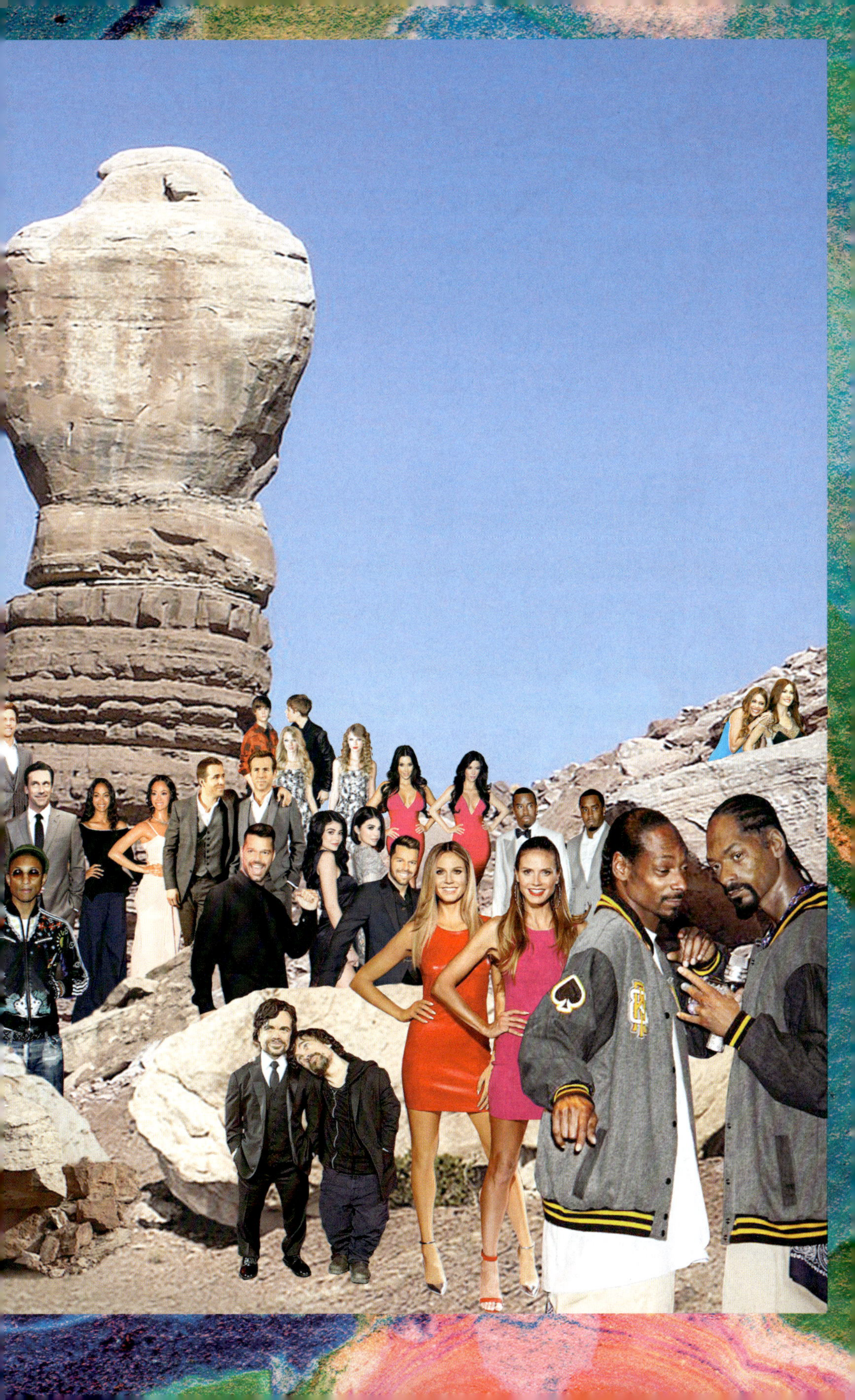

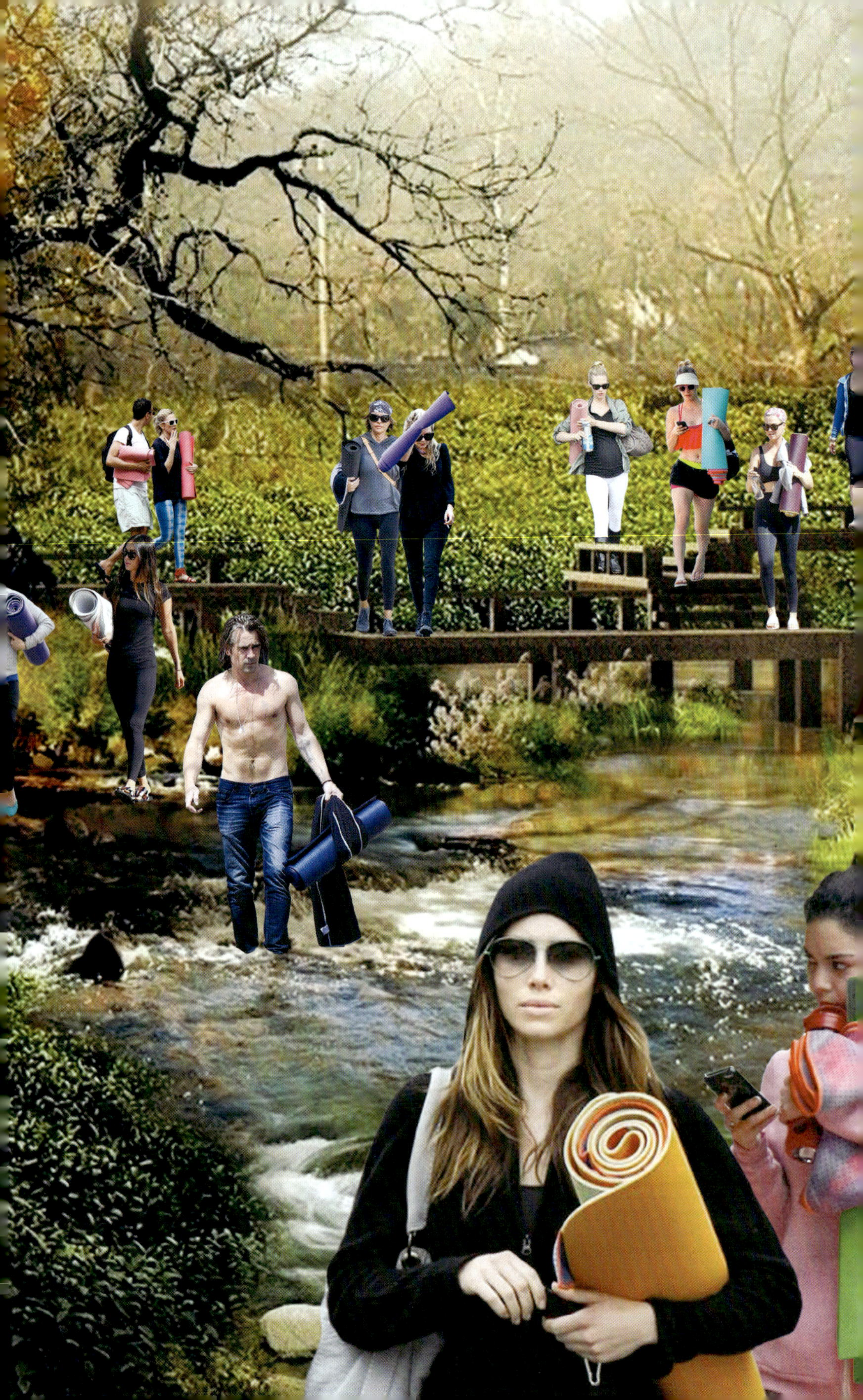

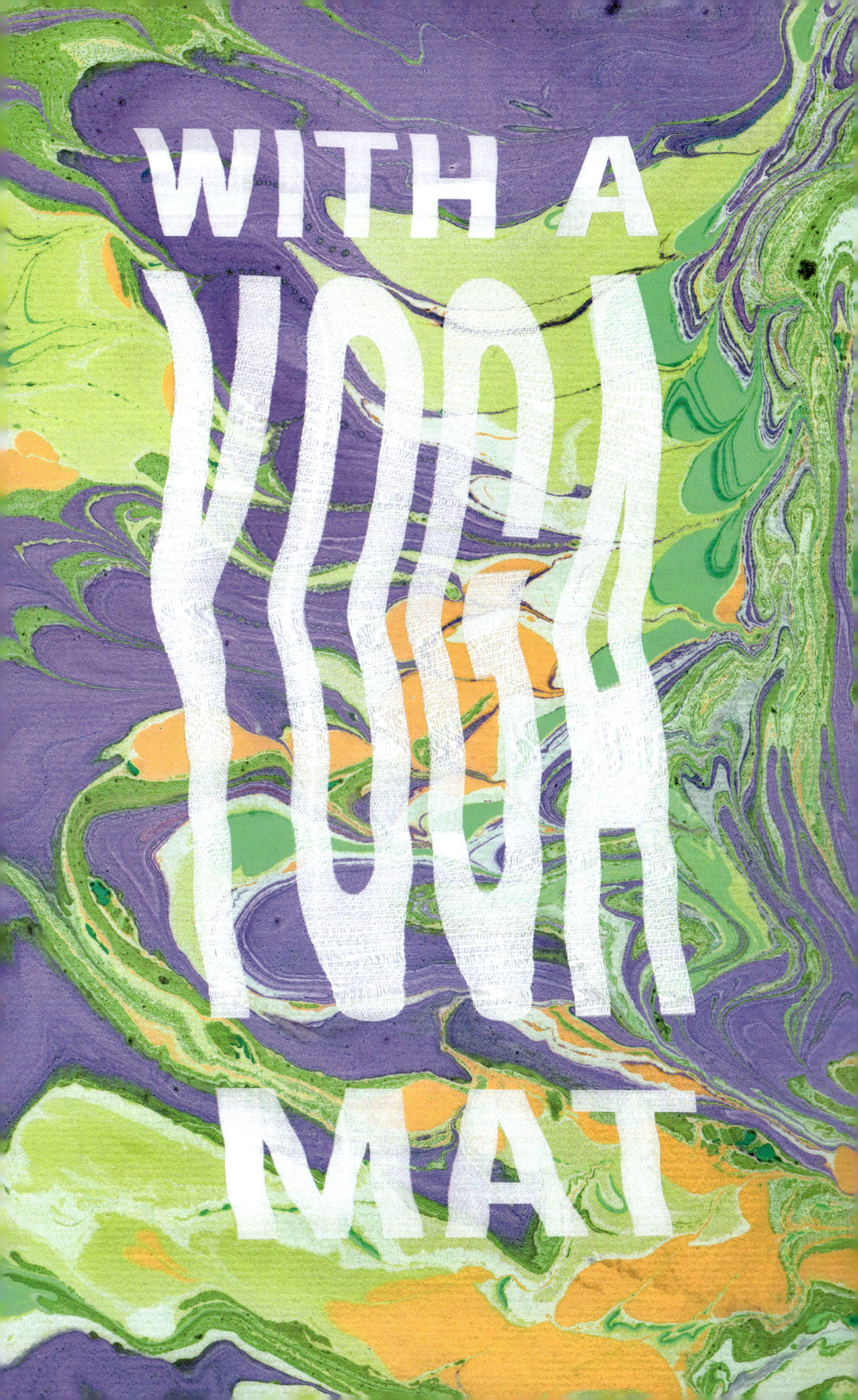
WITH A
YOGA
MAT

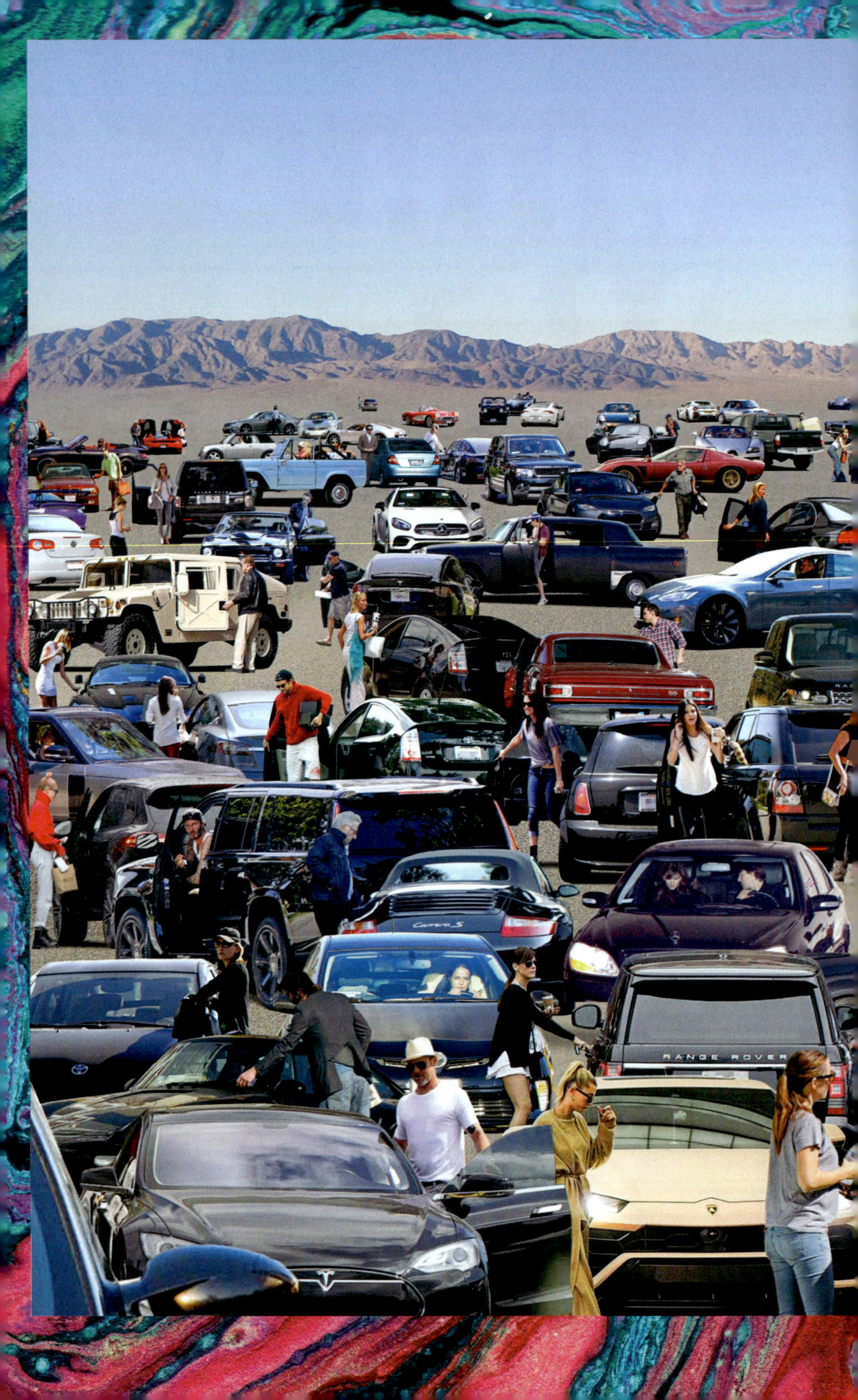
Carrera S
RANGE ROVER

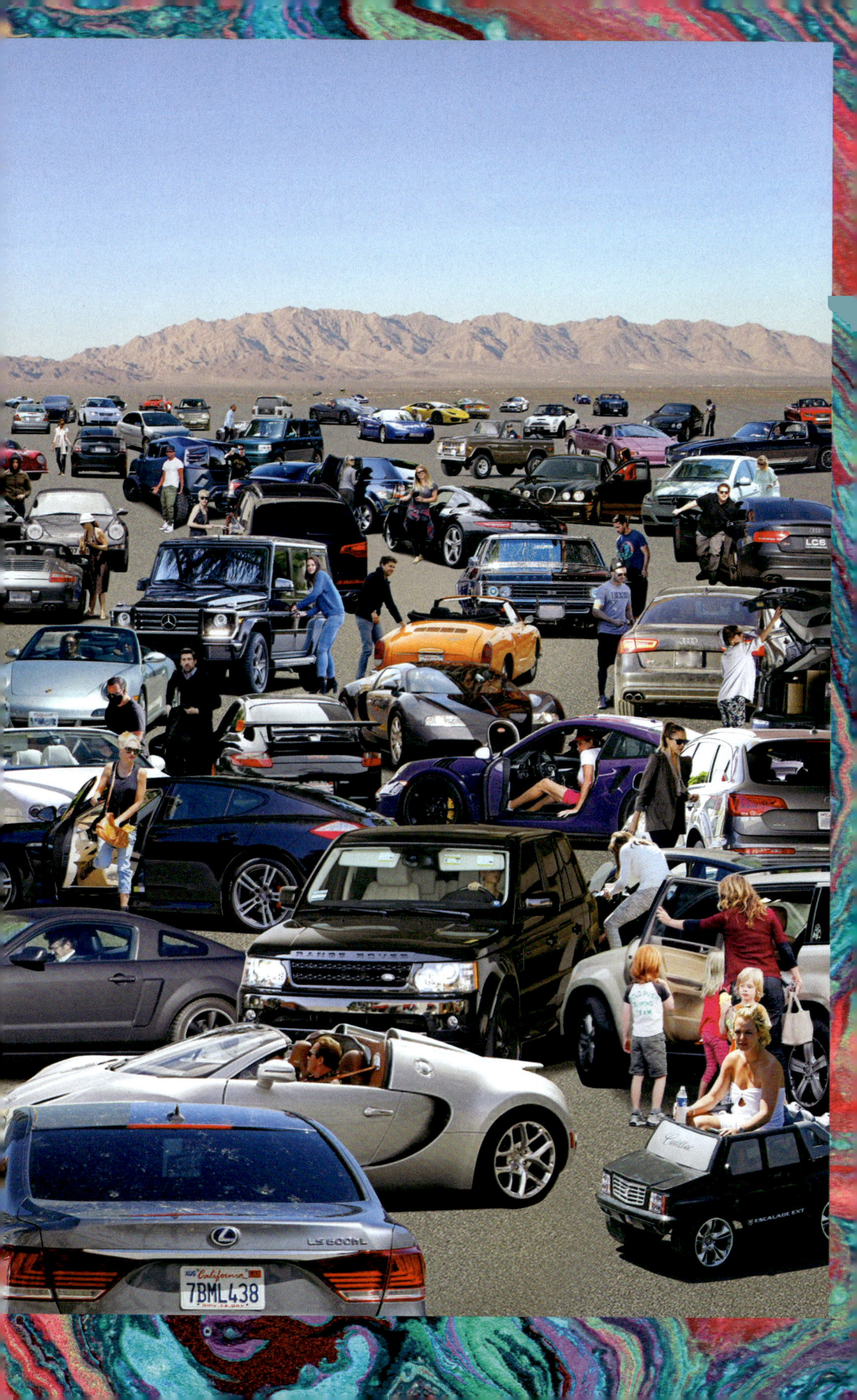
LS600hL
California
7BML438

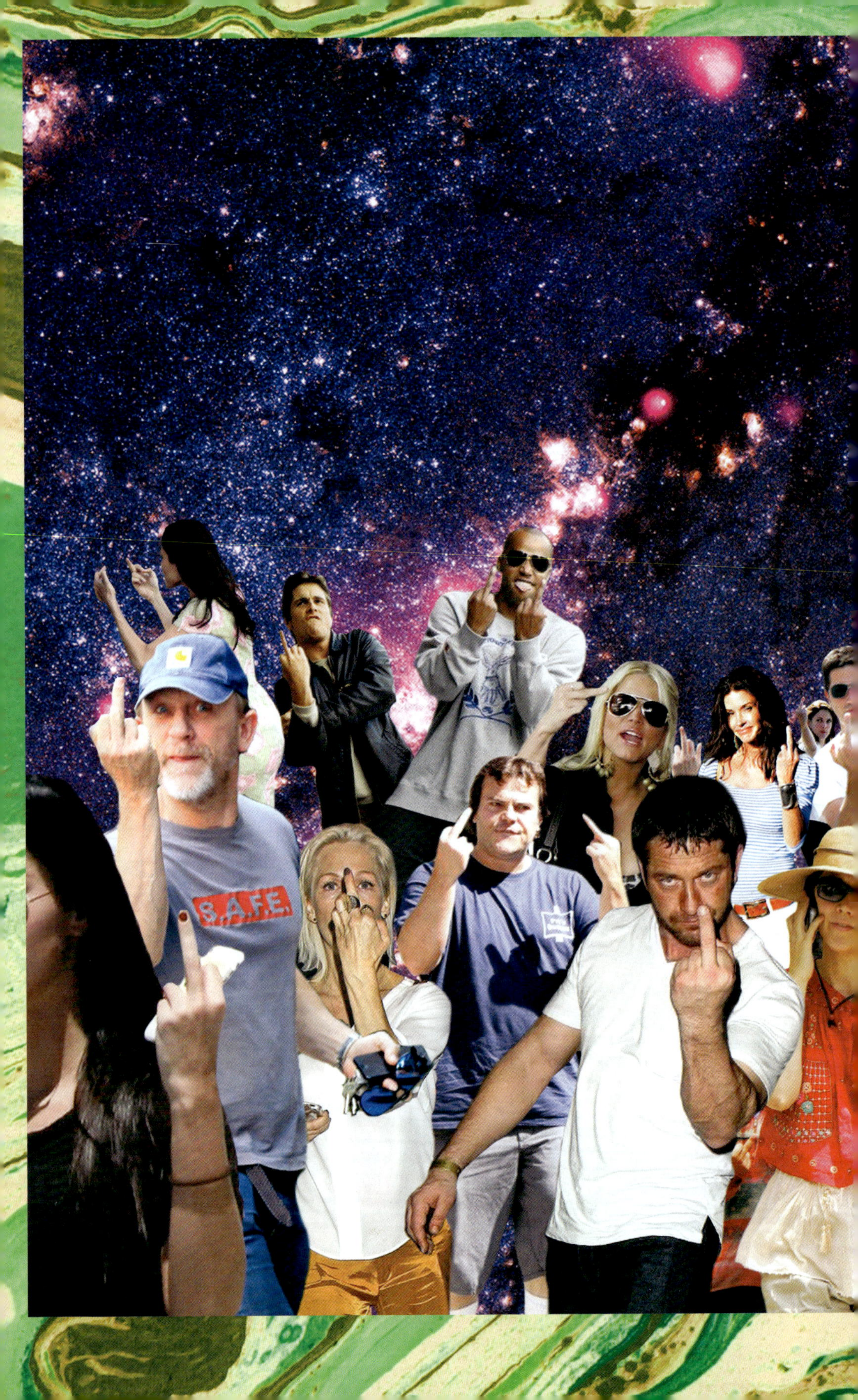
S.A.F.E.

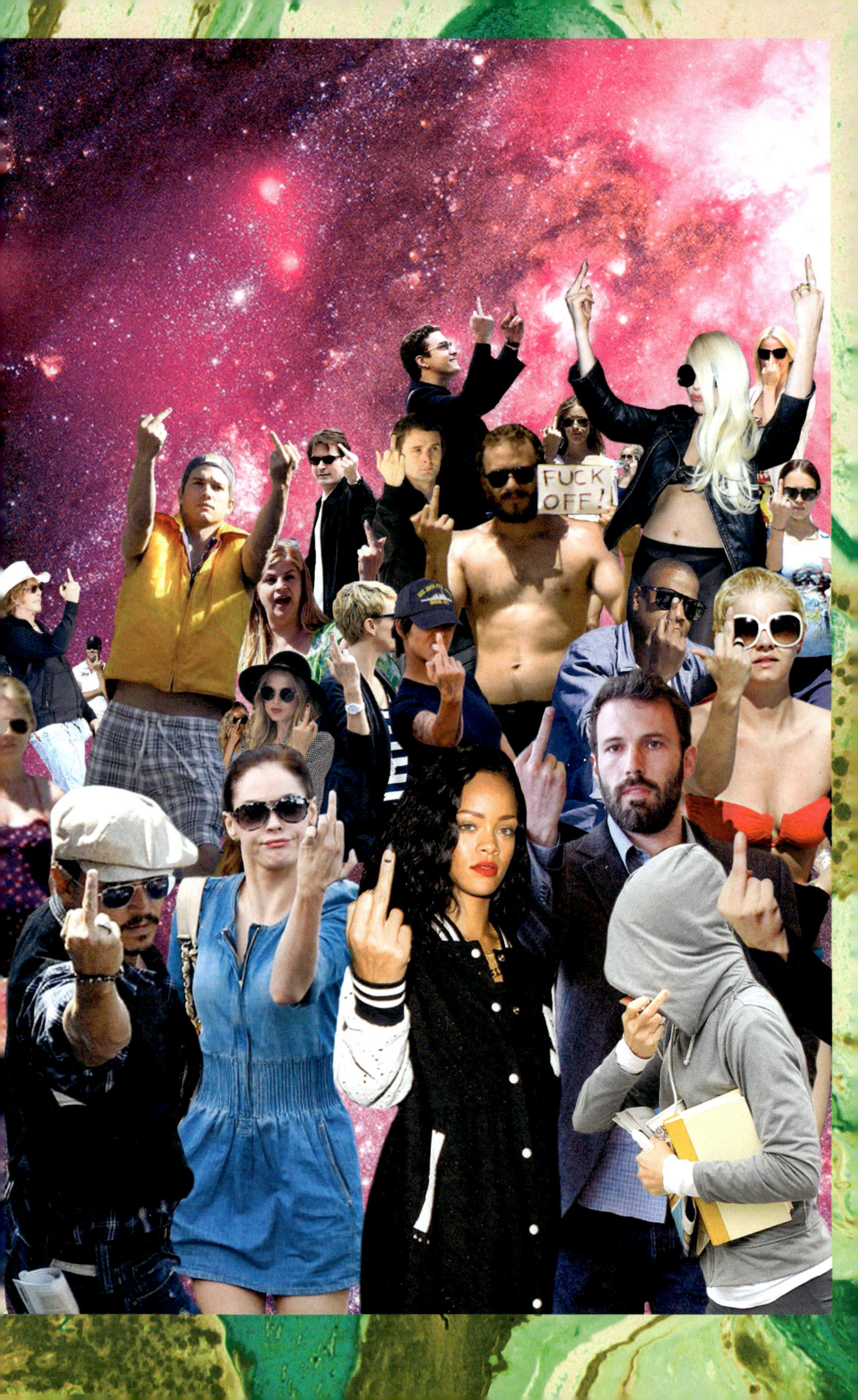
FUCK
OFF!

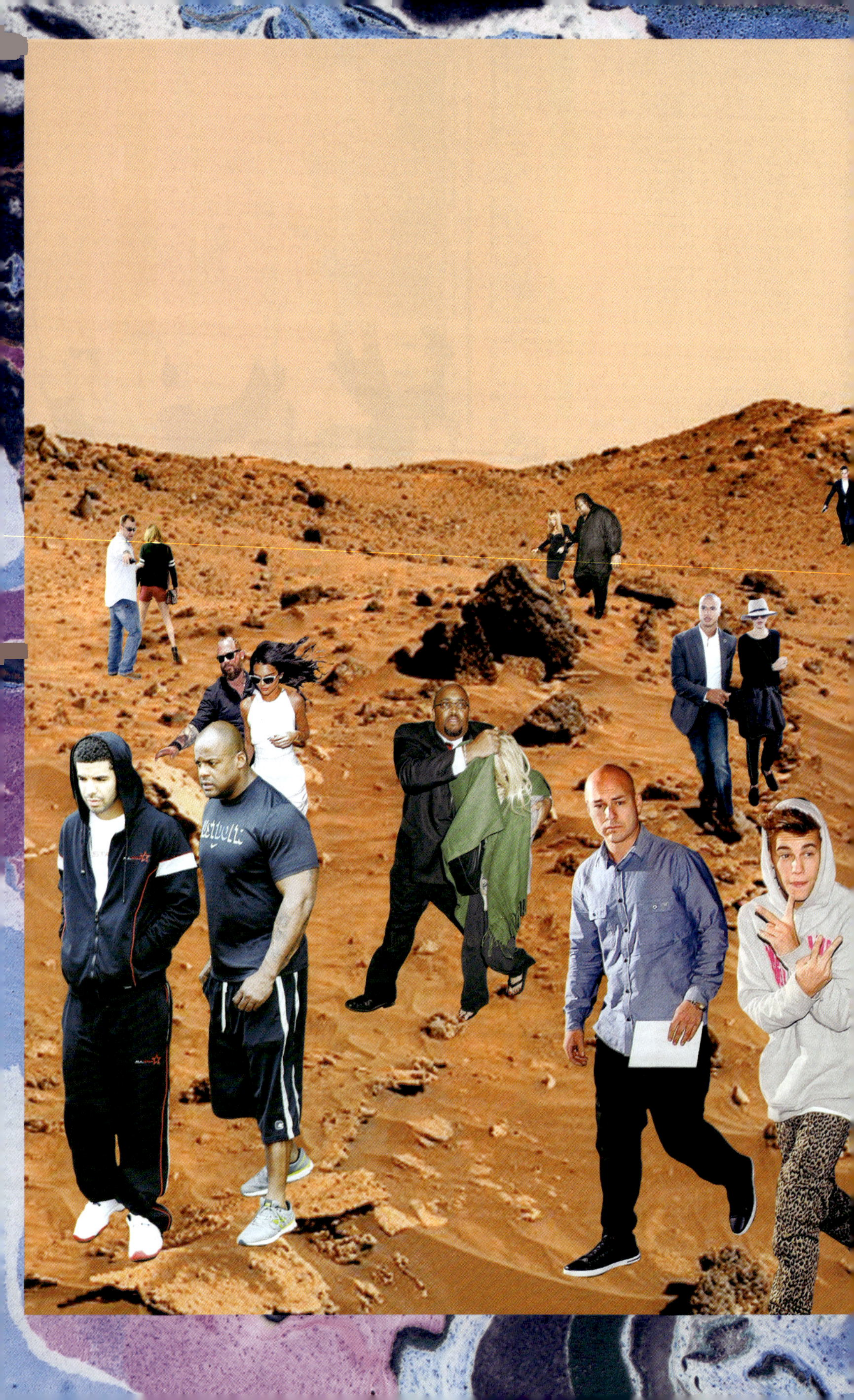

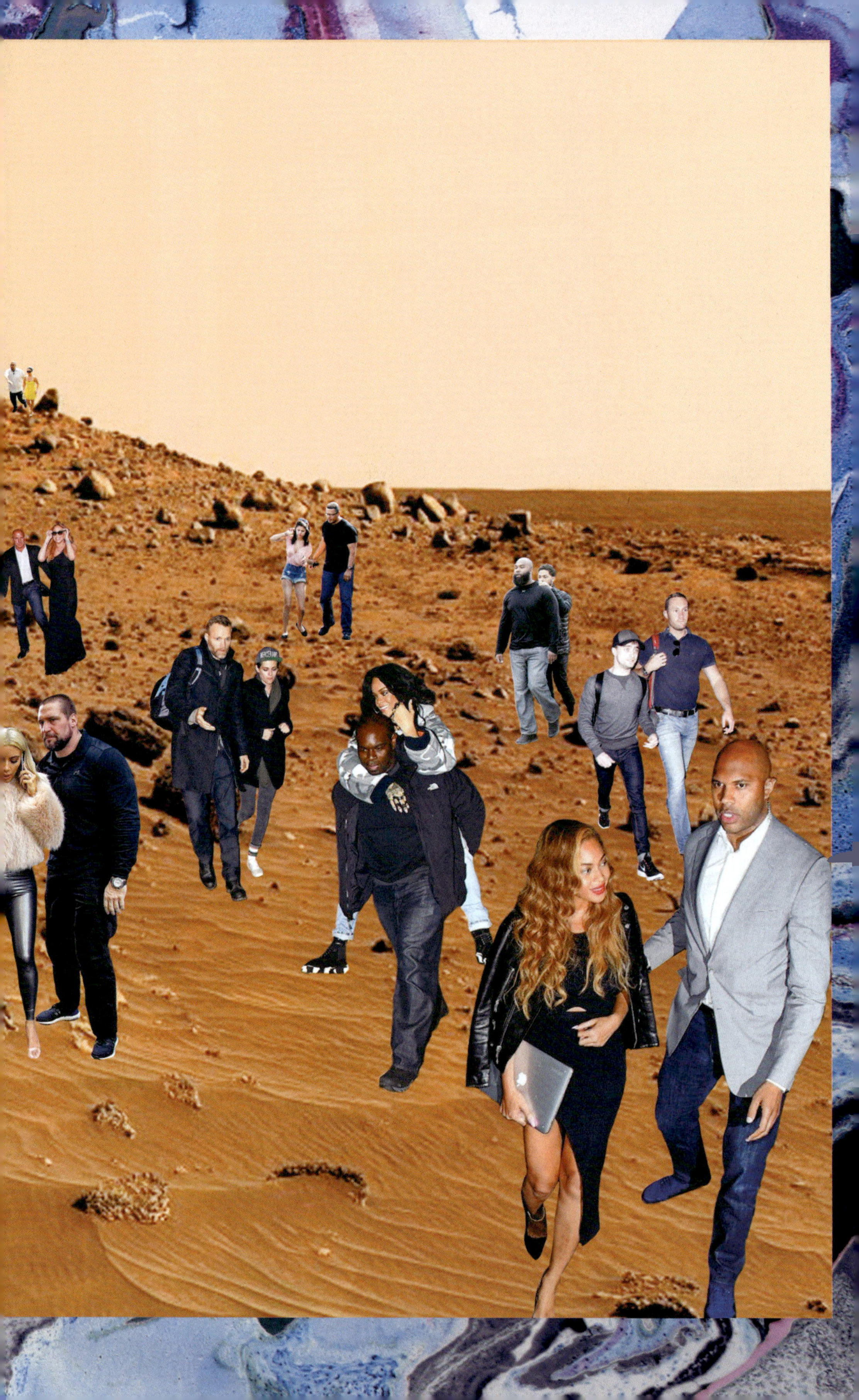

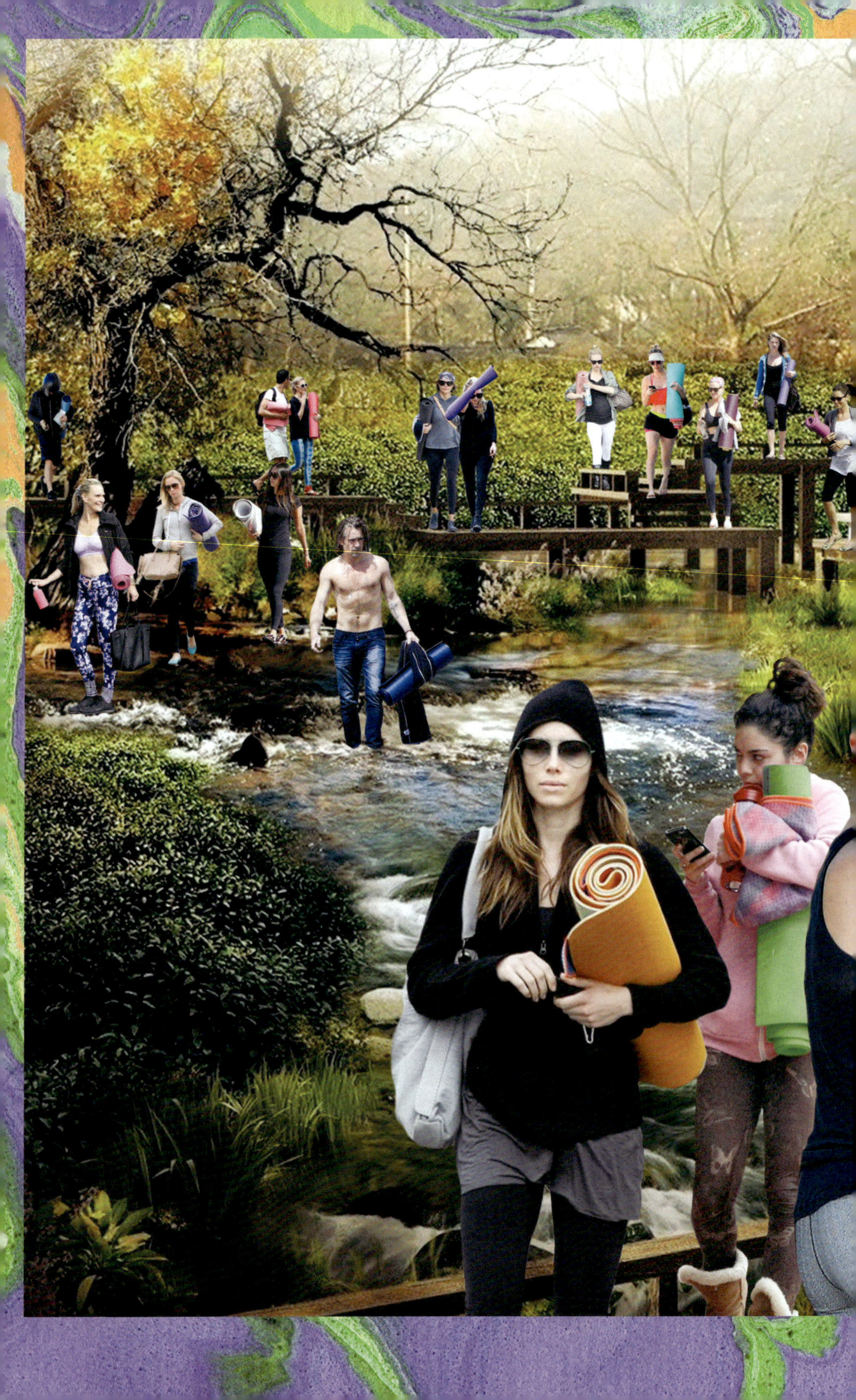

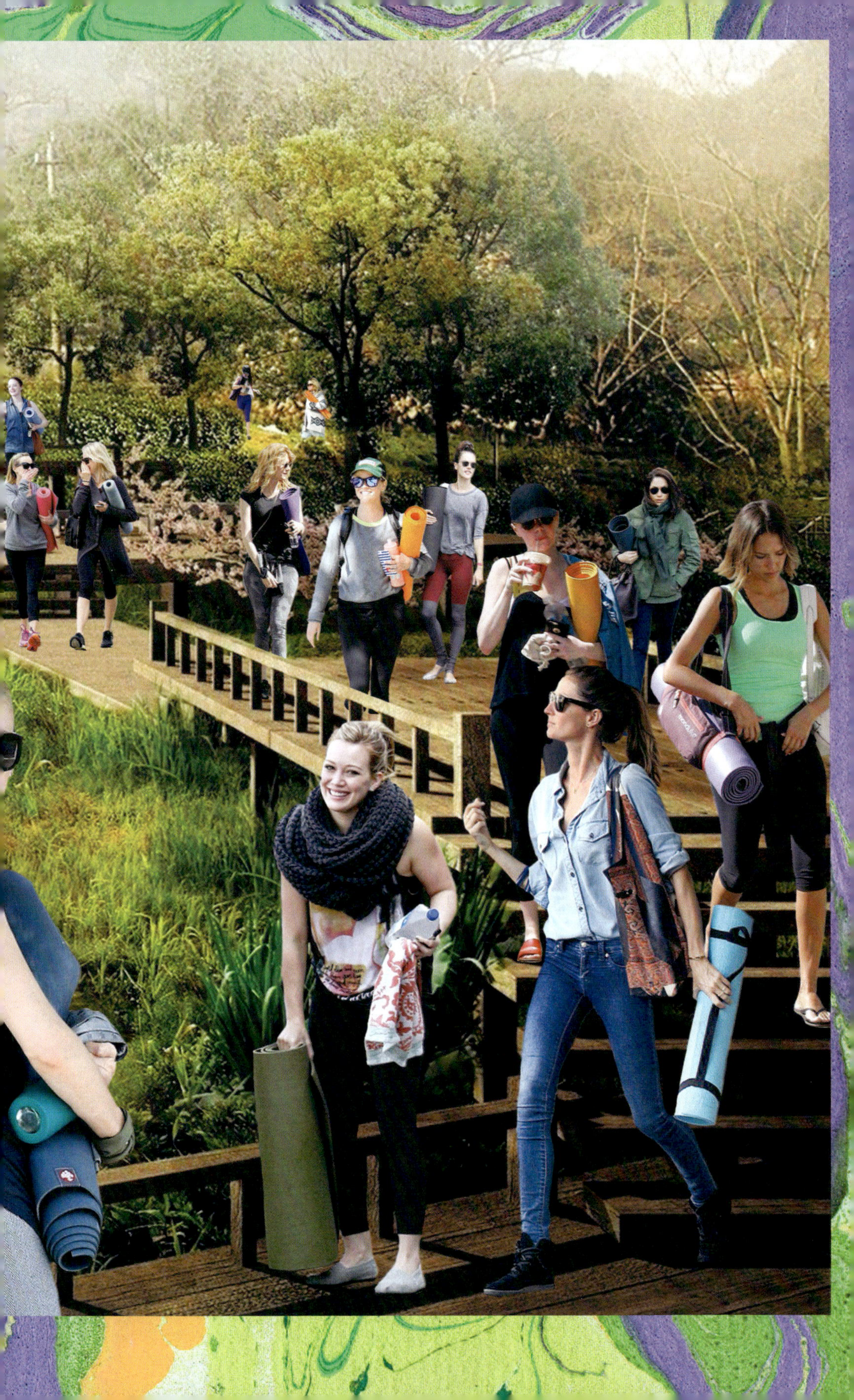

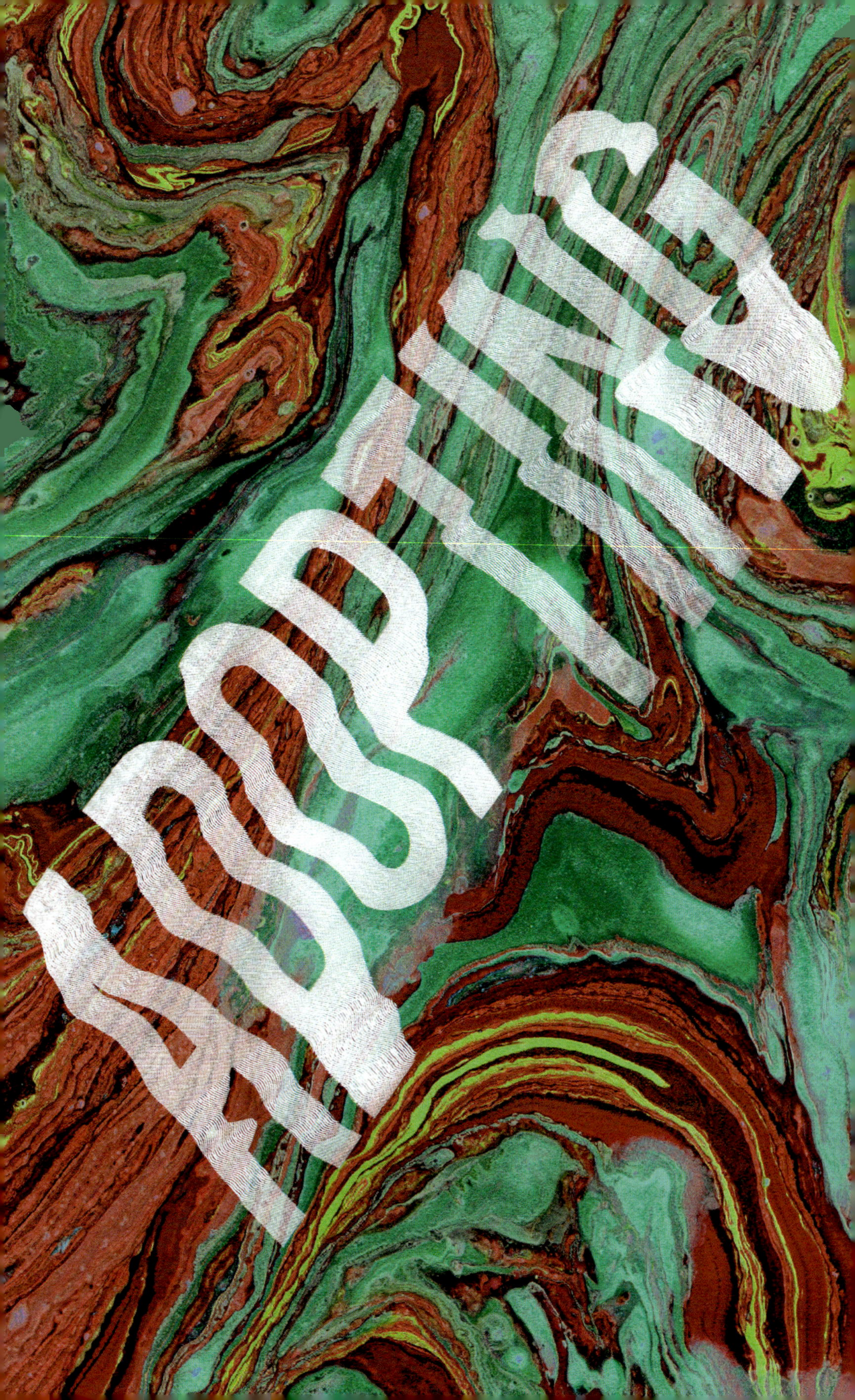
ADOPTING

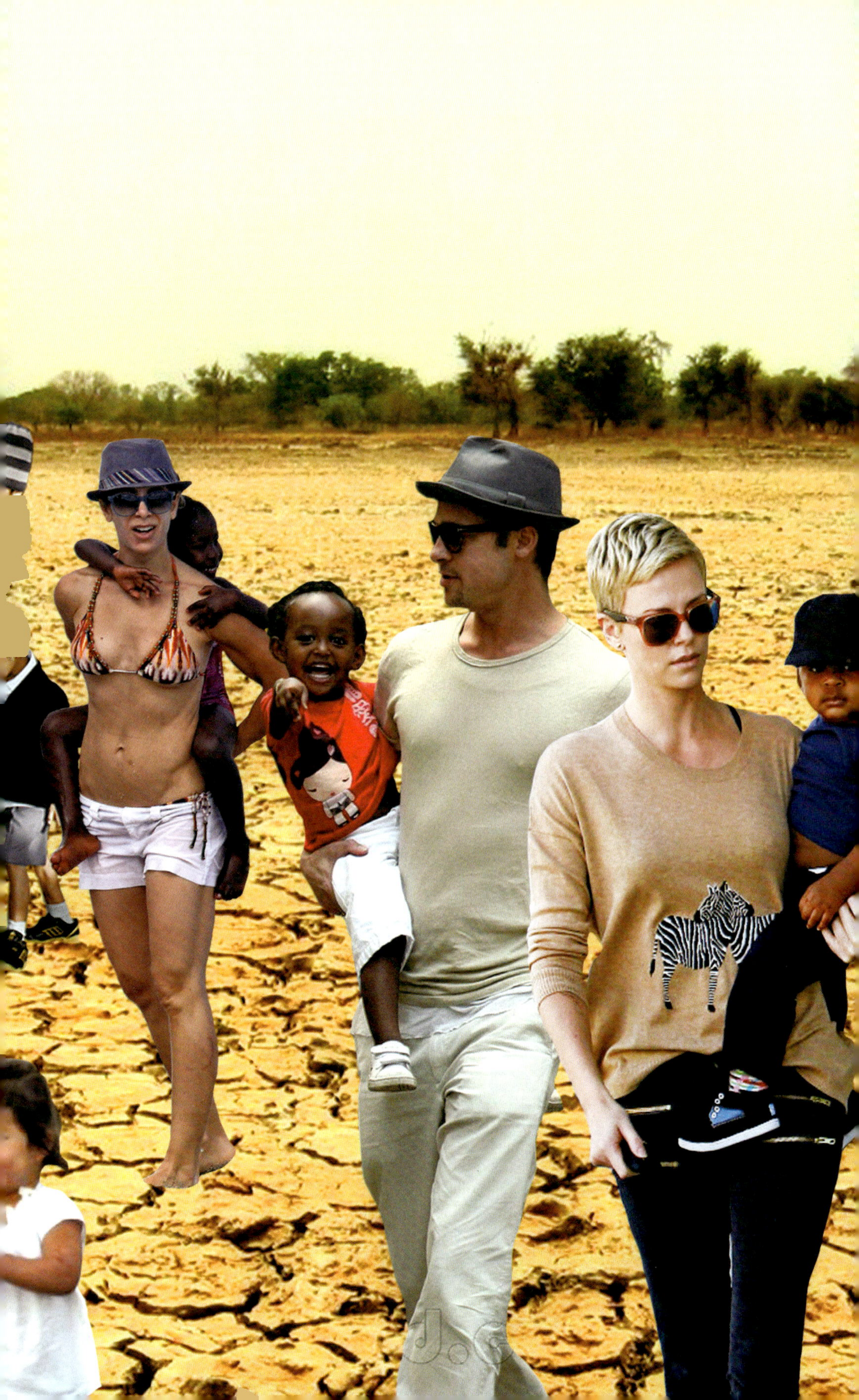

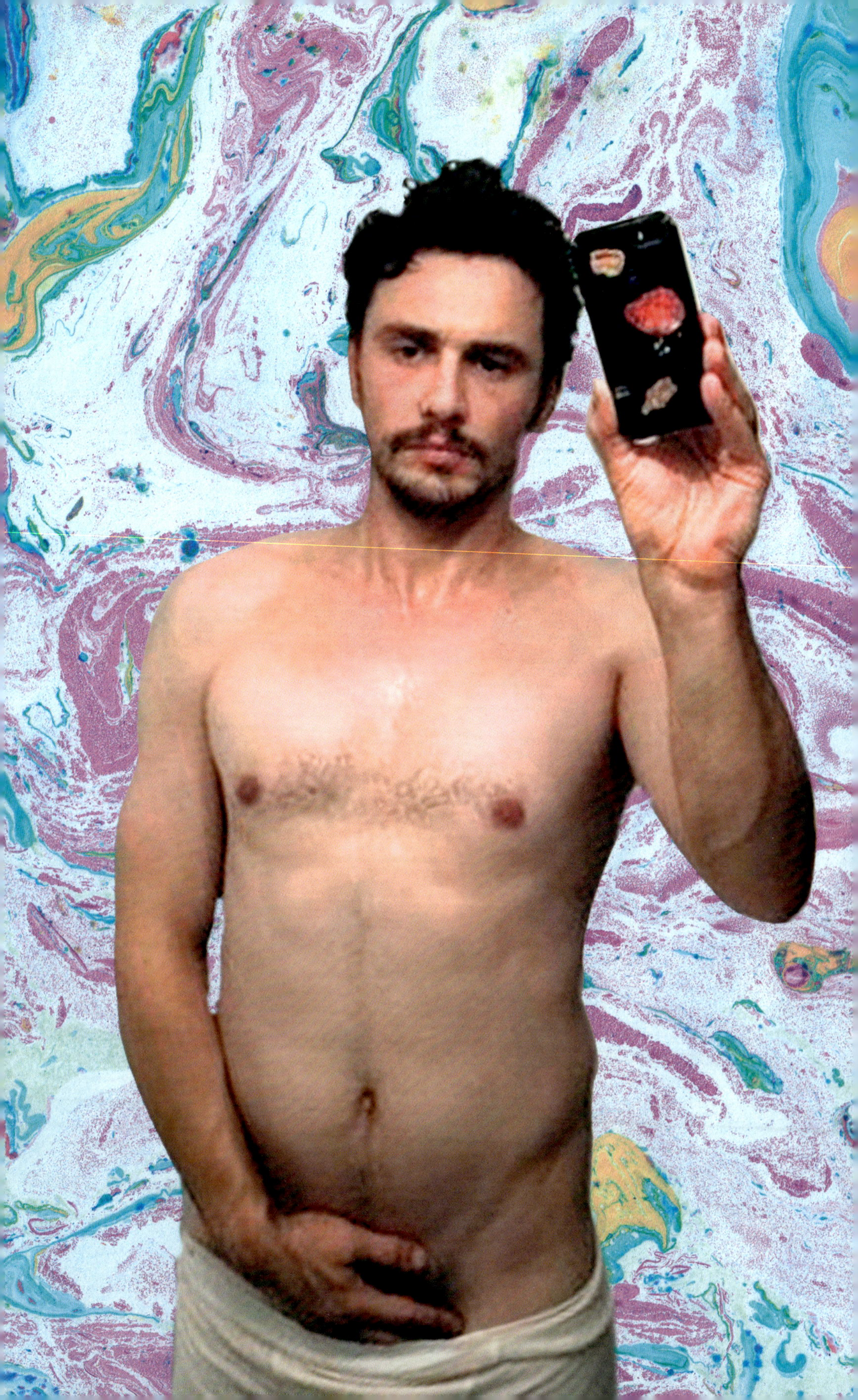

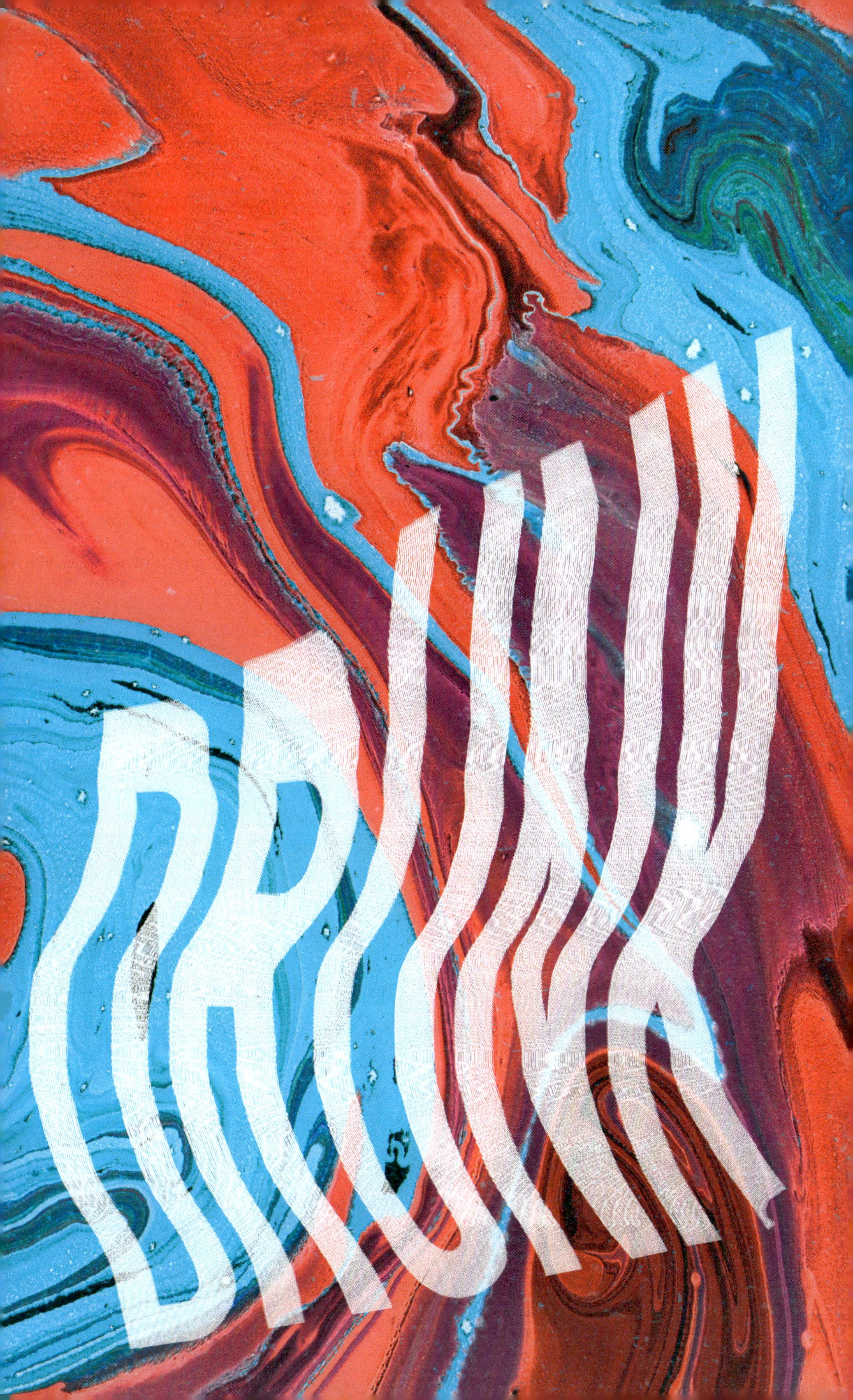
DRUNK

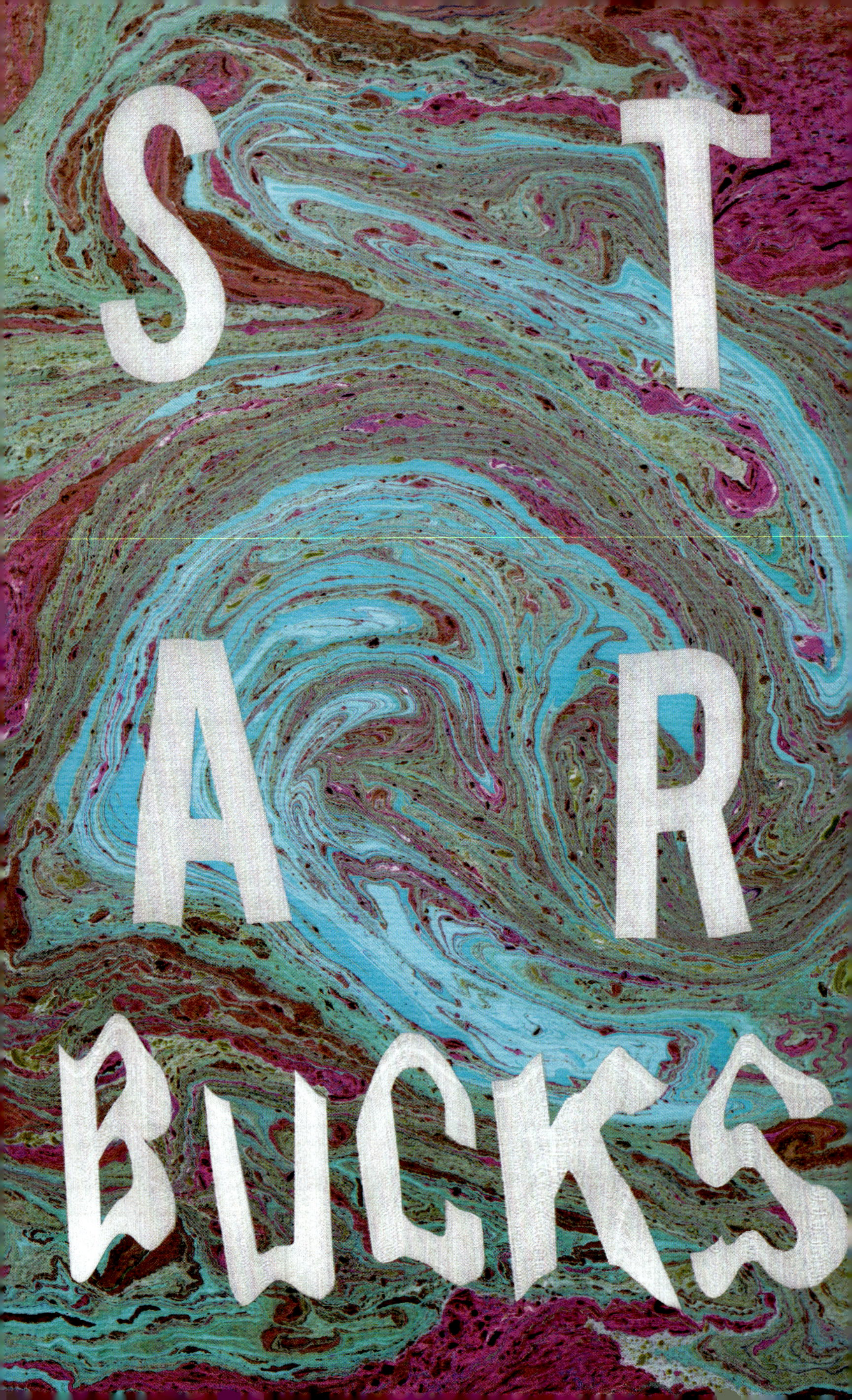
S T
A R
BUCKS

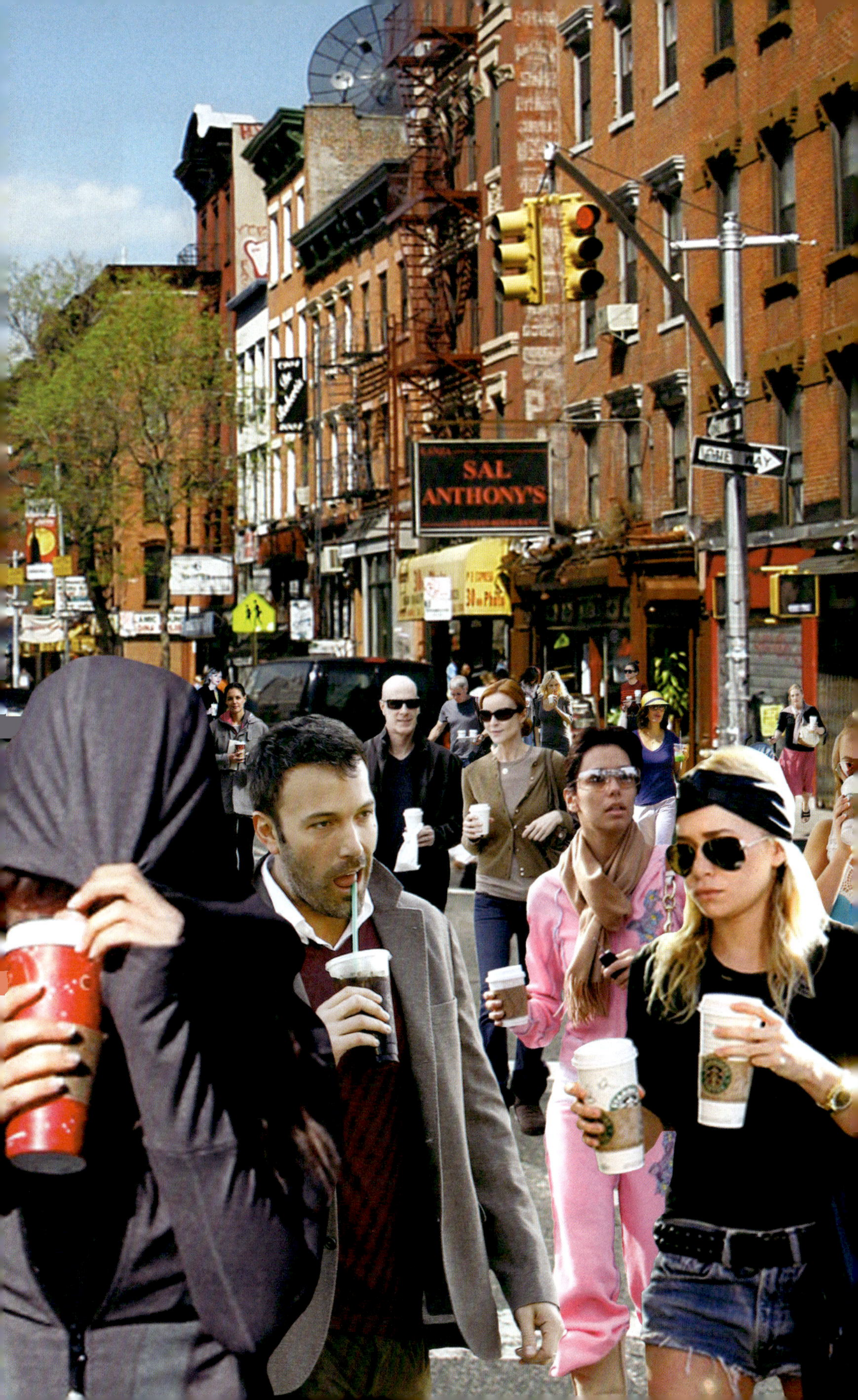
SAL
ANTHONY'S

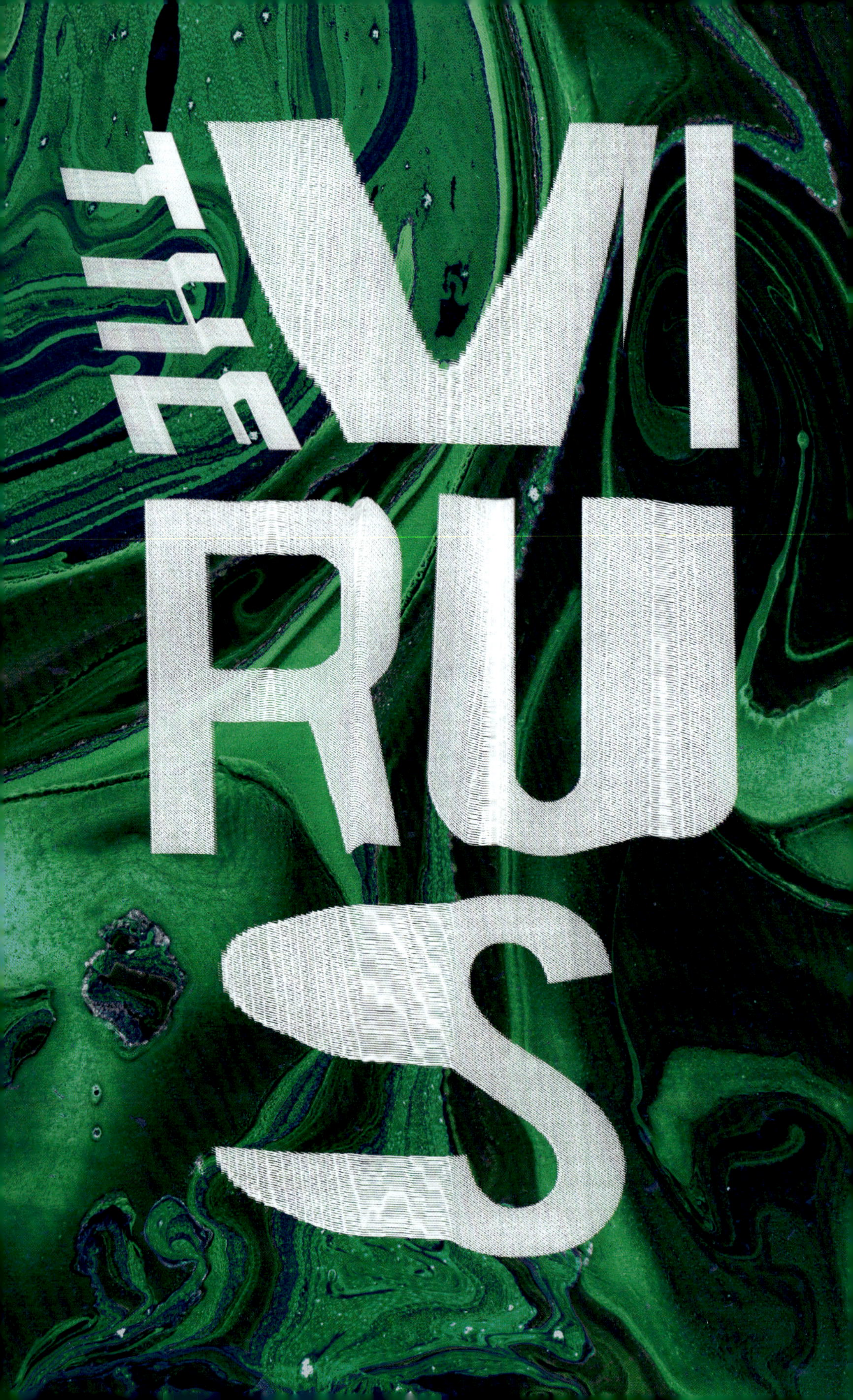
THE
VI
RU
S

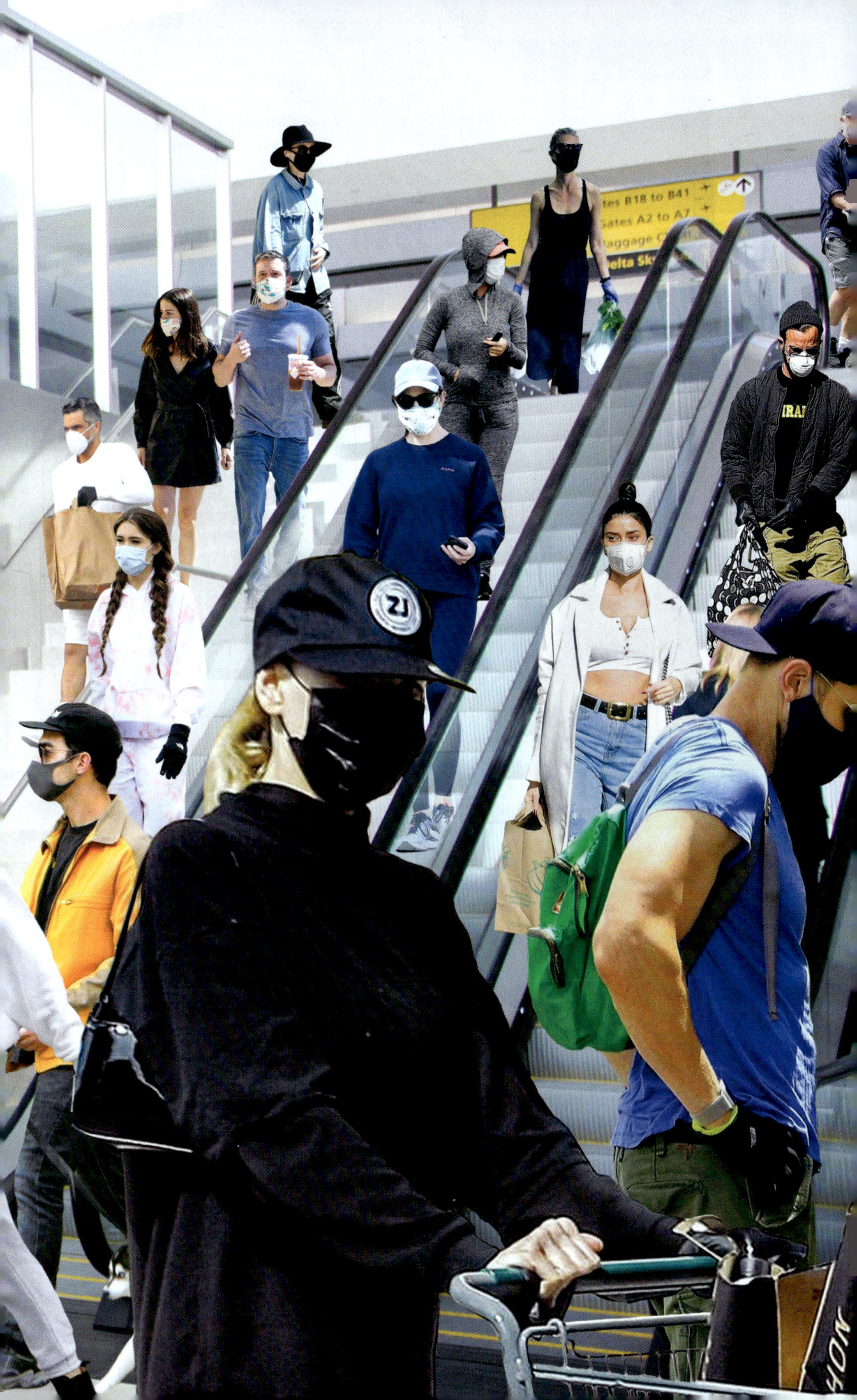
tes B18 to B41
Gates A2 to A7

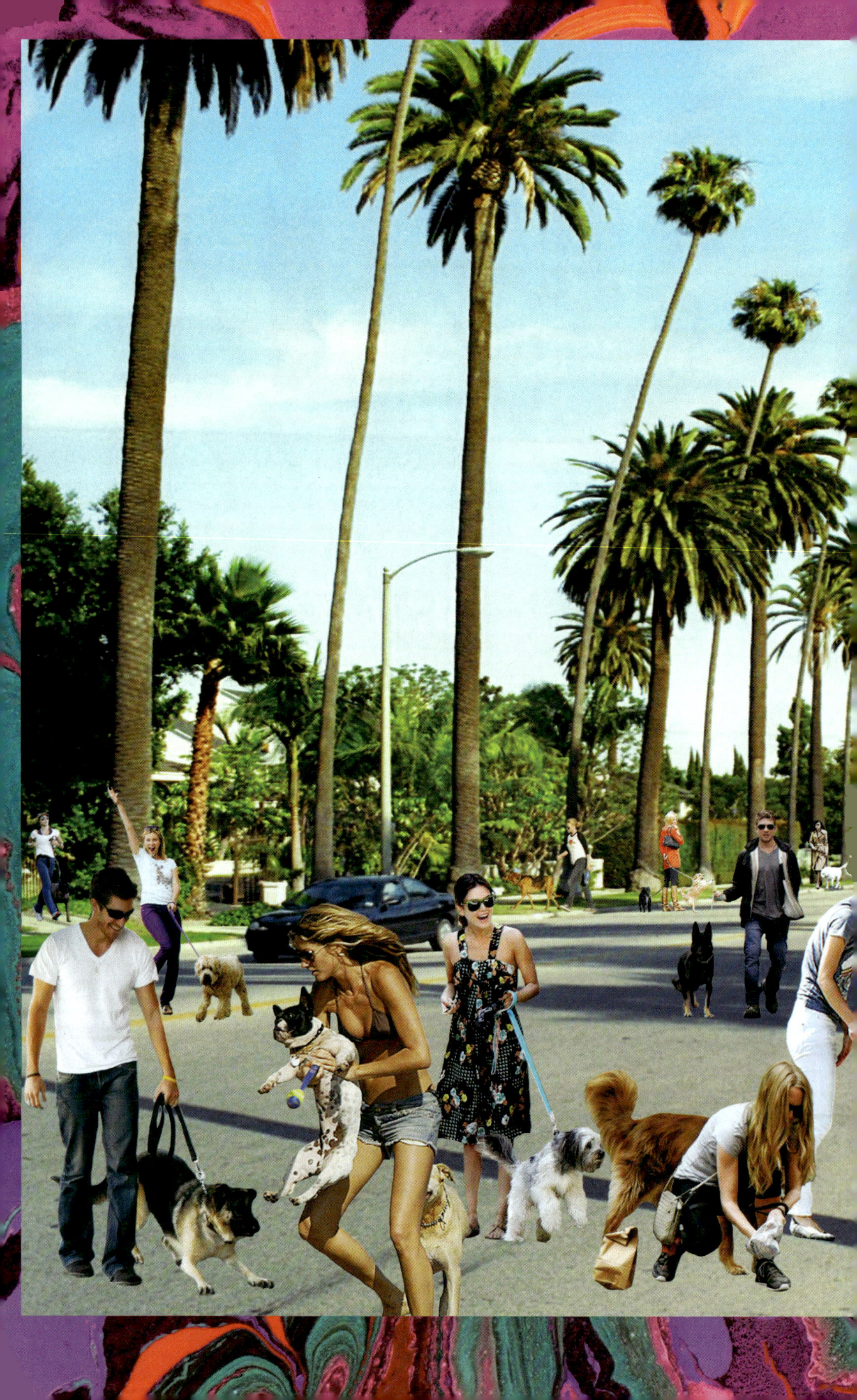

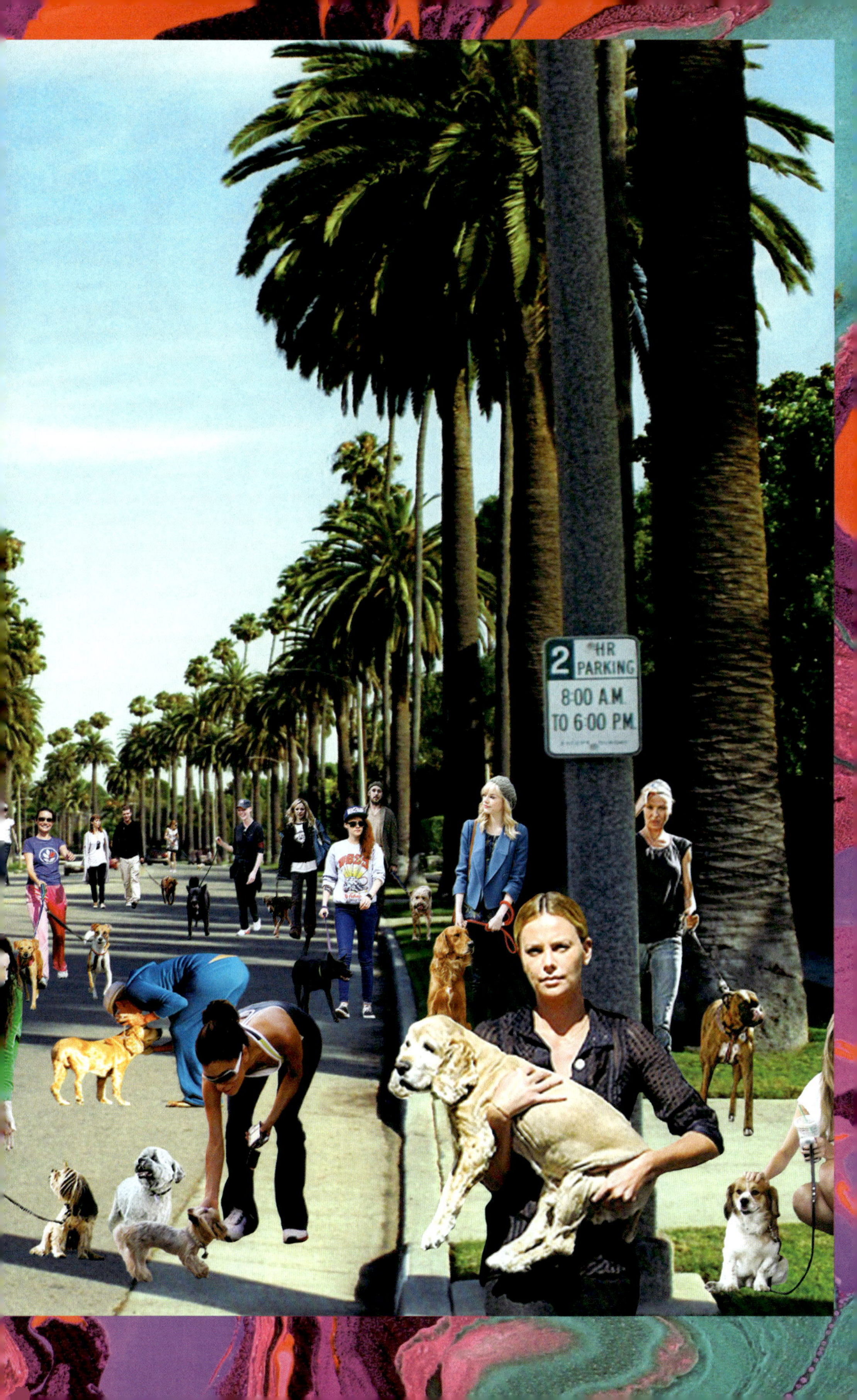
2 HR PARKING
8:00 A.M.
TO 6:00 P.M.

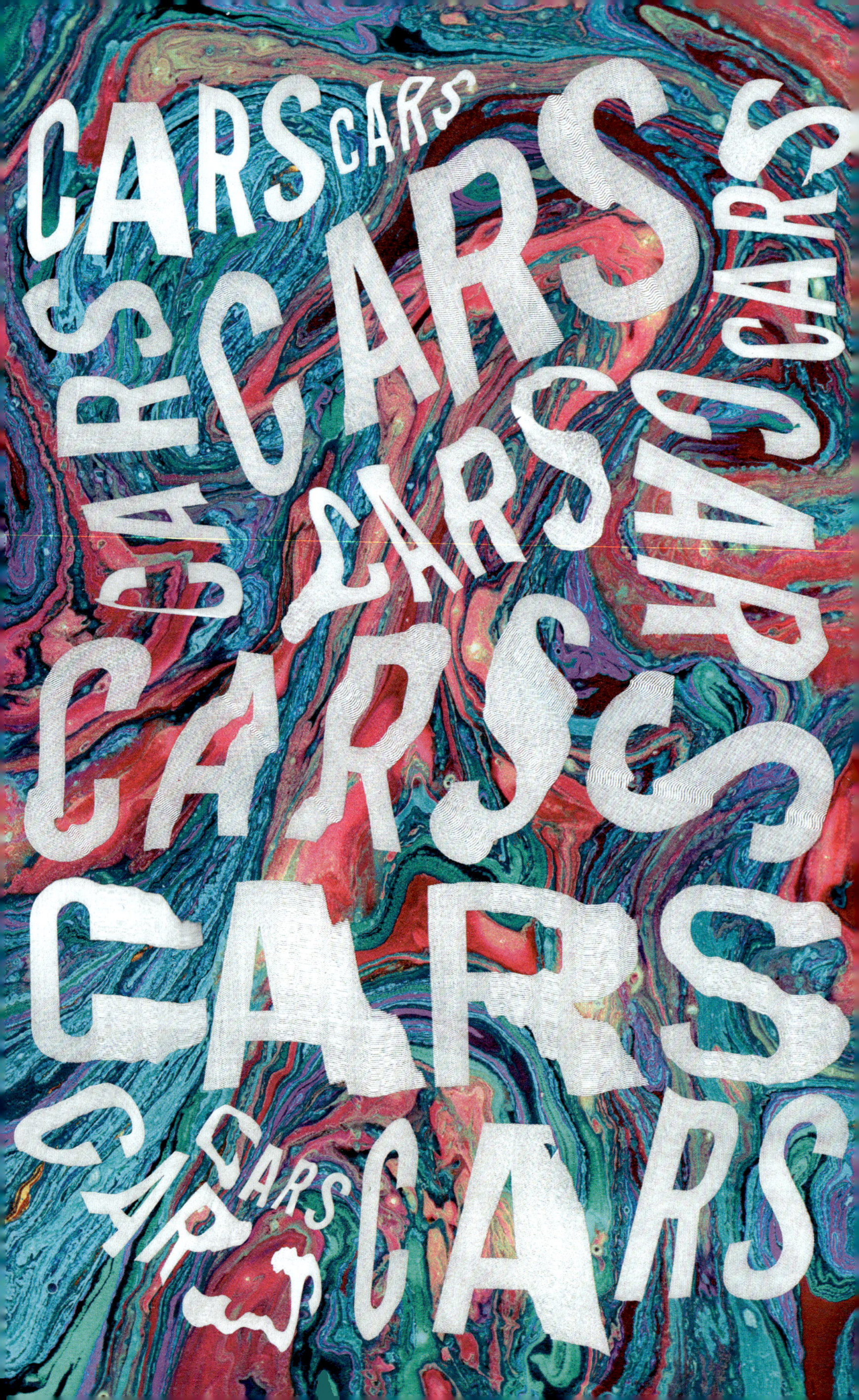
CARS
CARS
CARS
CARS
CARS
CARS
CARS
CARS
CARS
CARS

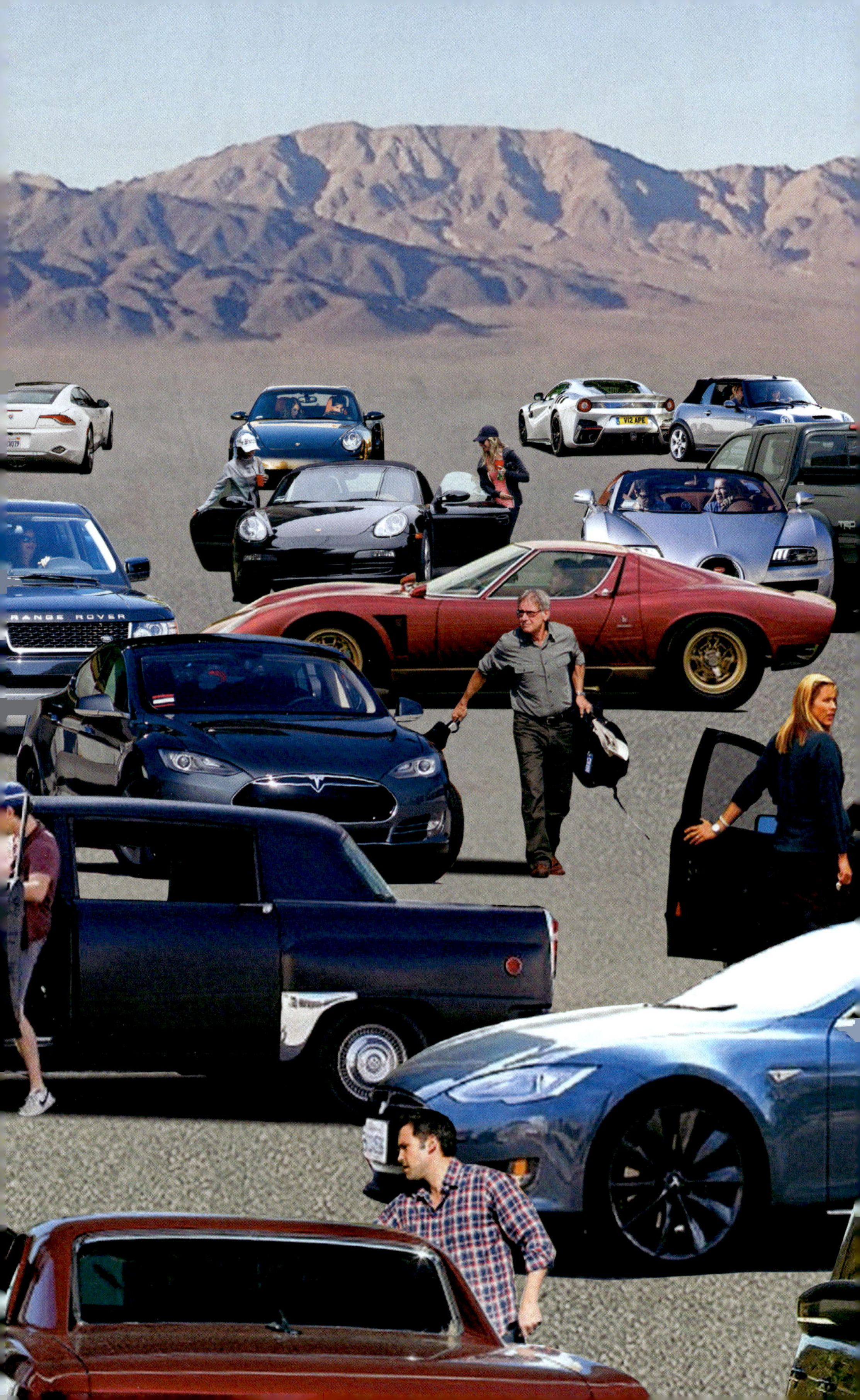
V12 APE
RANGE ROVER

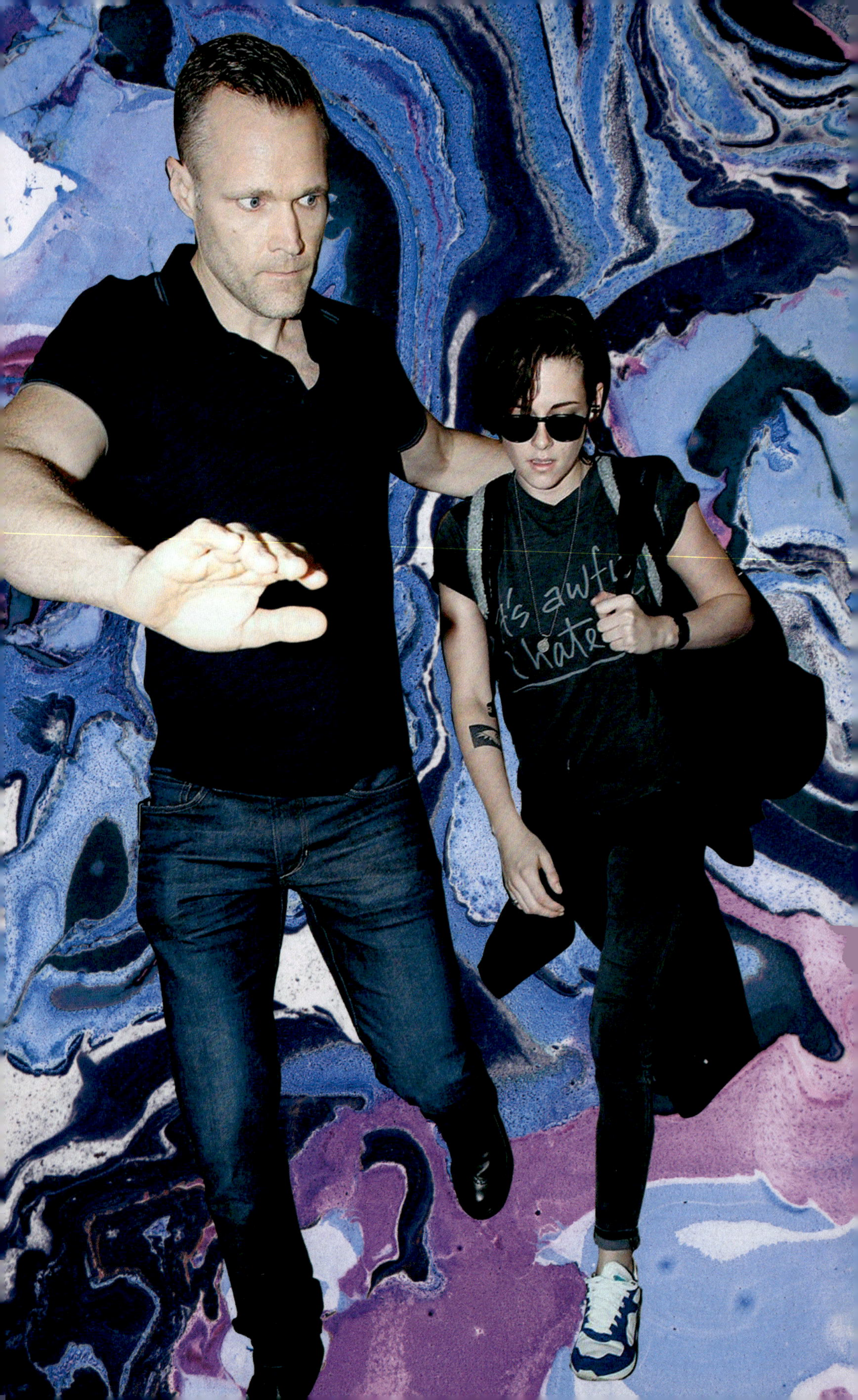

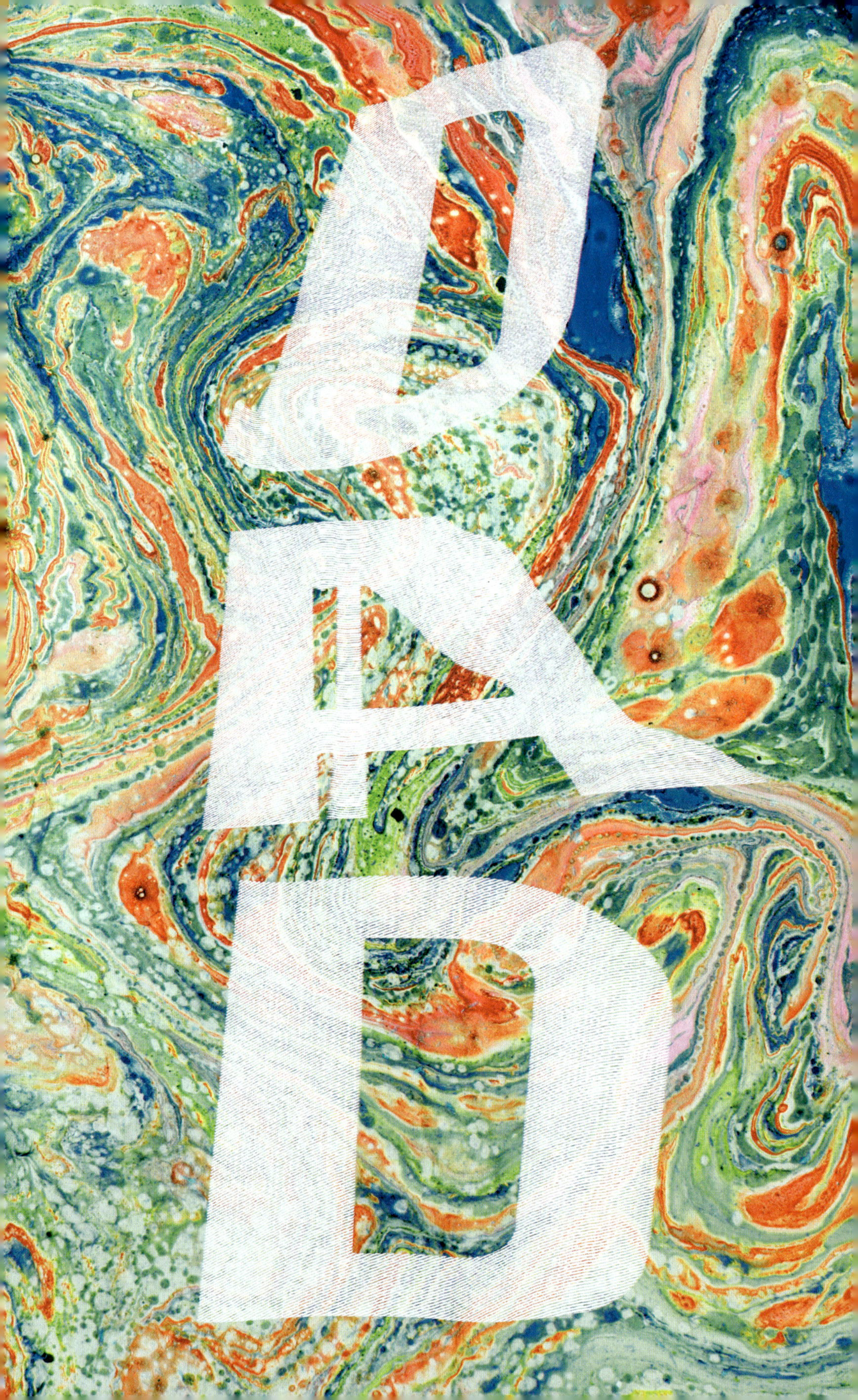
DAD

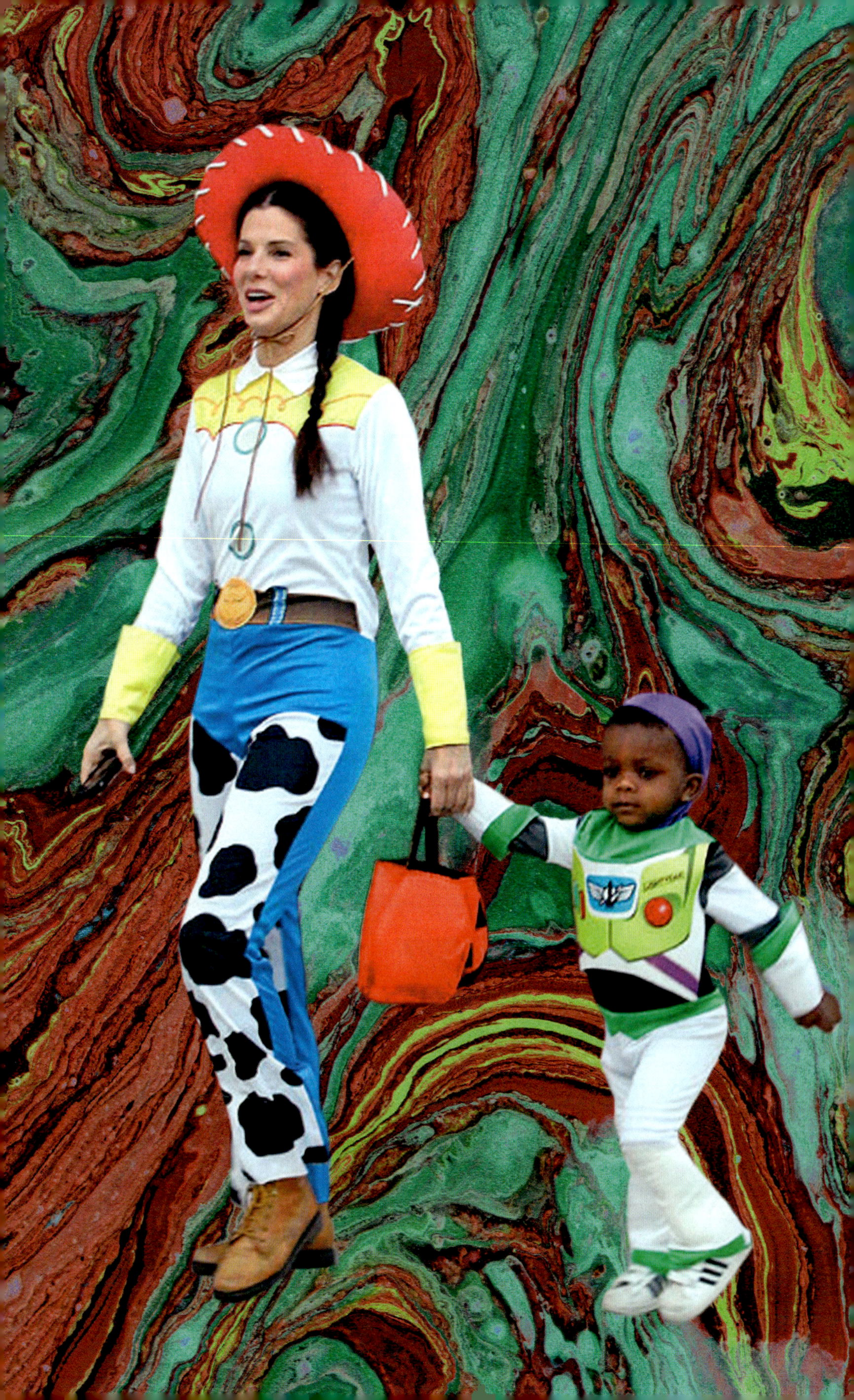

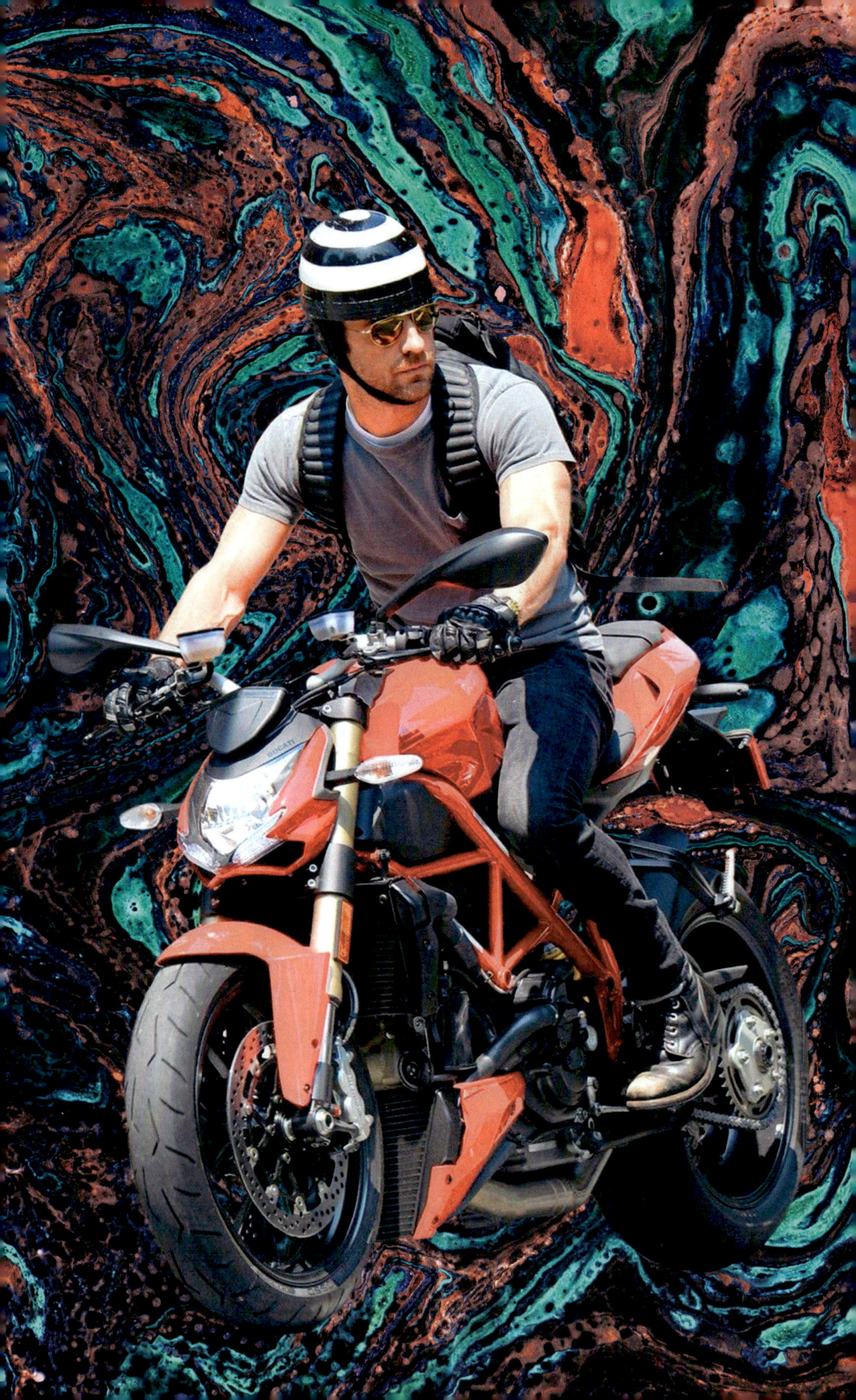

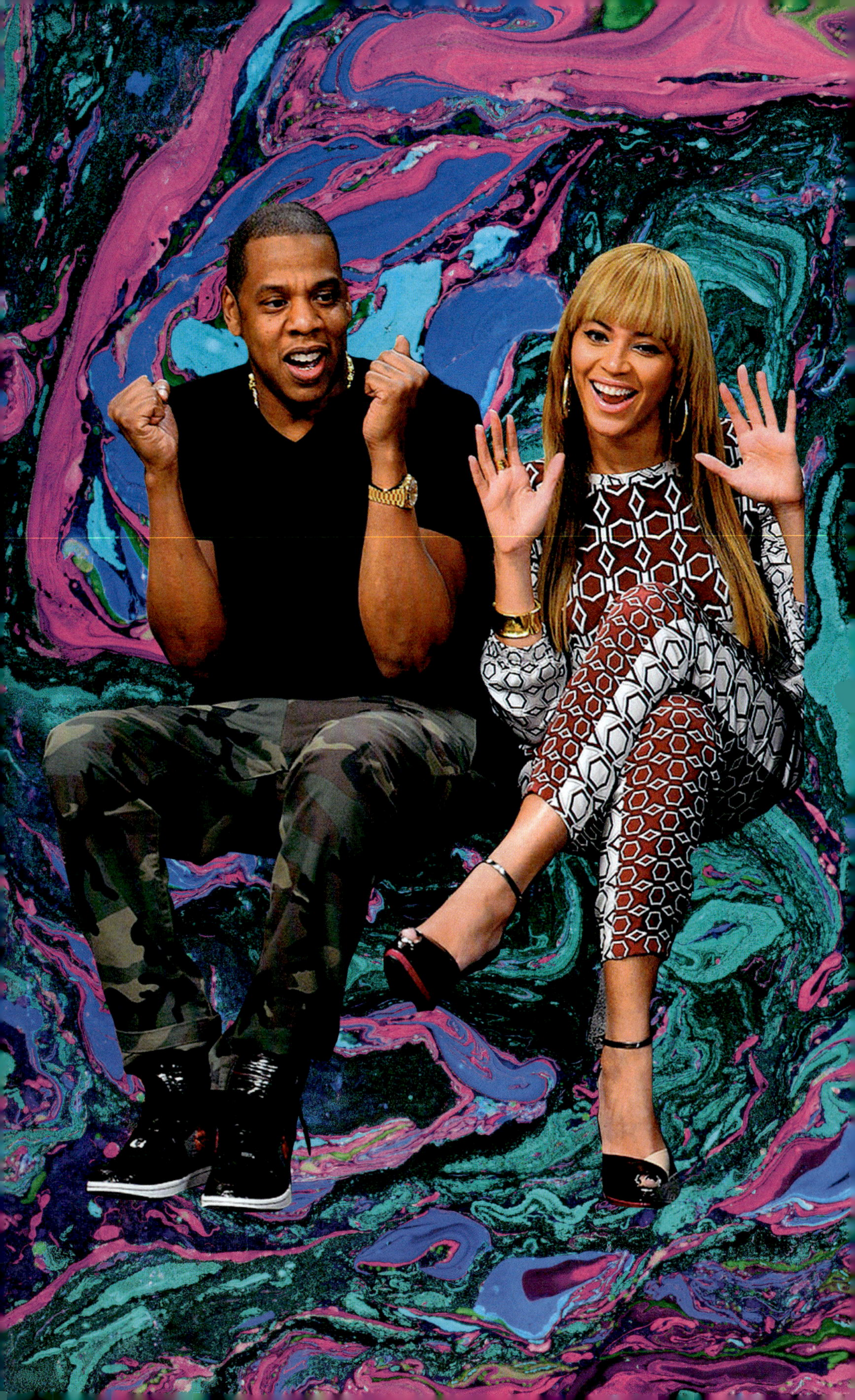

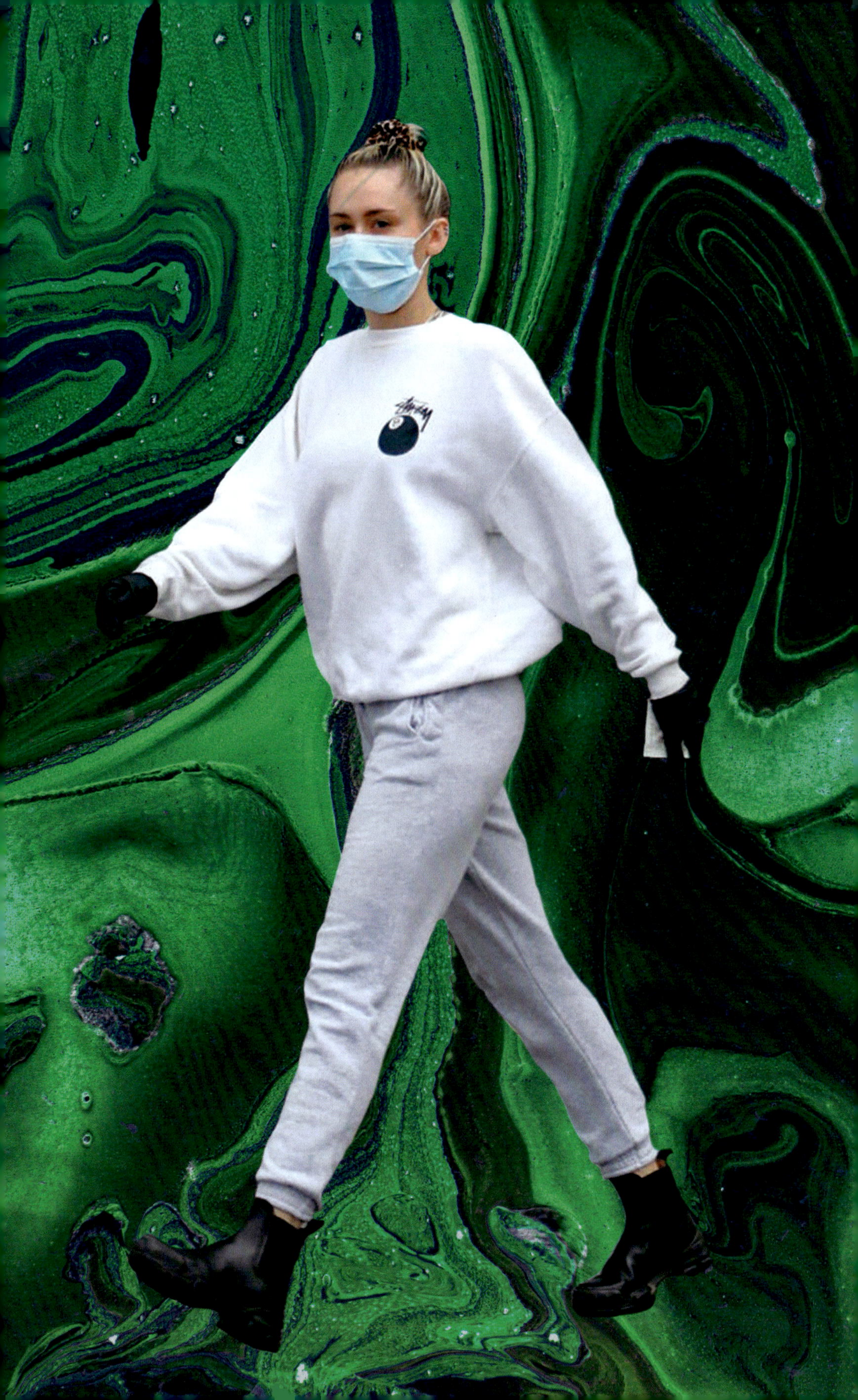

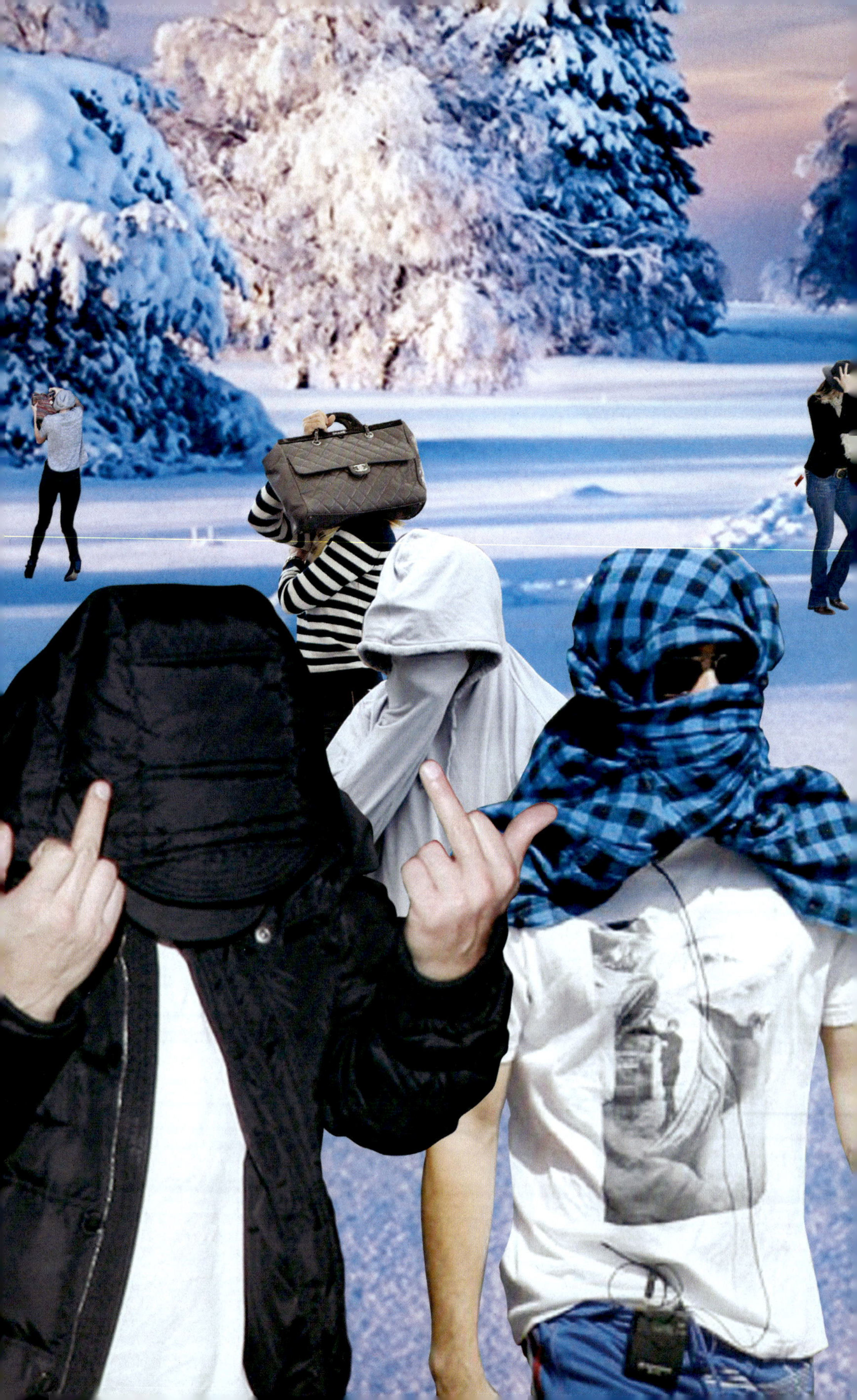

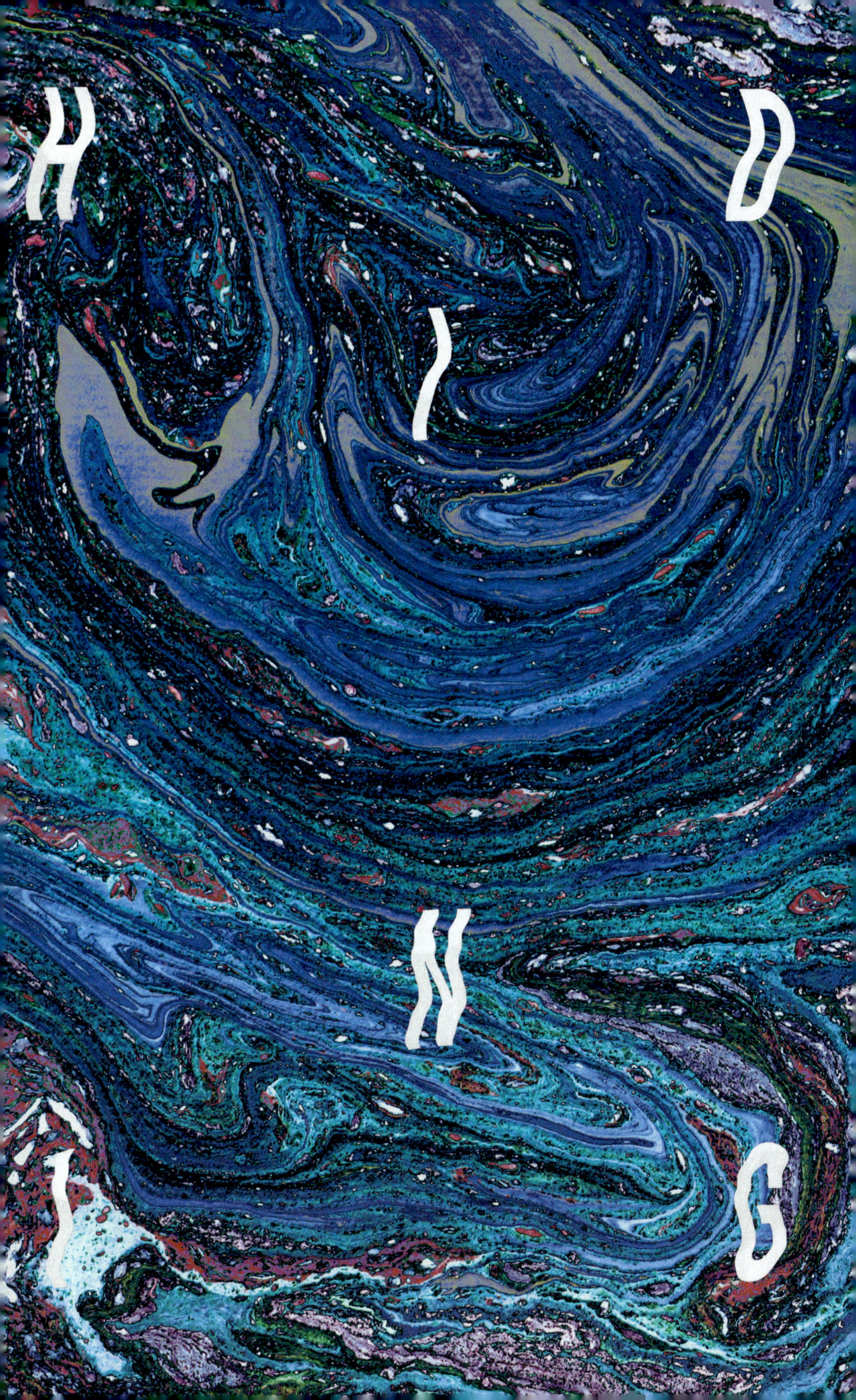
H
D
I
N
I
G

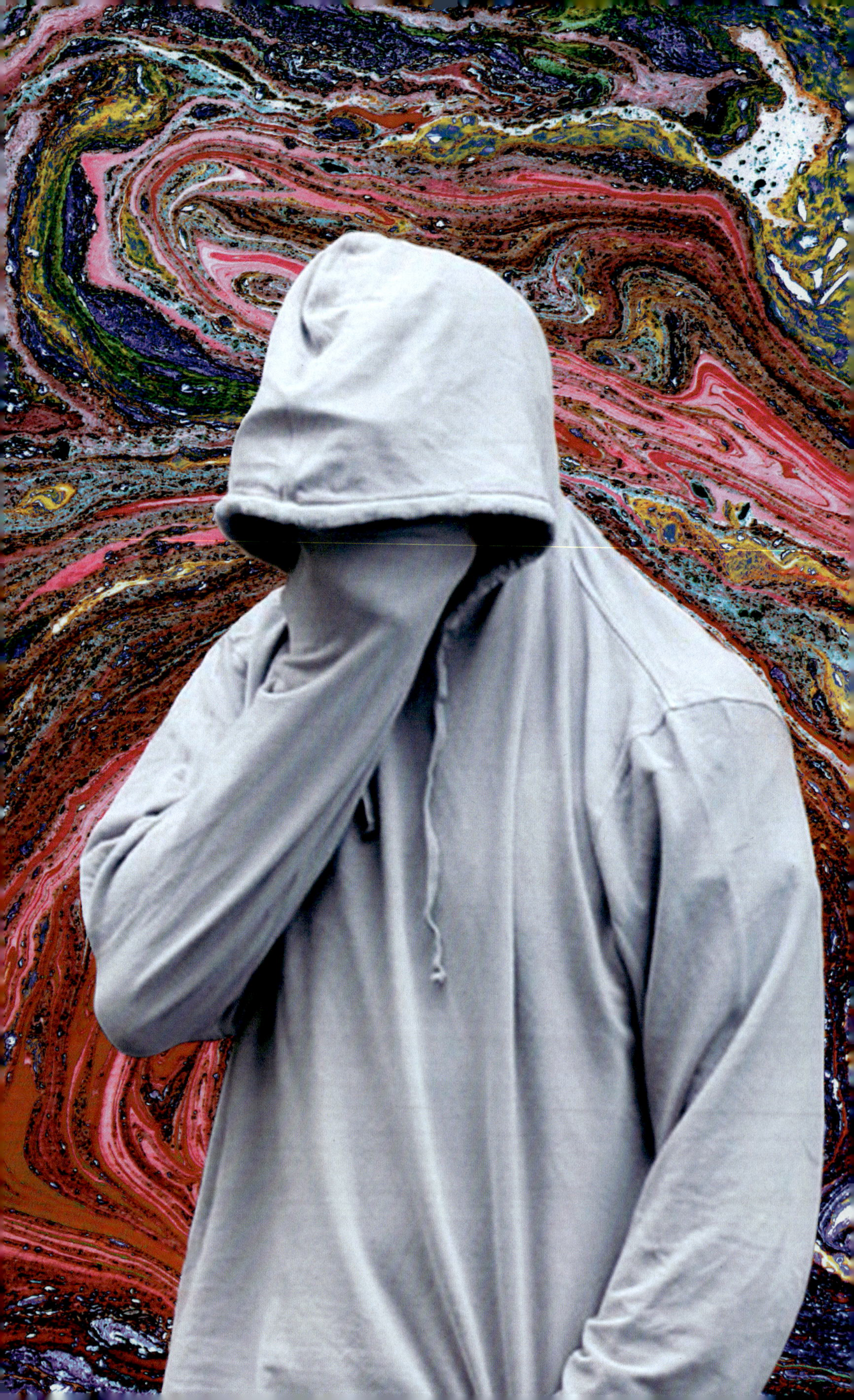

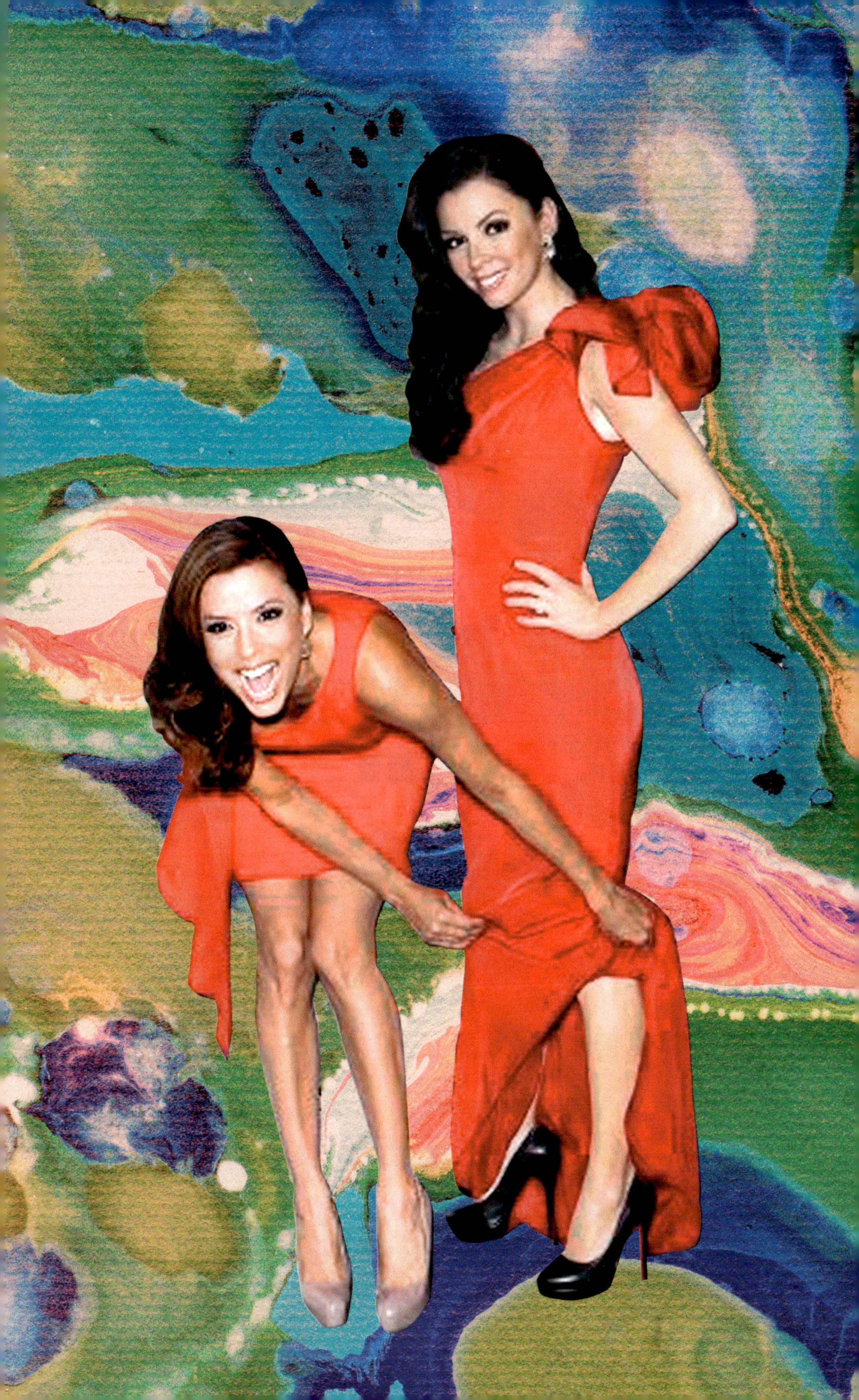

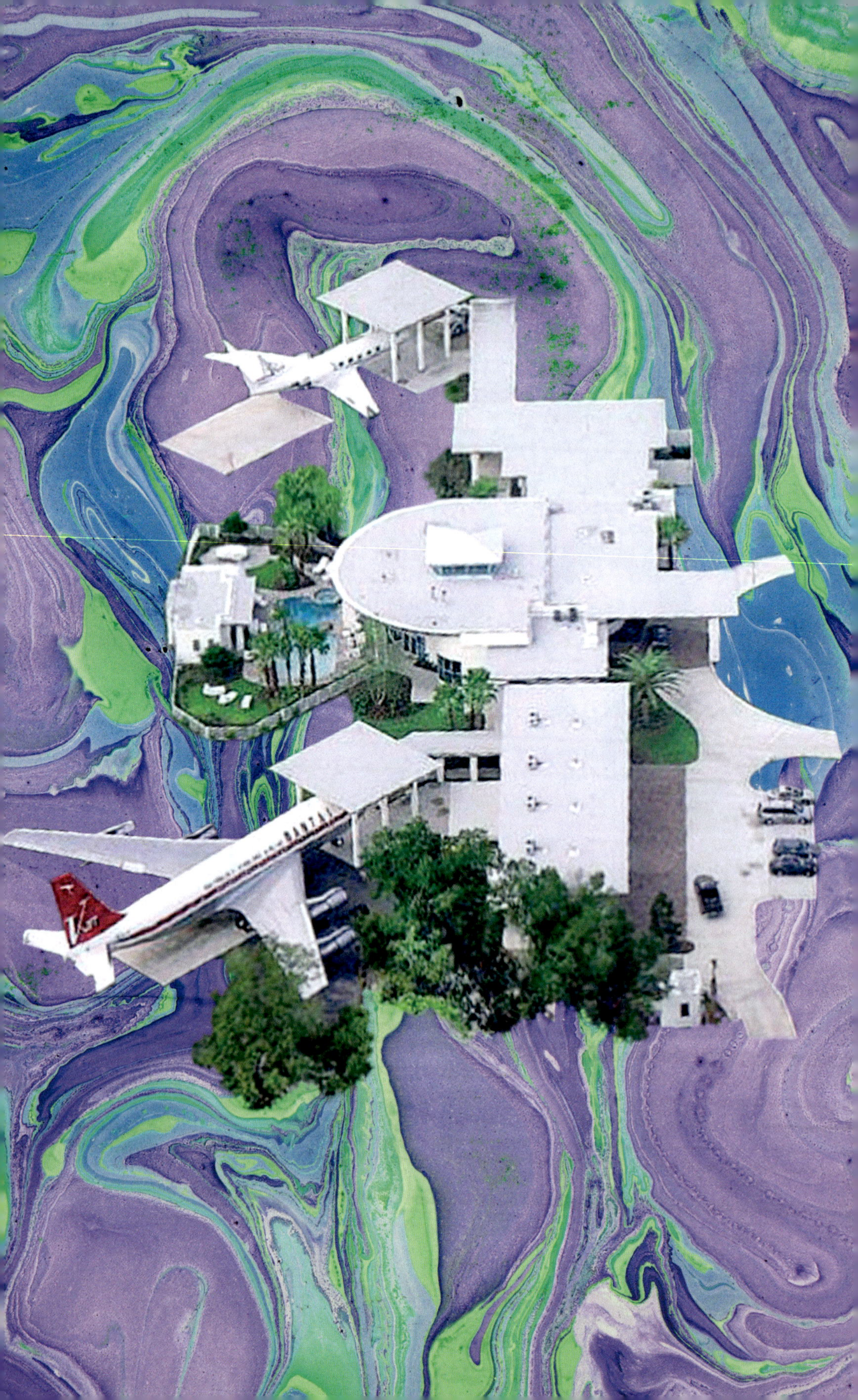

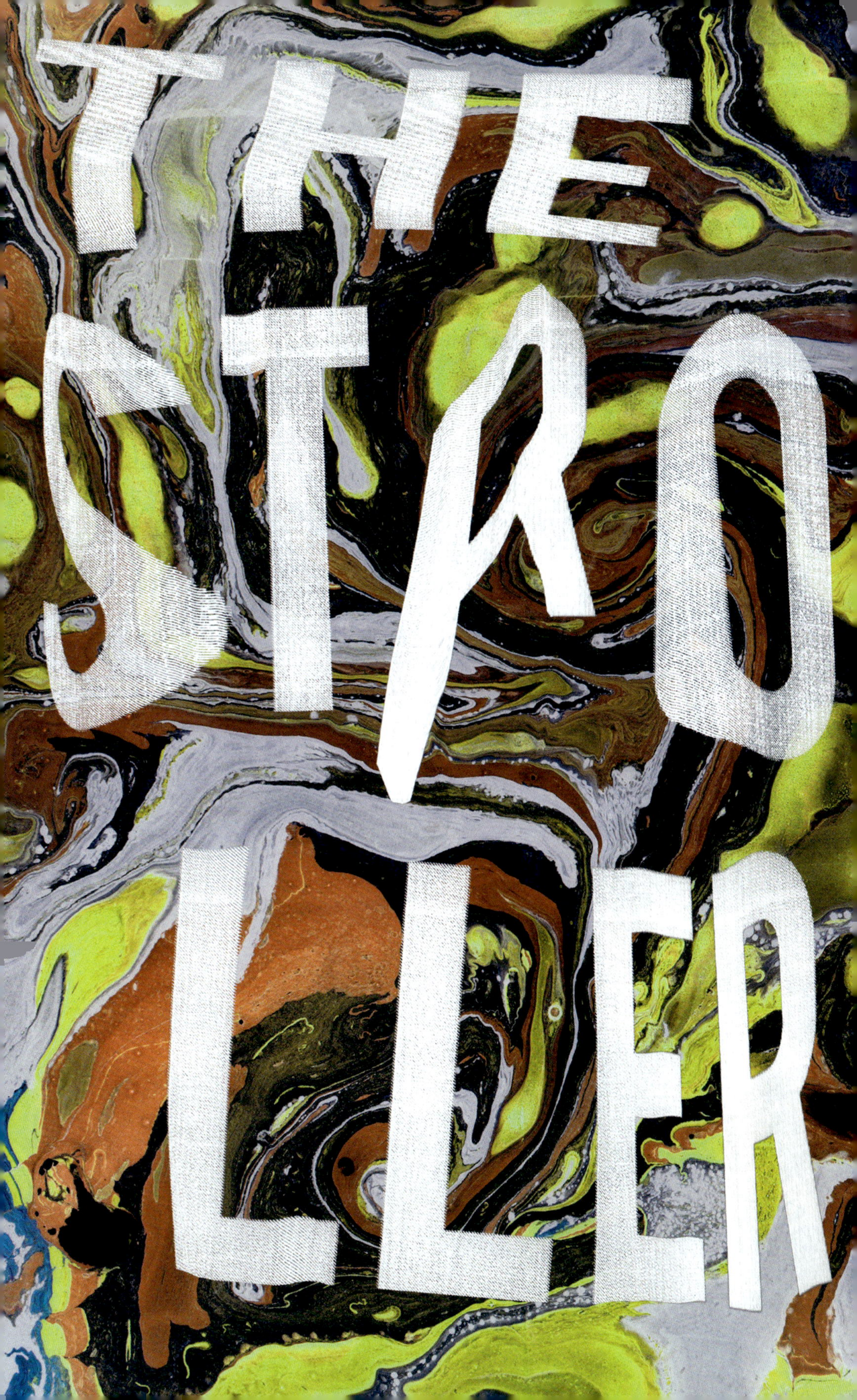
THE
STRO
LLER

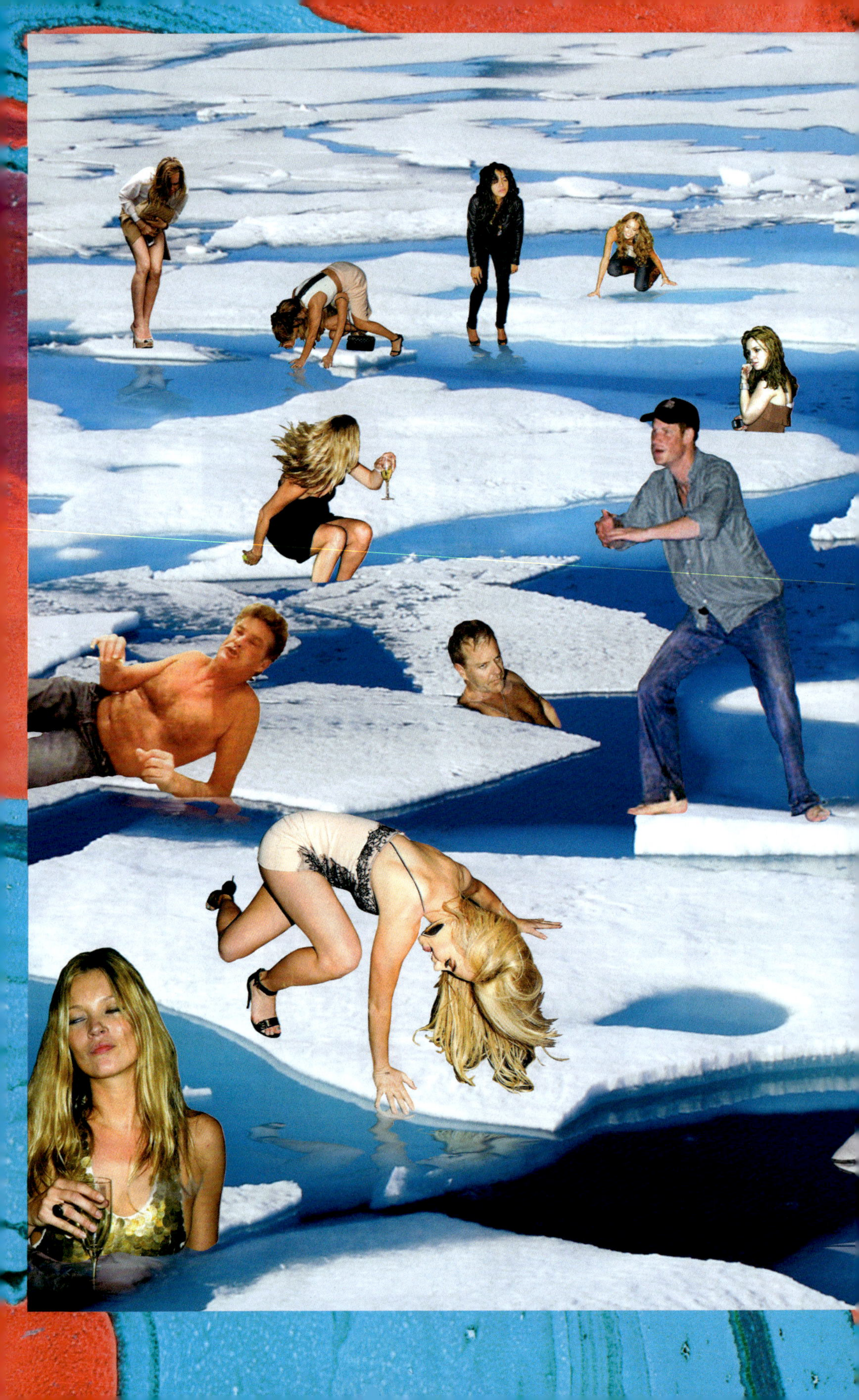

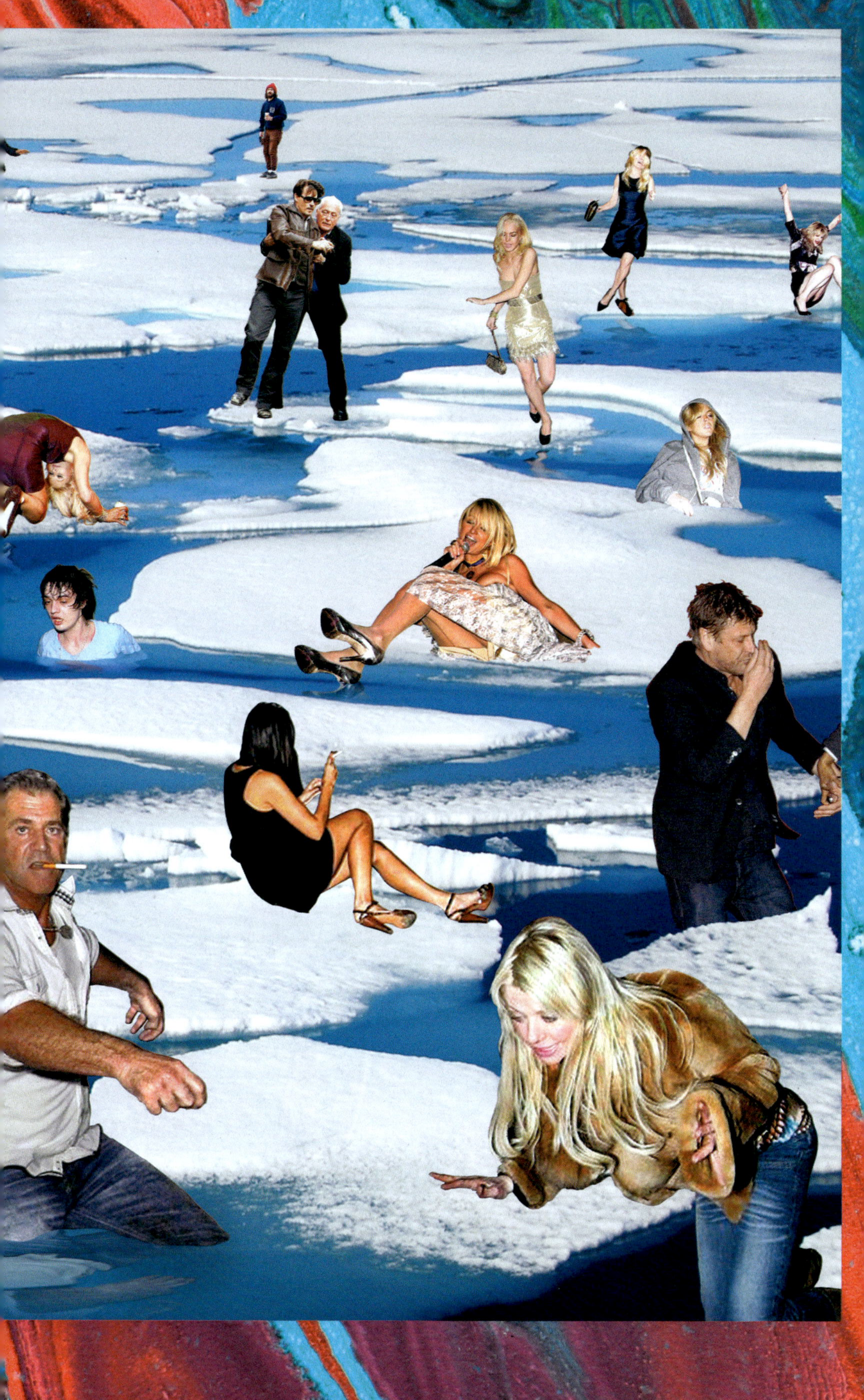

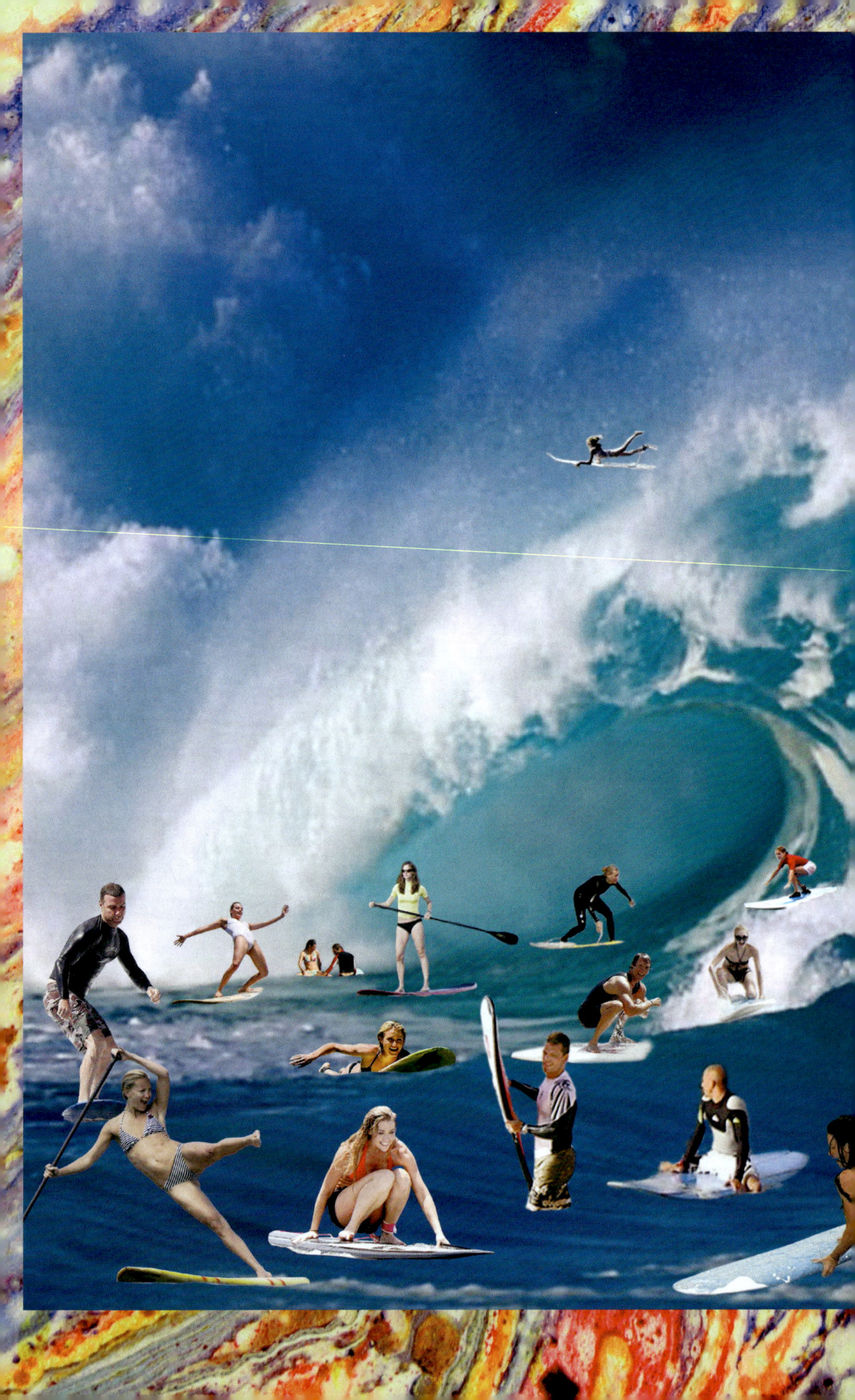

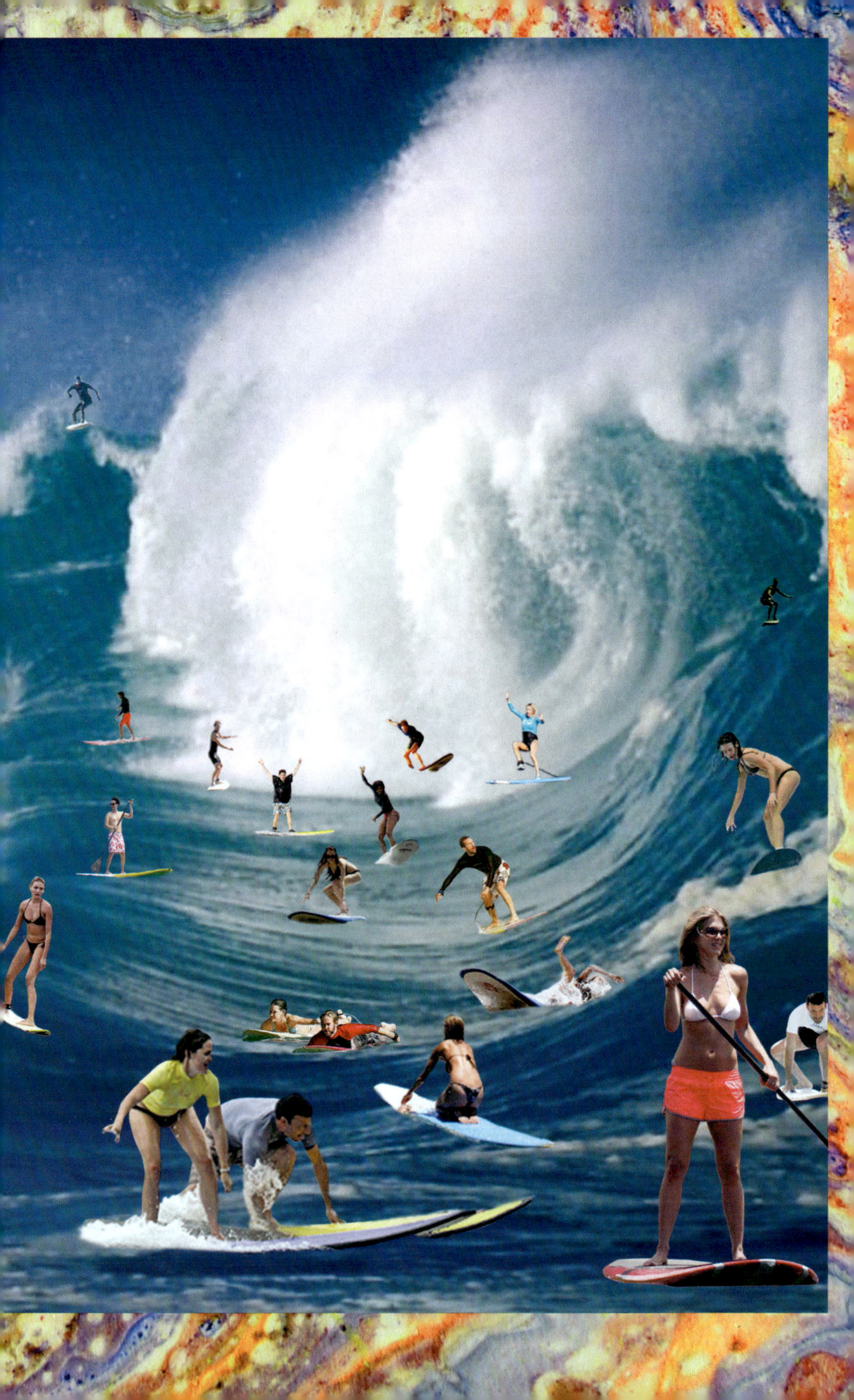

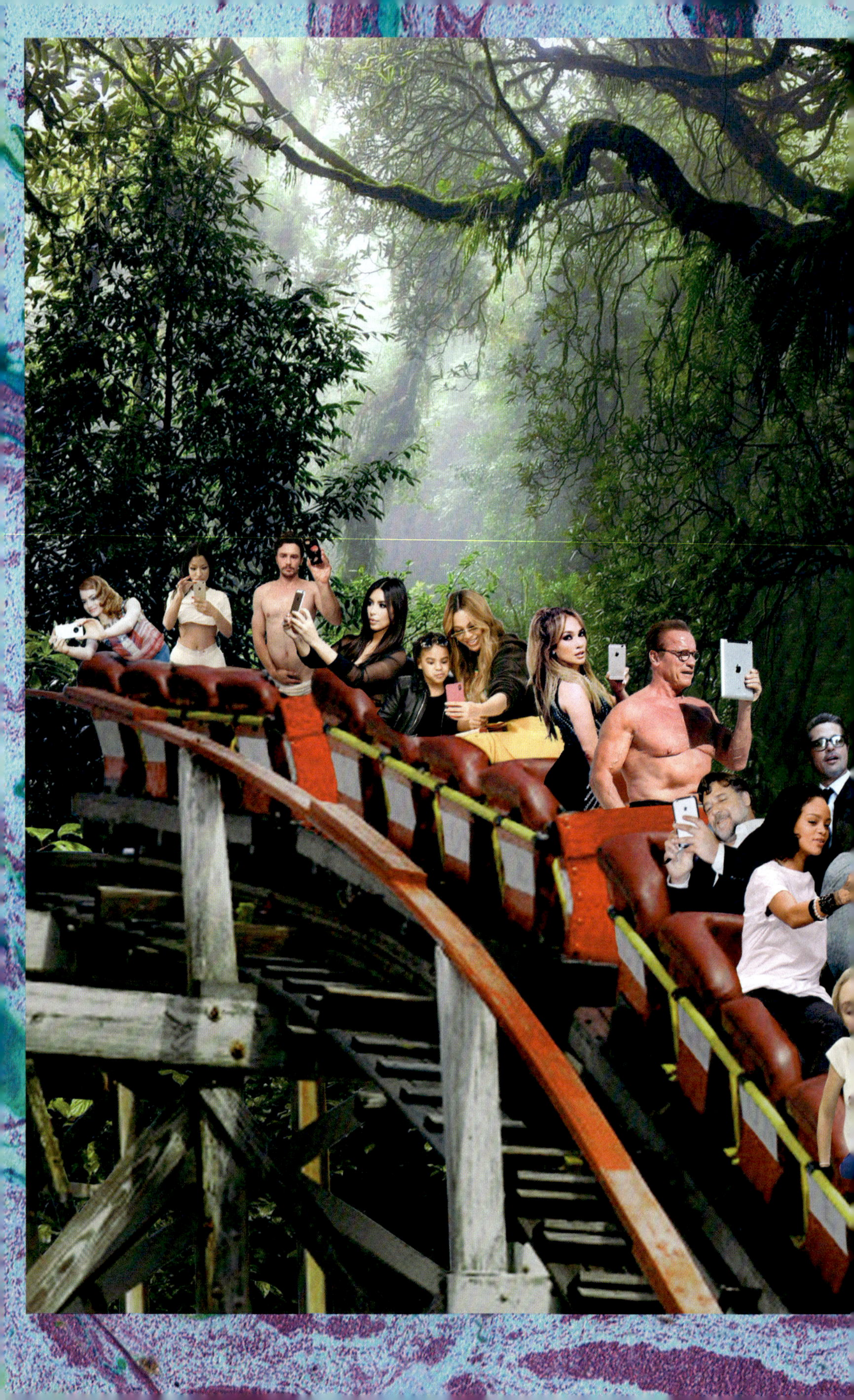

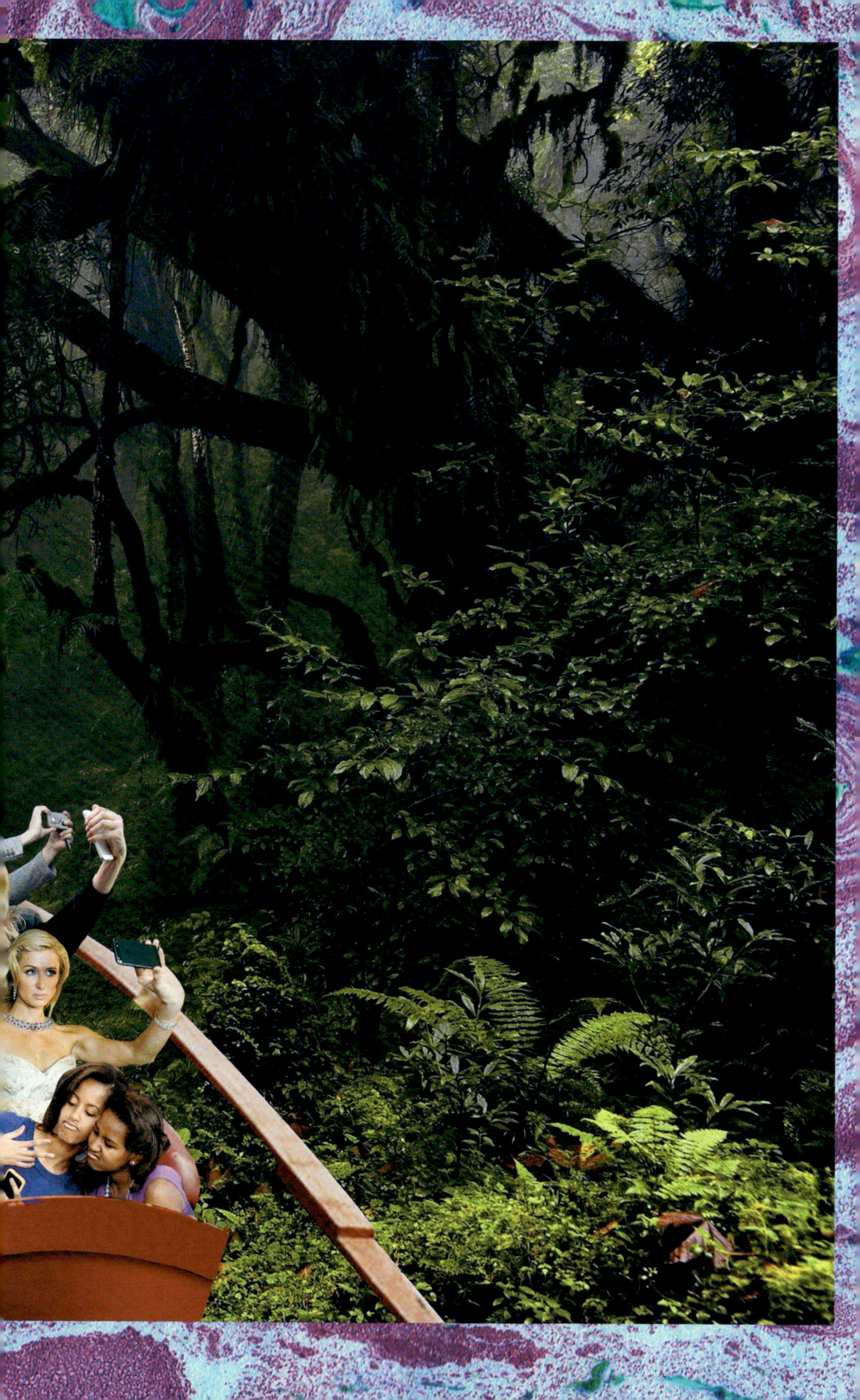

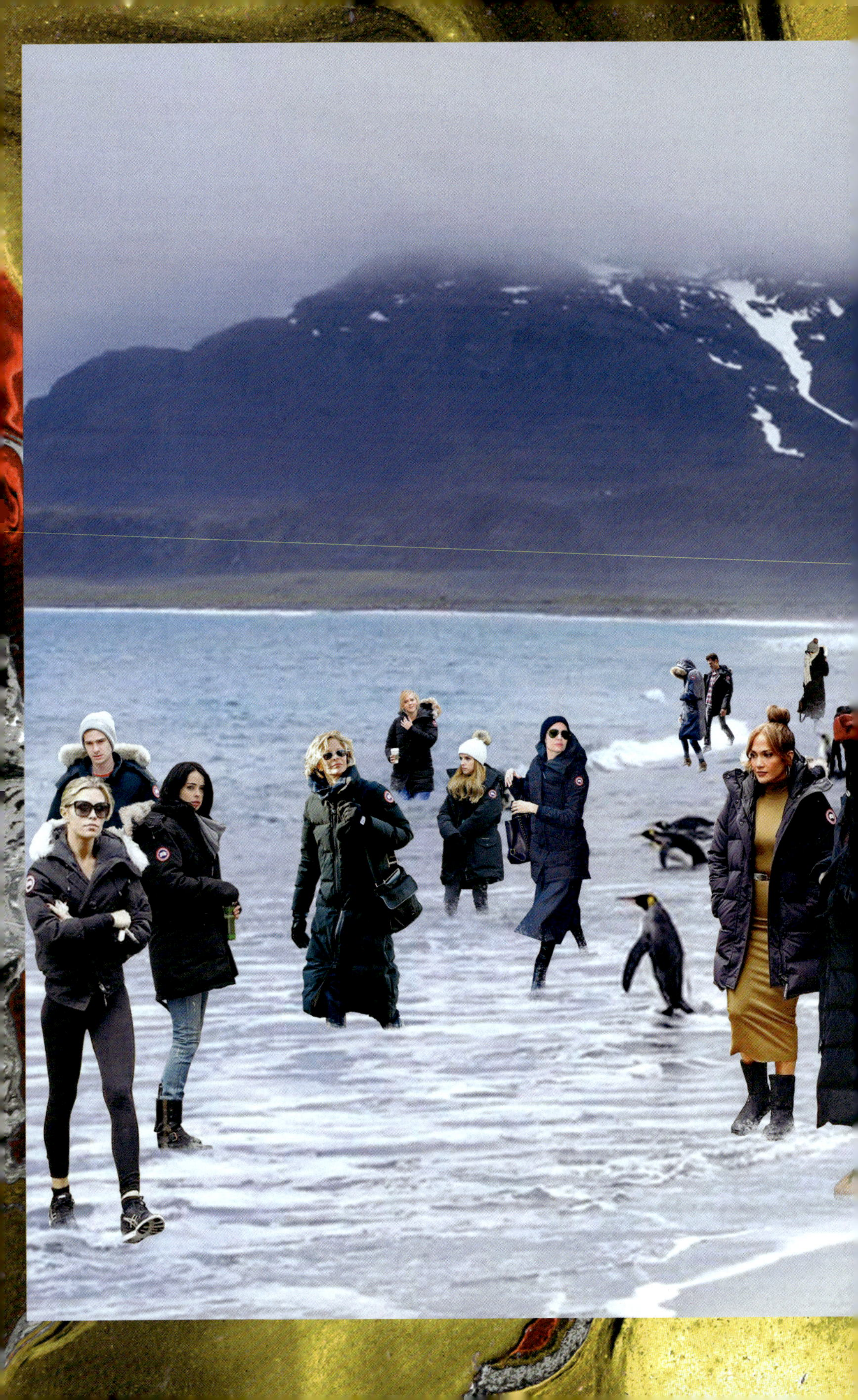

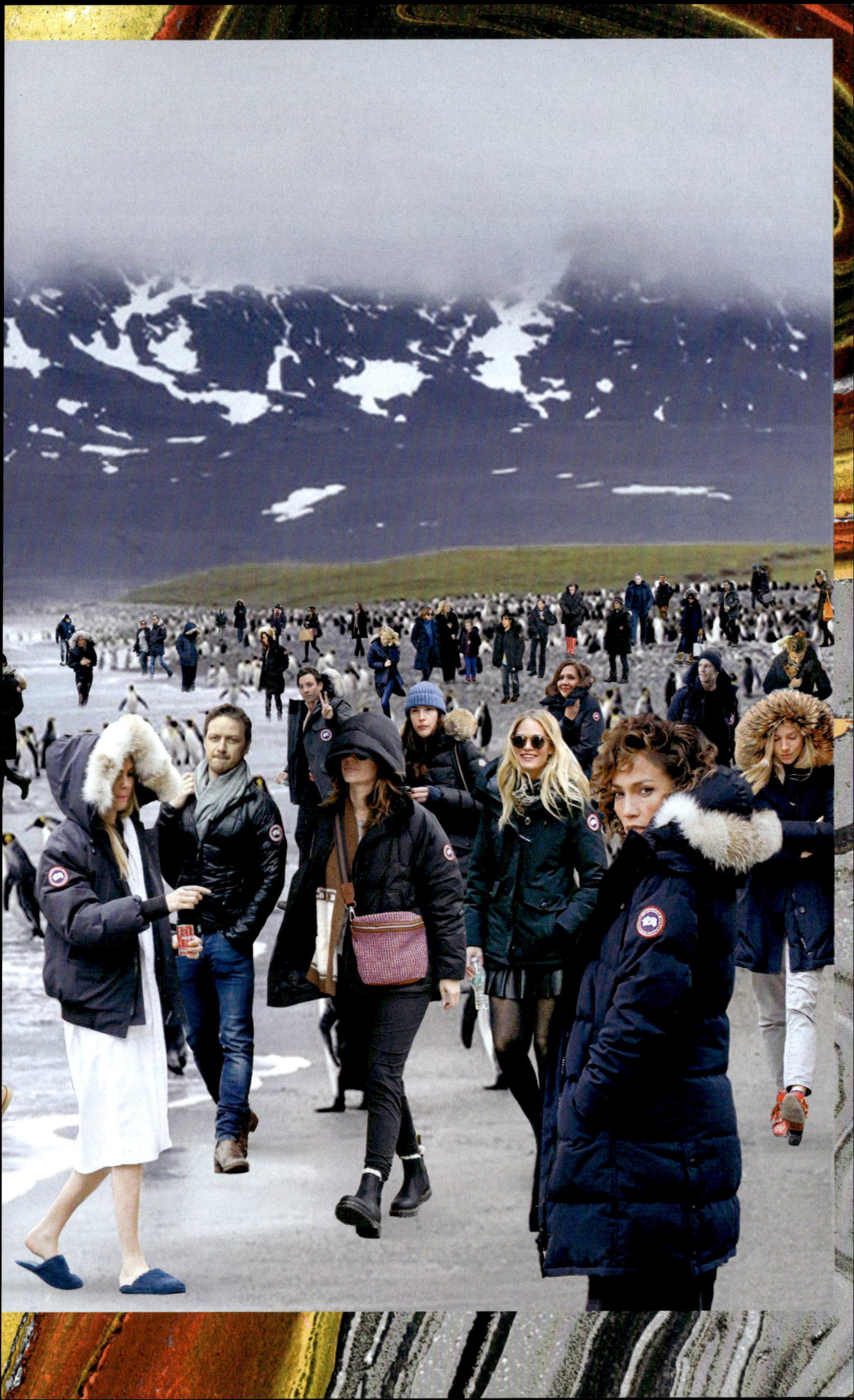

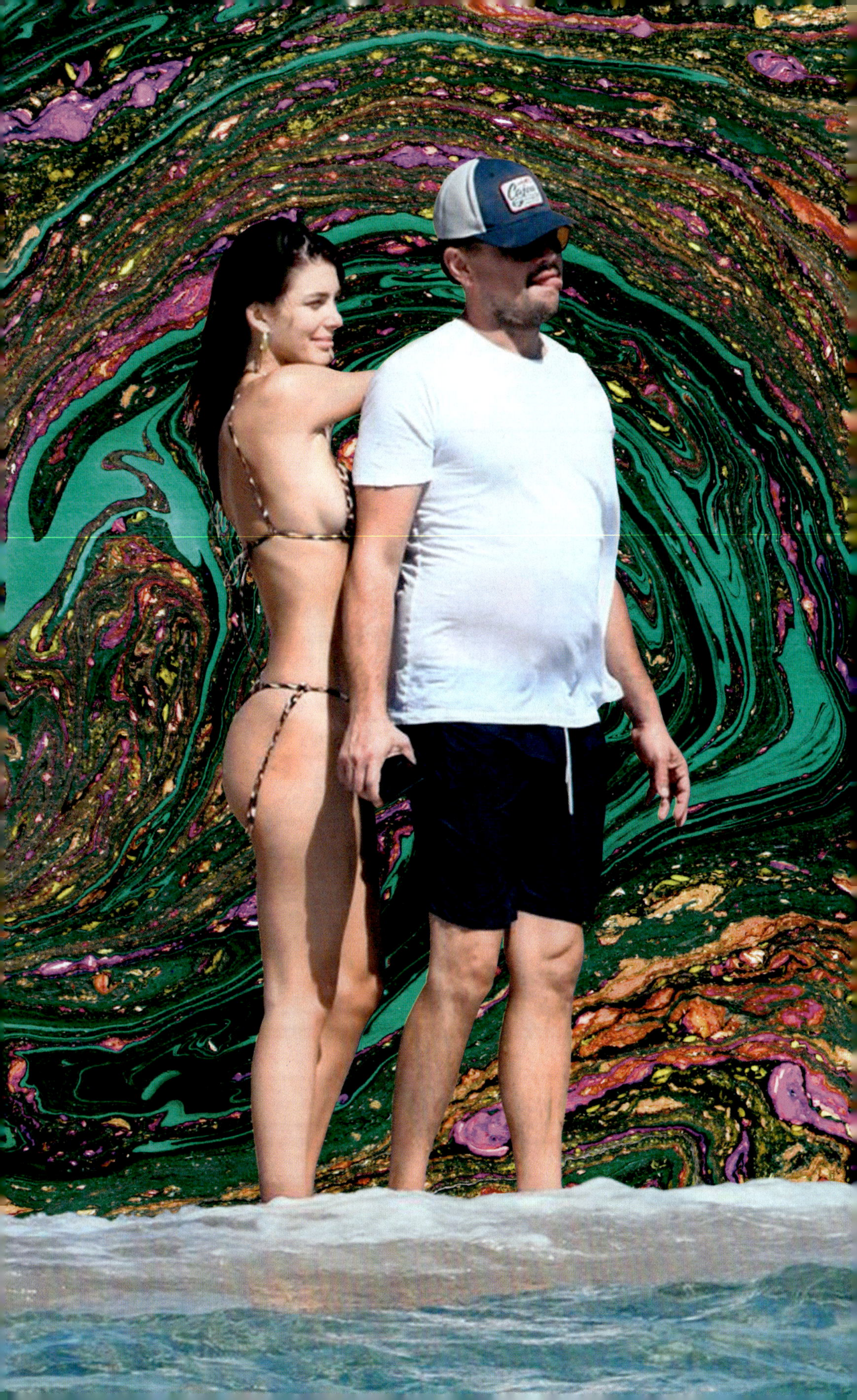

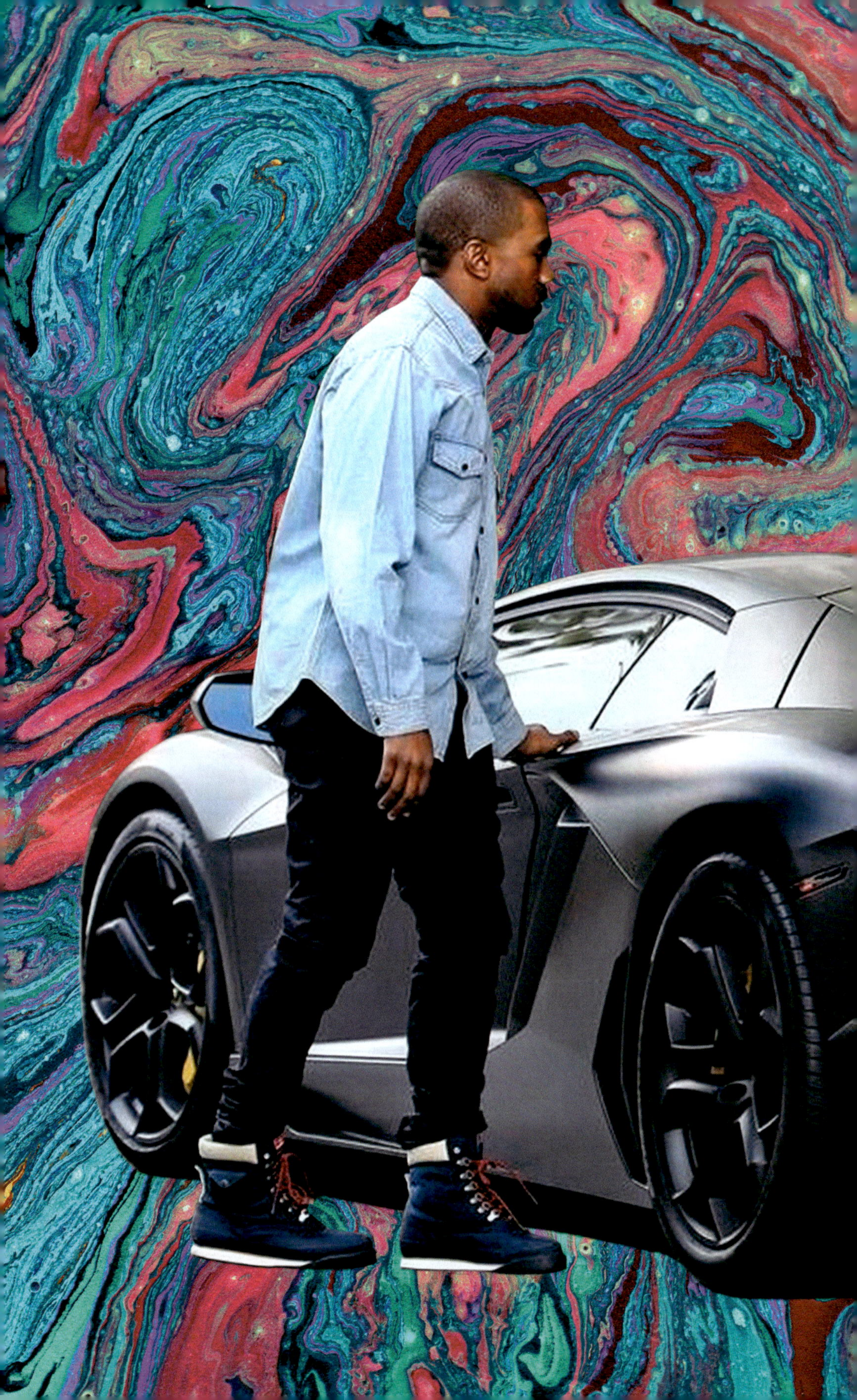

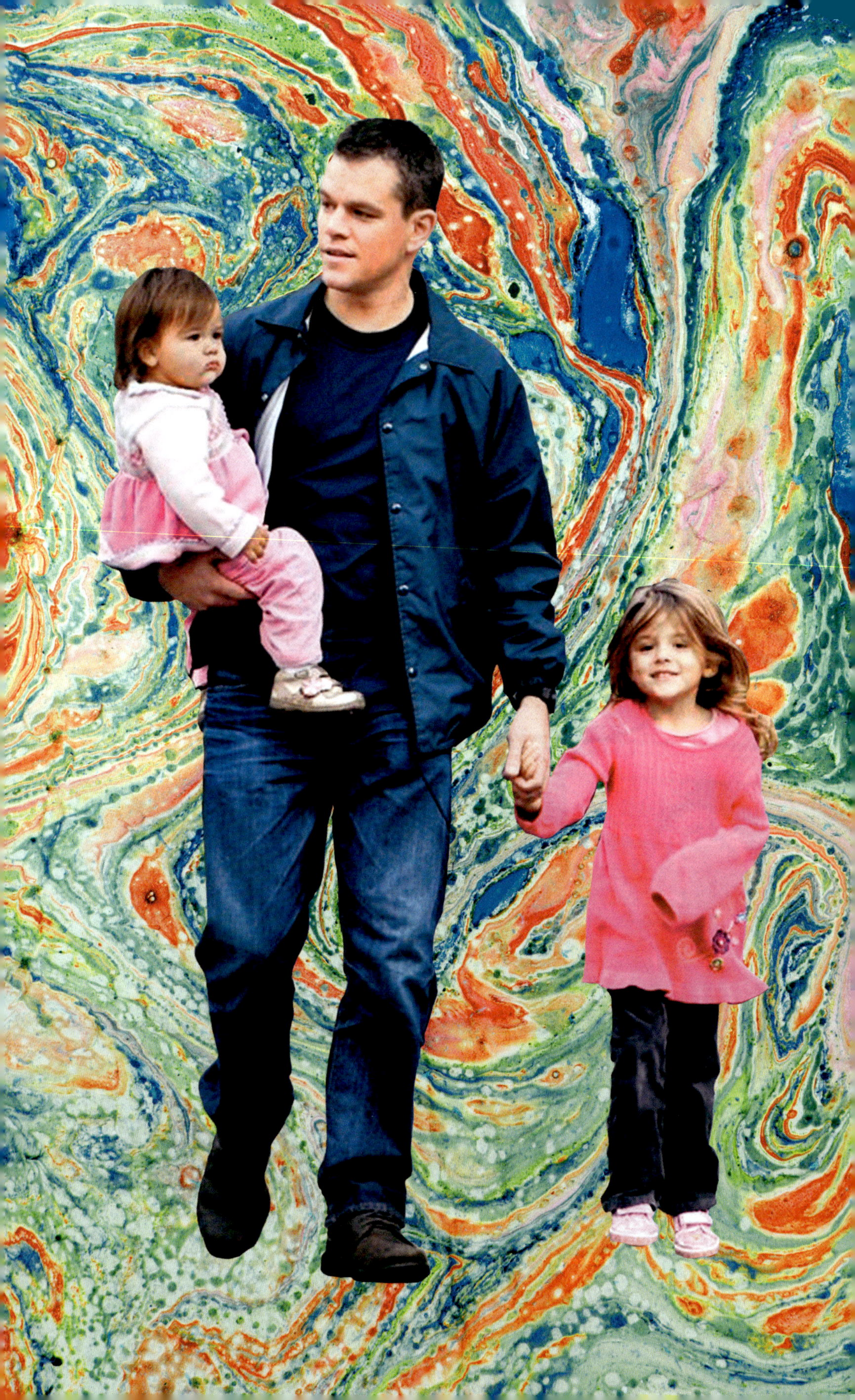

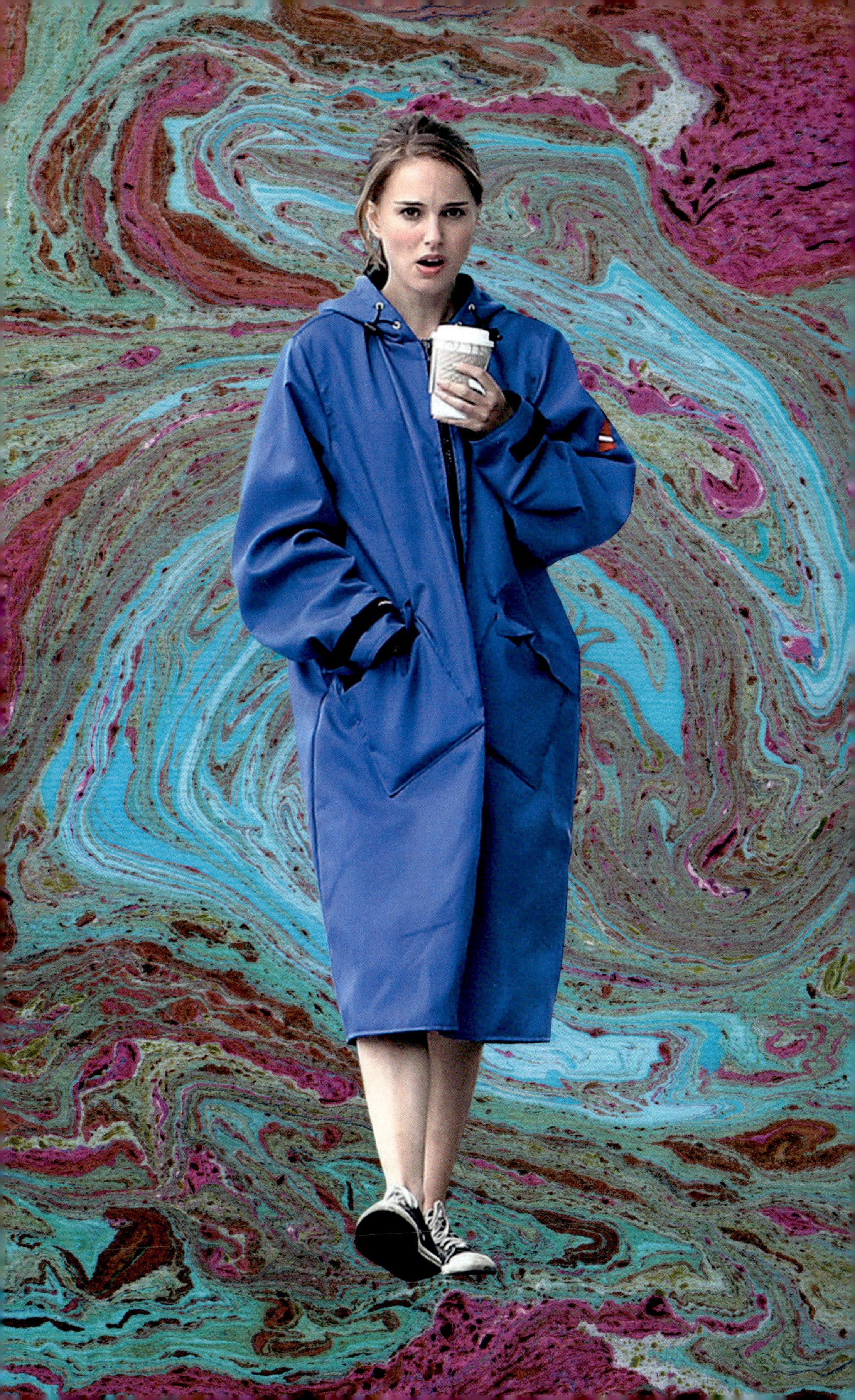

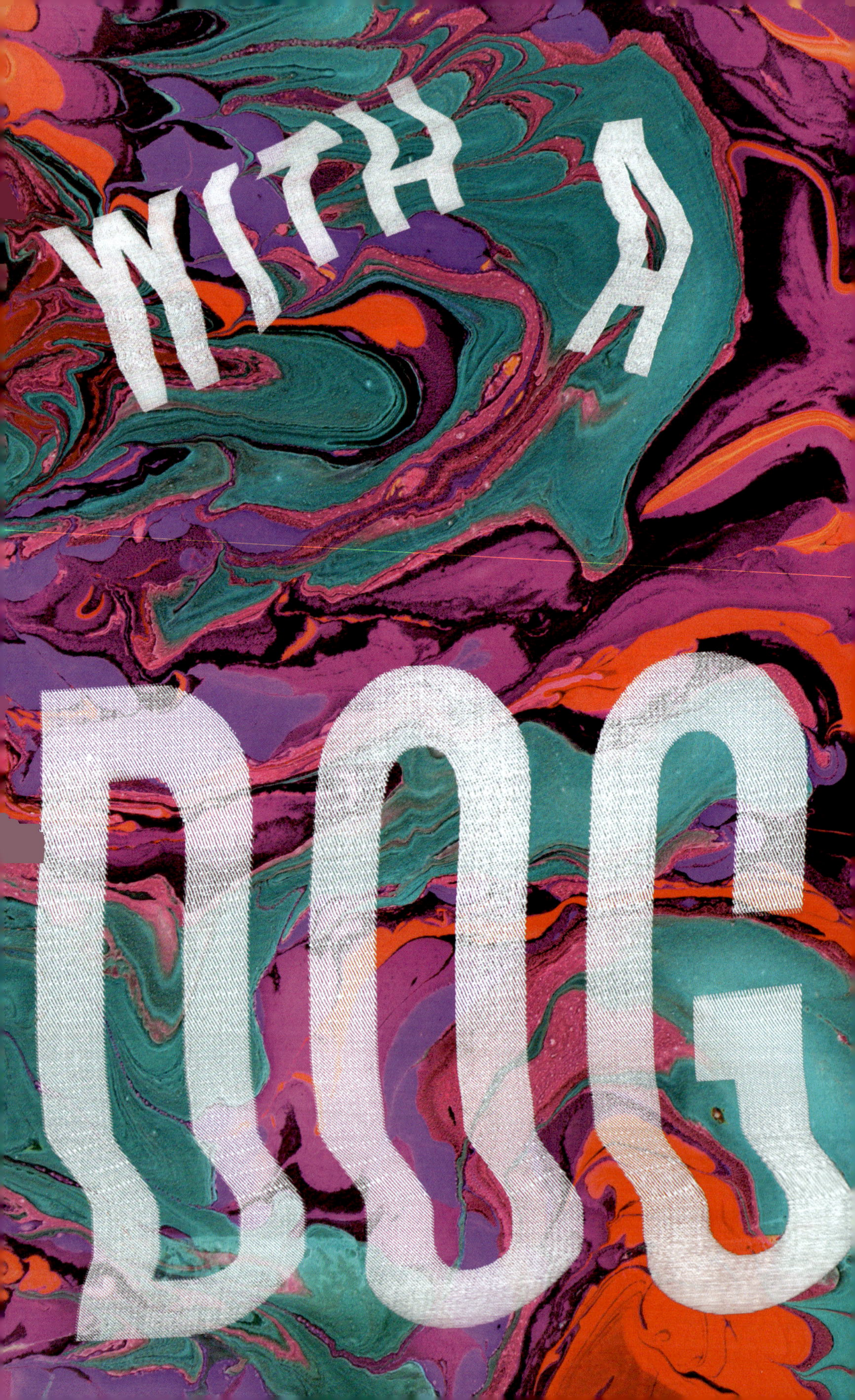
WITH A
DOG

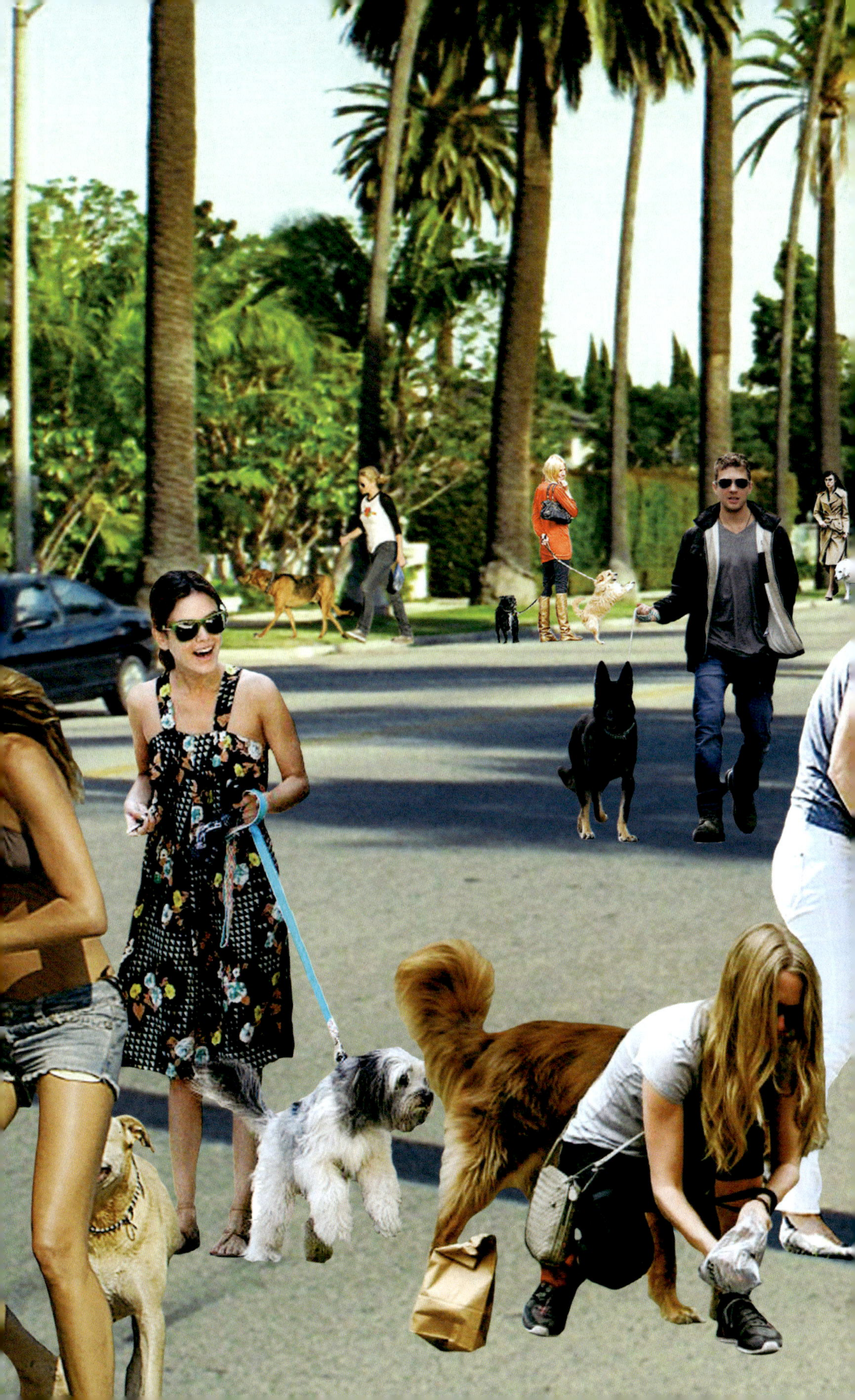

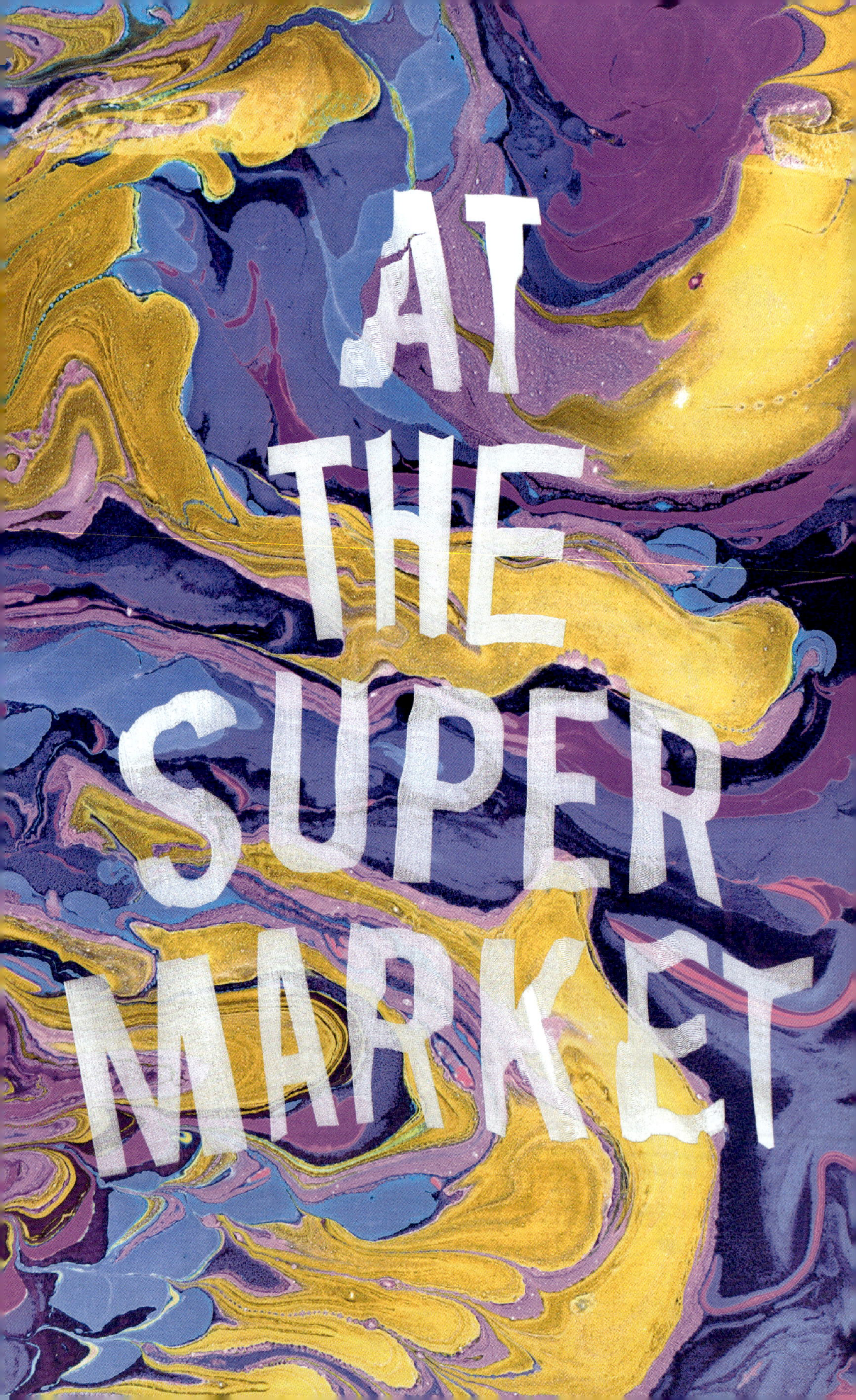
AT
THE
SUPER
MARKET

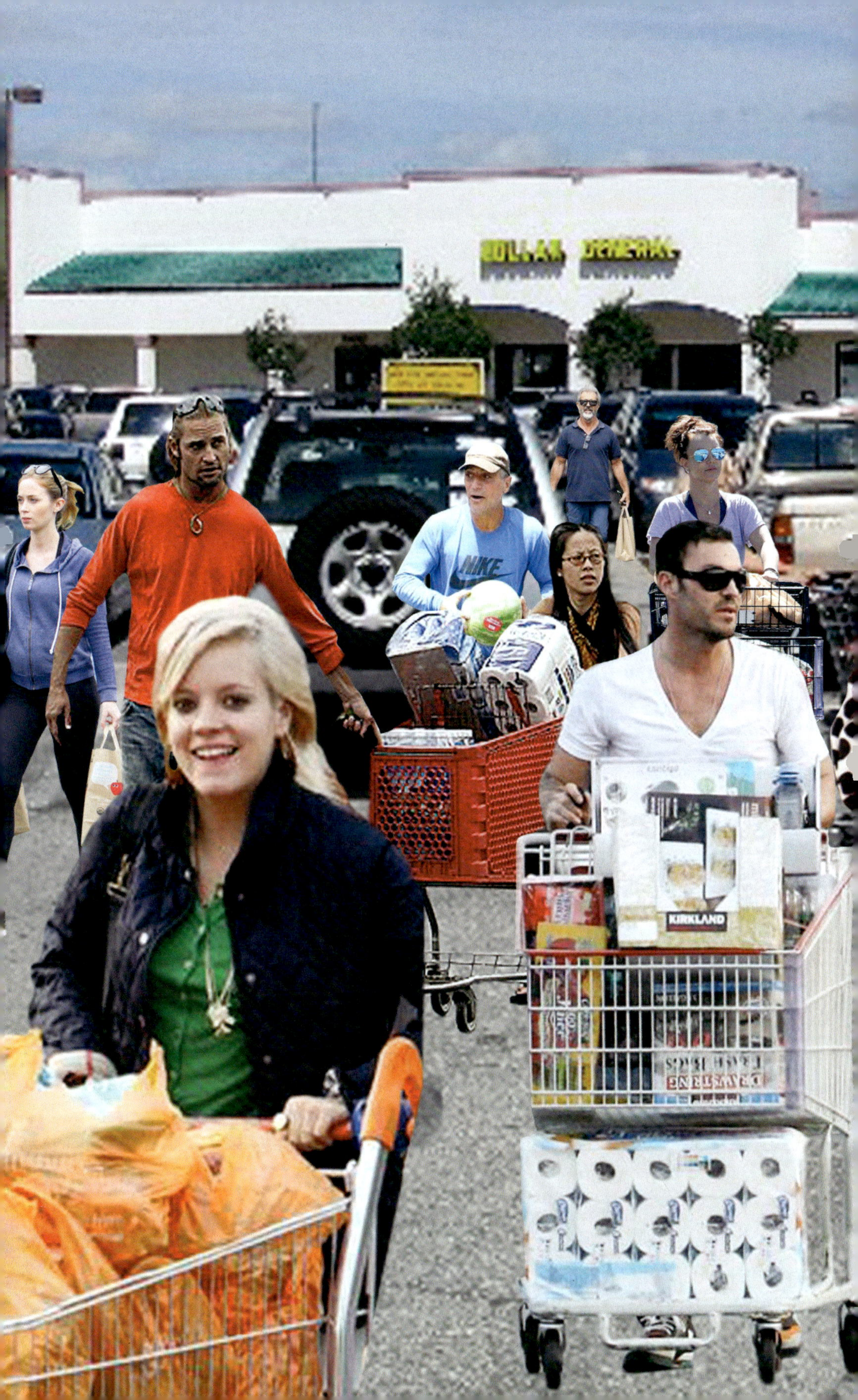
NIKE
KIRKLAND

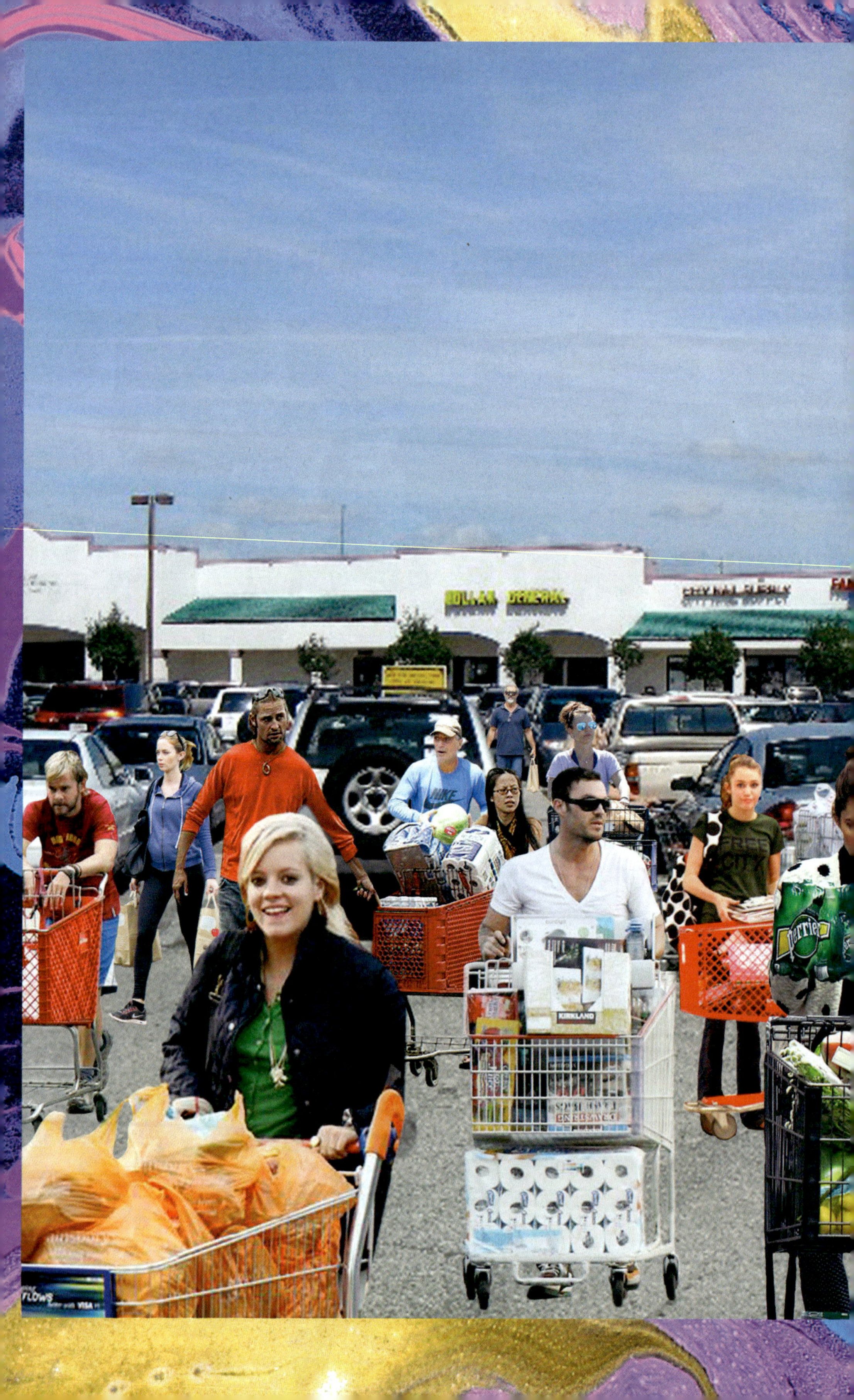
DOLLAR GENERAL
FREE CITY
KIRKLAND
Perrier

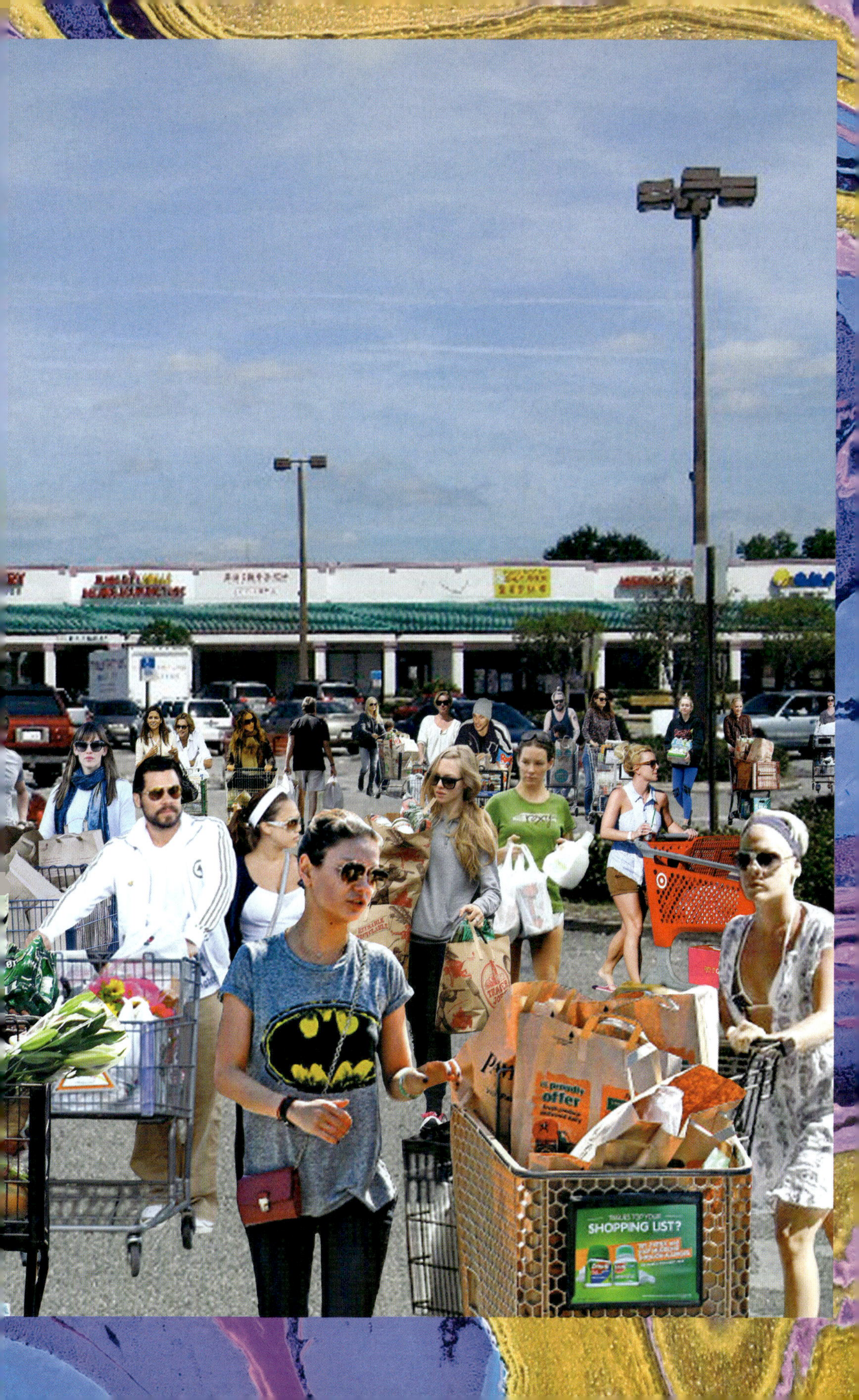

offer
SHOPPING LIST?

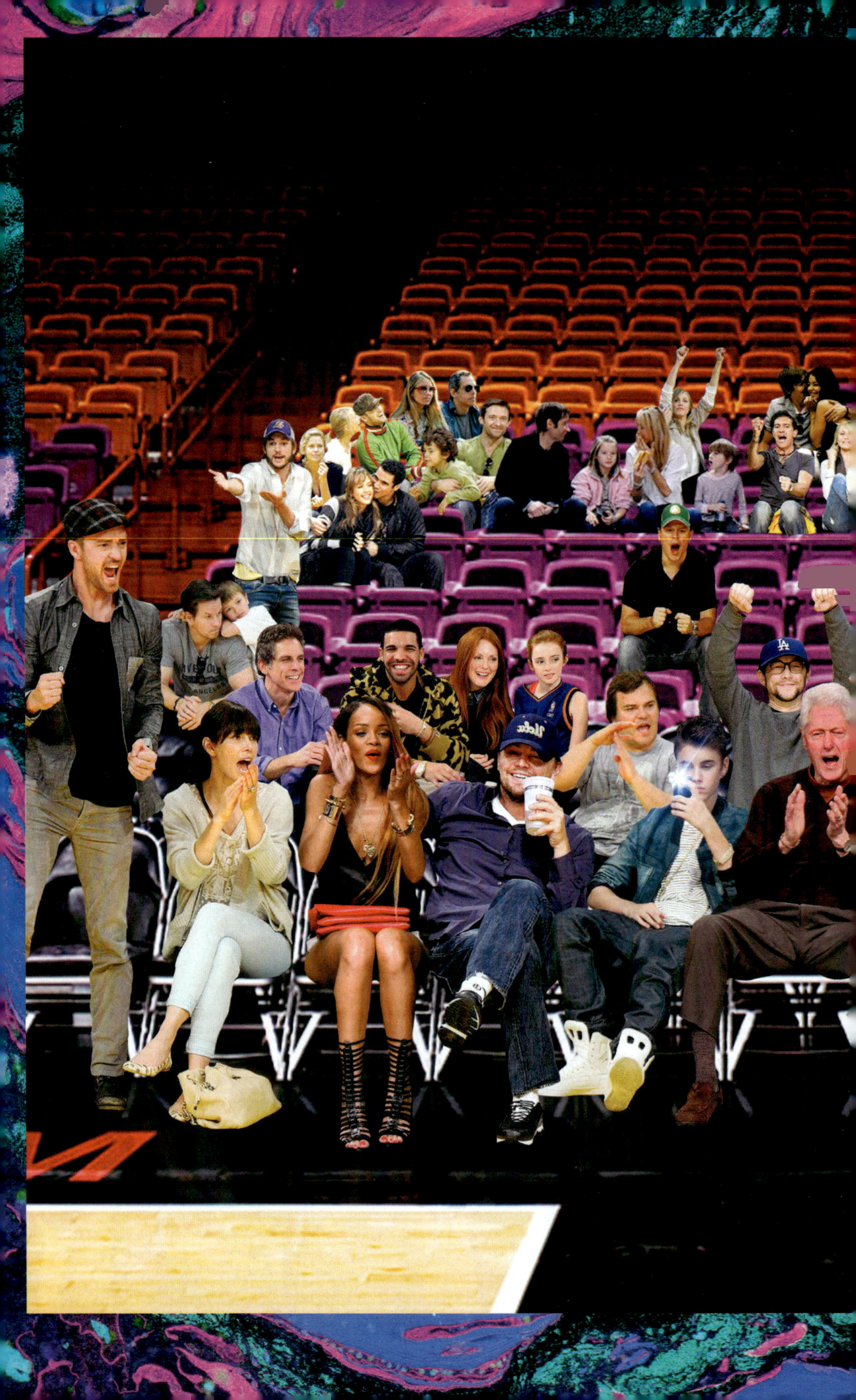

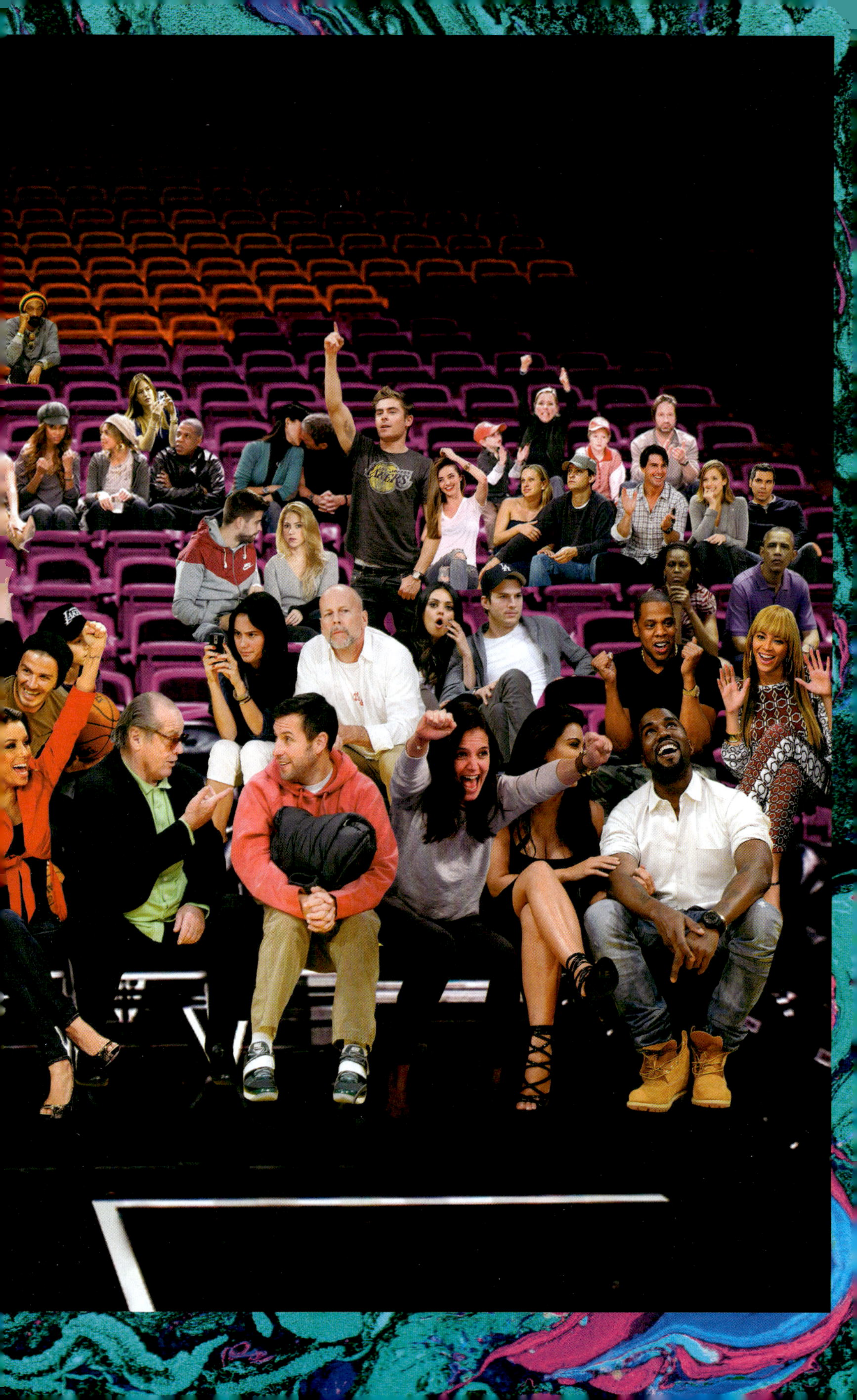
LAKERS

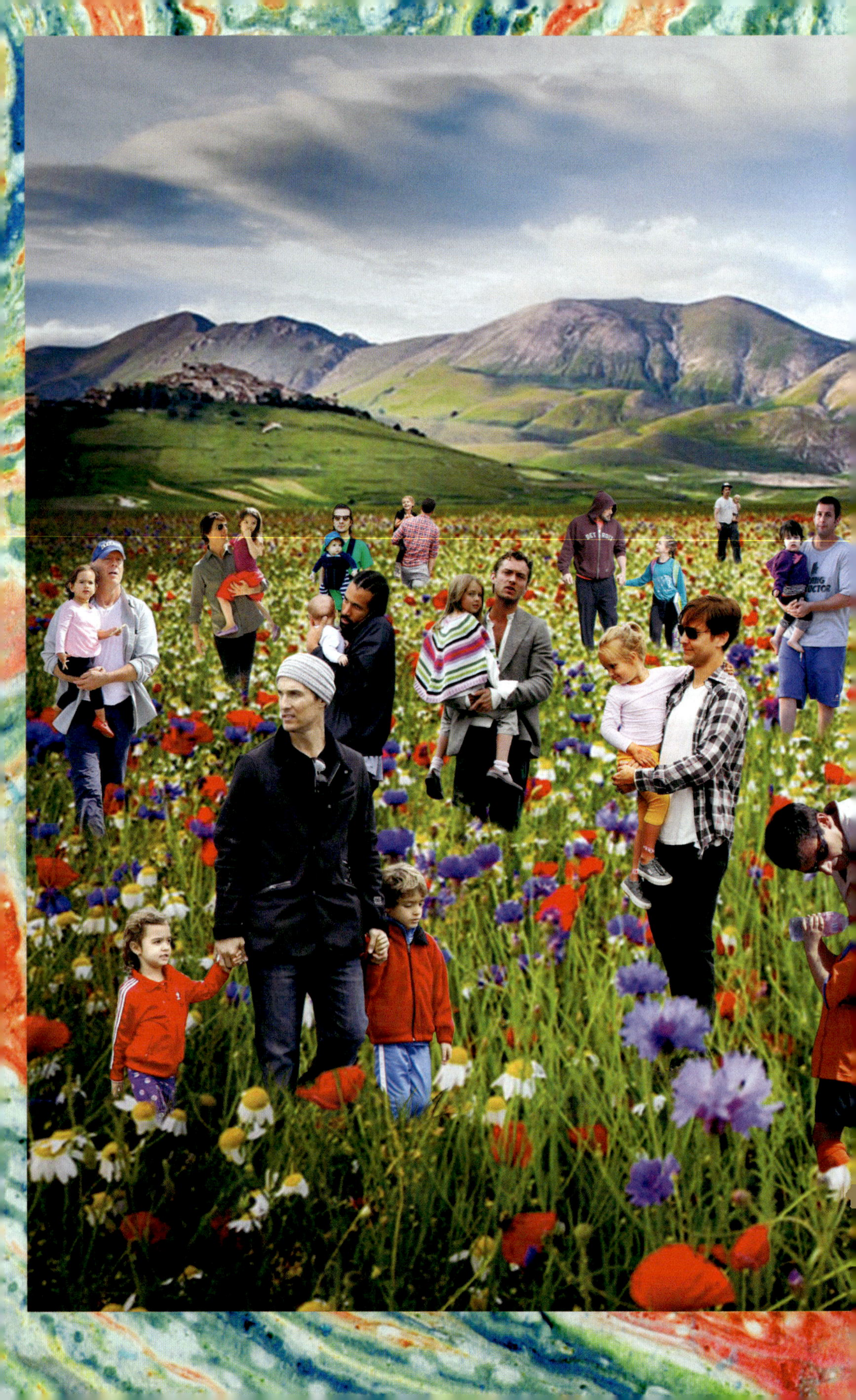

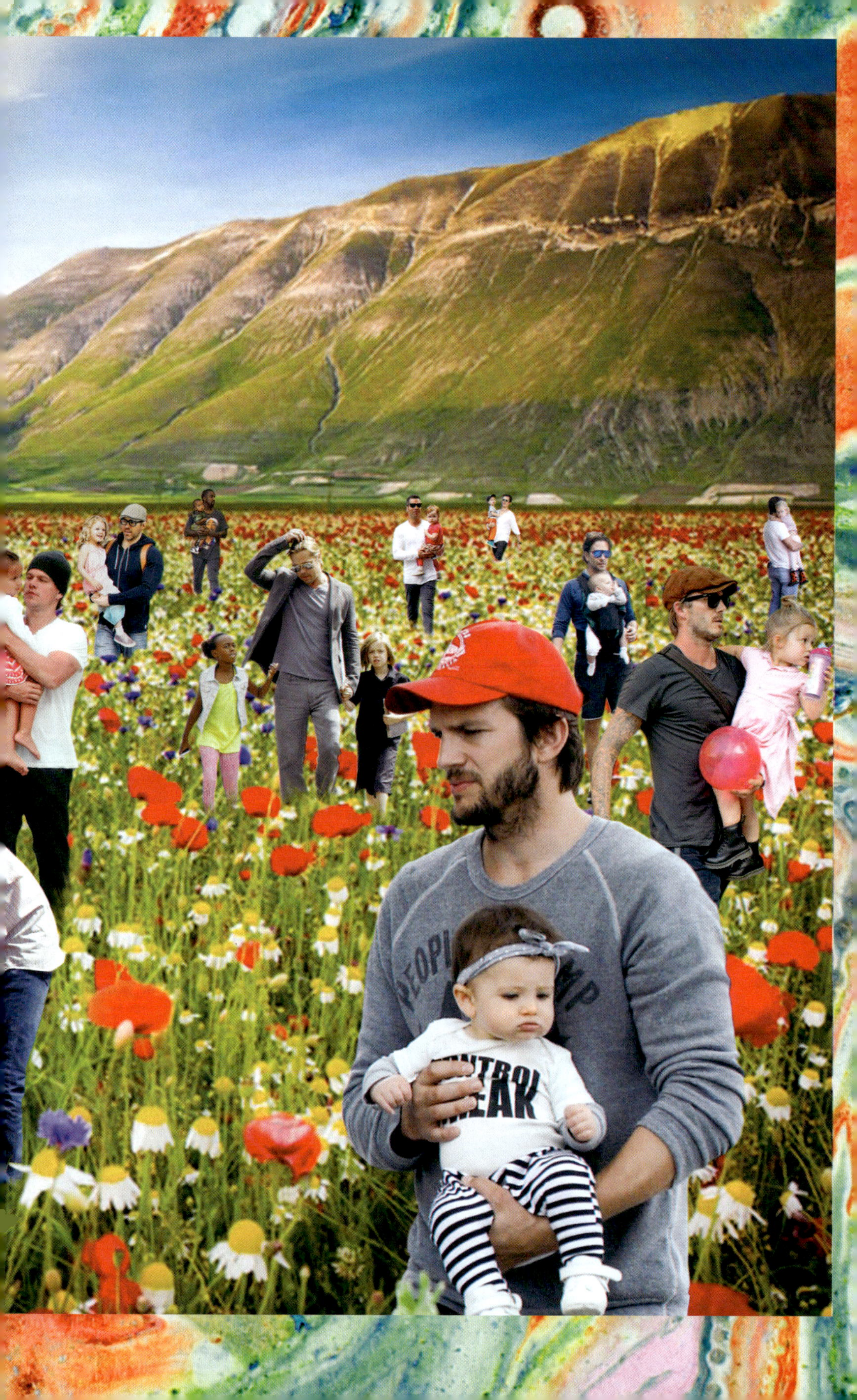

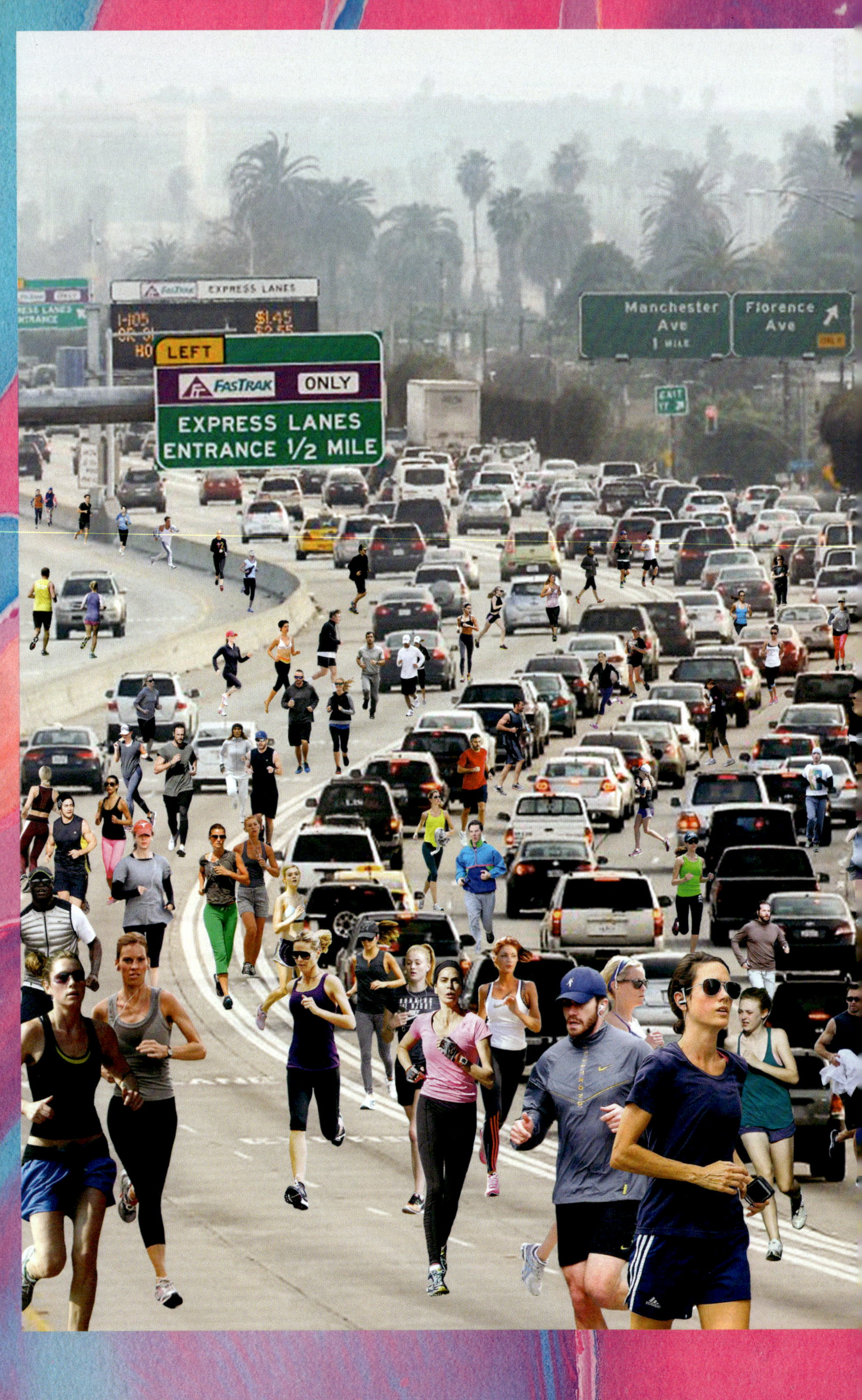

EXPRESS LANES
LEFT
FasTrak ONLY
EXPRESS LANES
ENTRANCE 1/2 MILE
Manchester
Ave
1 MILE
Florence
Ave

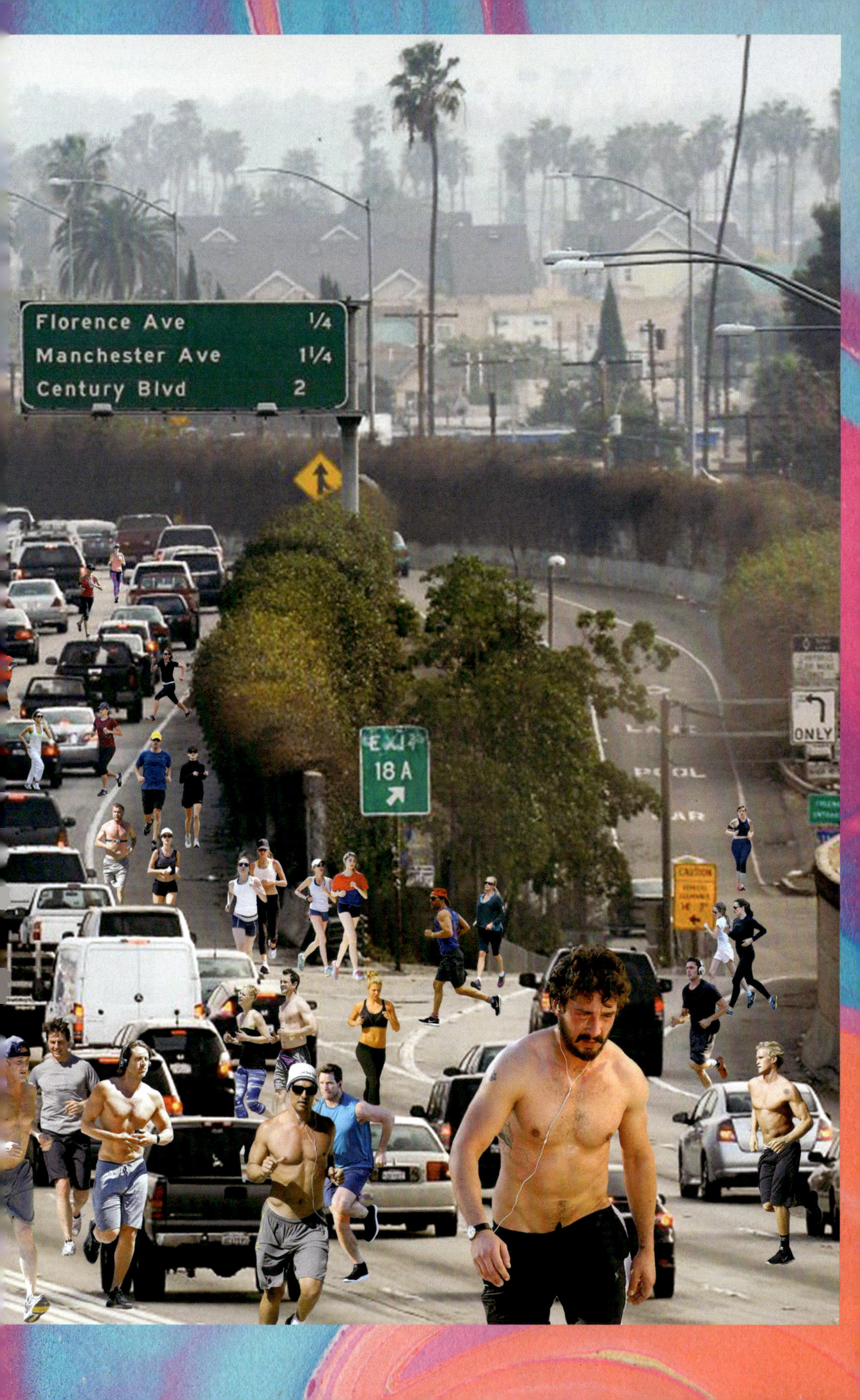
Florence Ave 1/4
Manchester Ave 1 1/4
Century Blvd 2
EXIT
18 A
ONLY

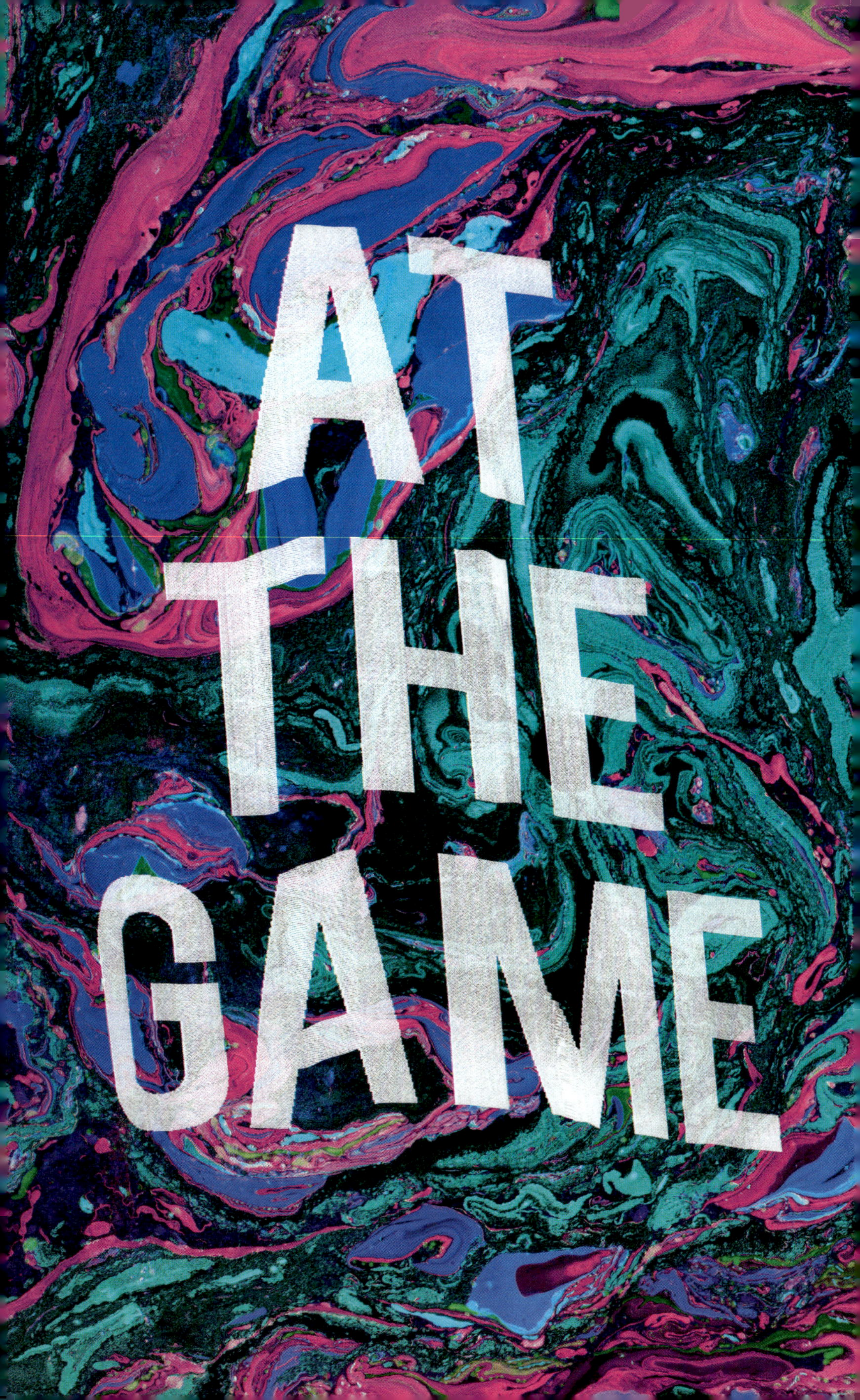
AT
THE
GAME

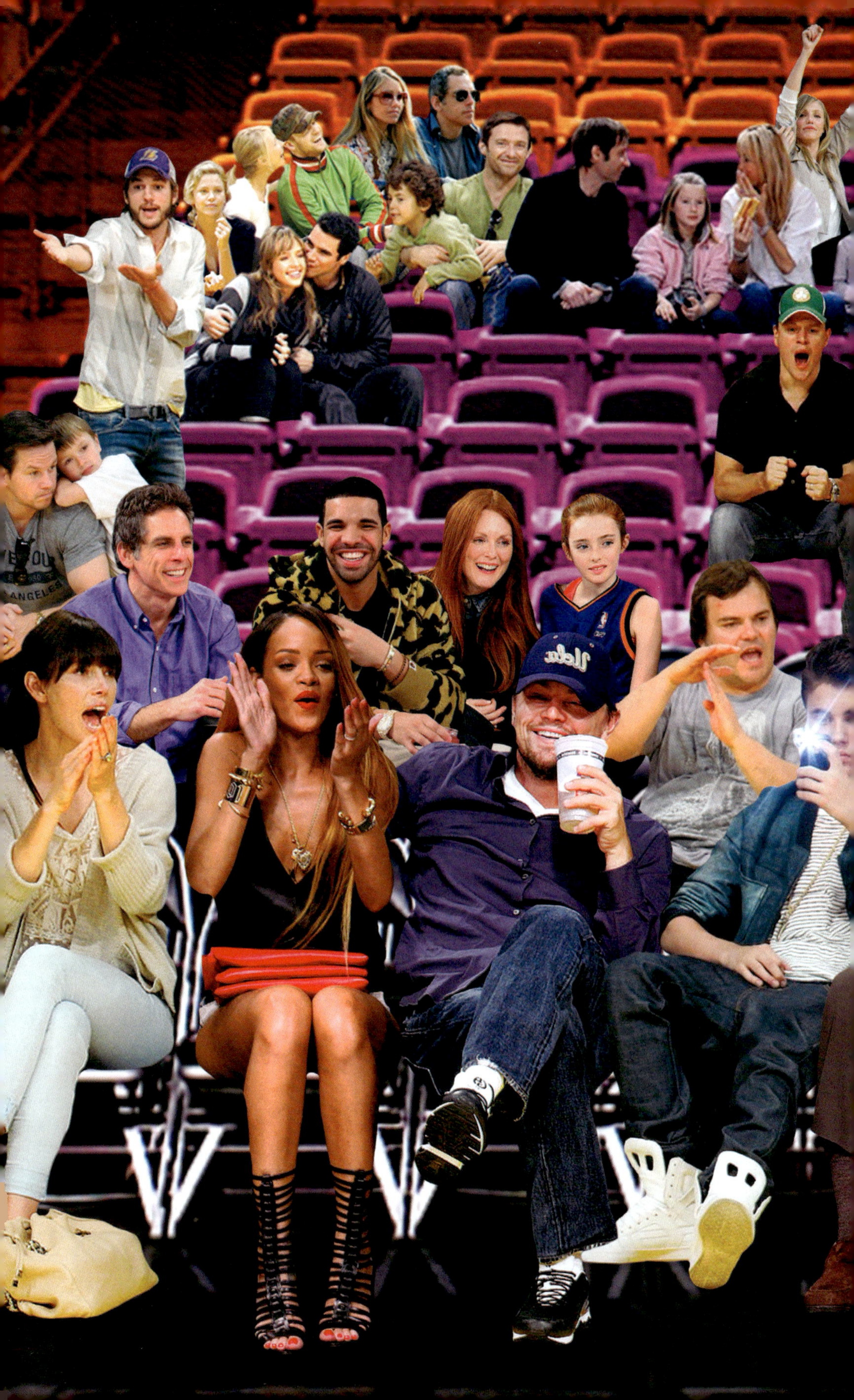

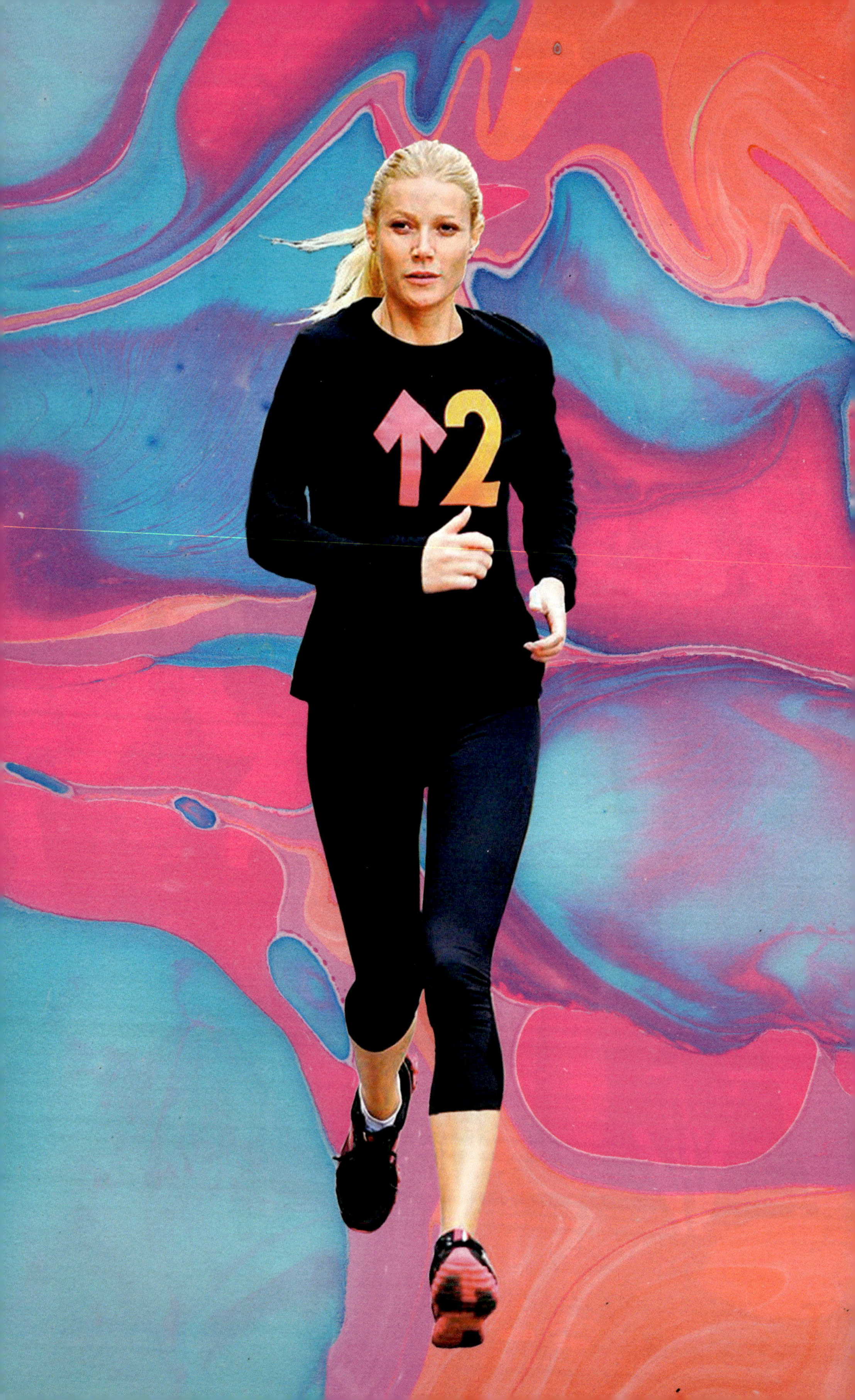

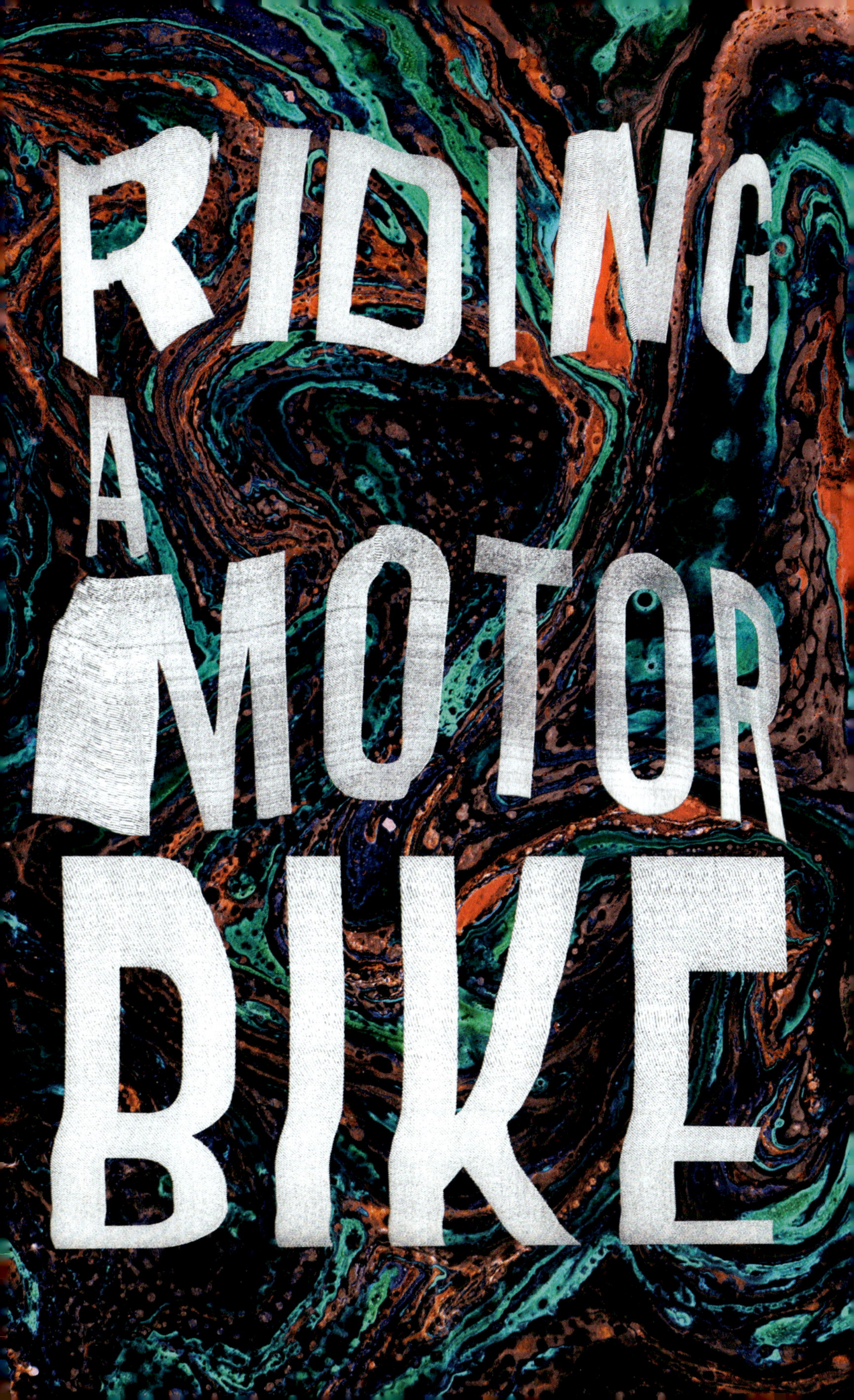
RIDING
A
MOTOR
BIKE

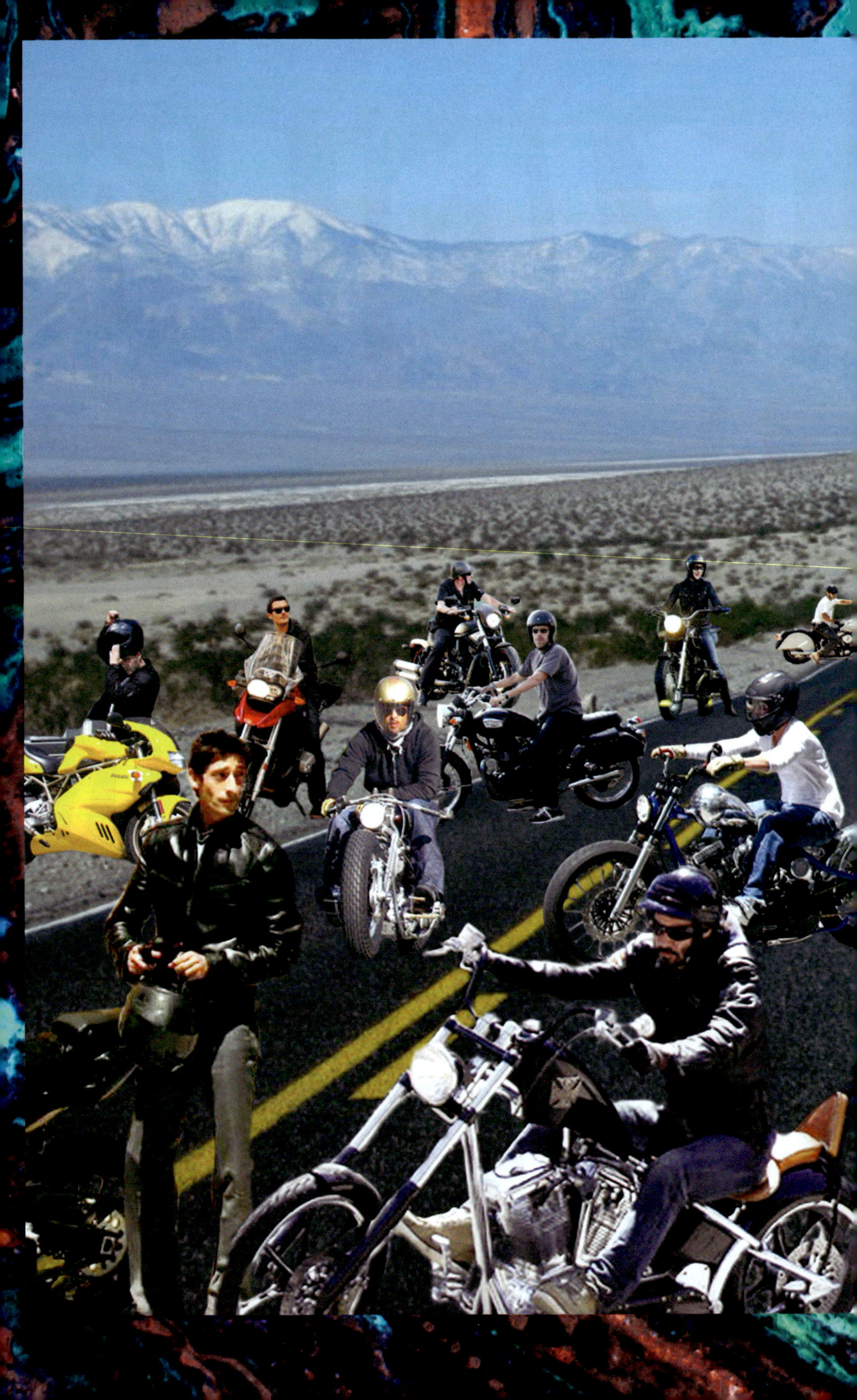

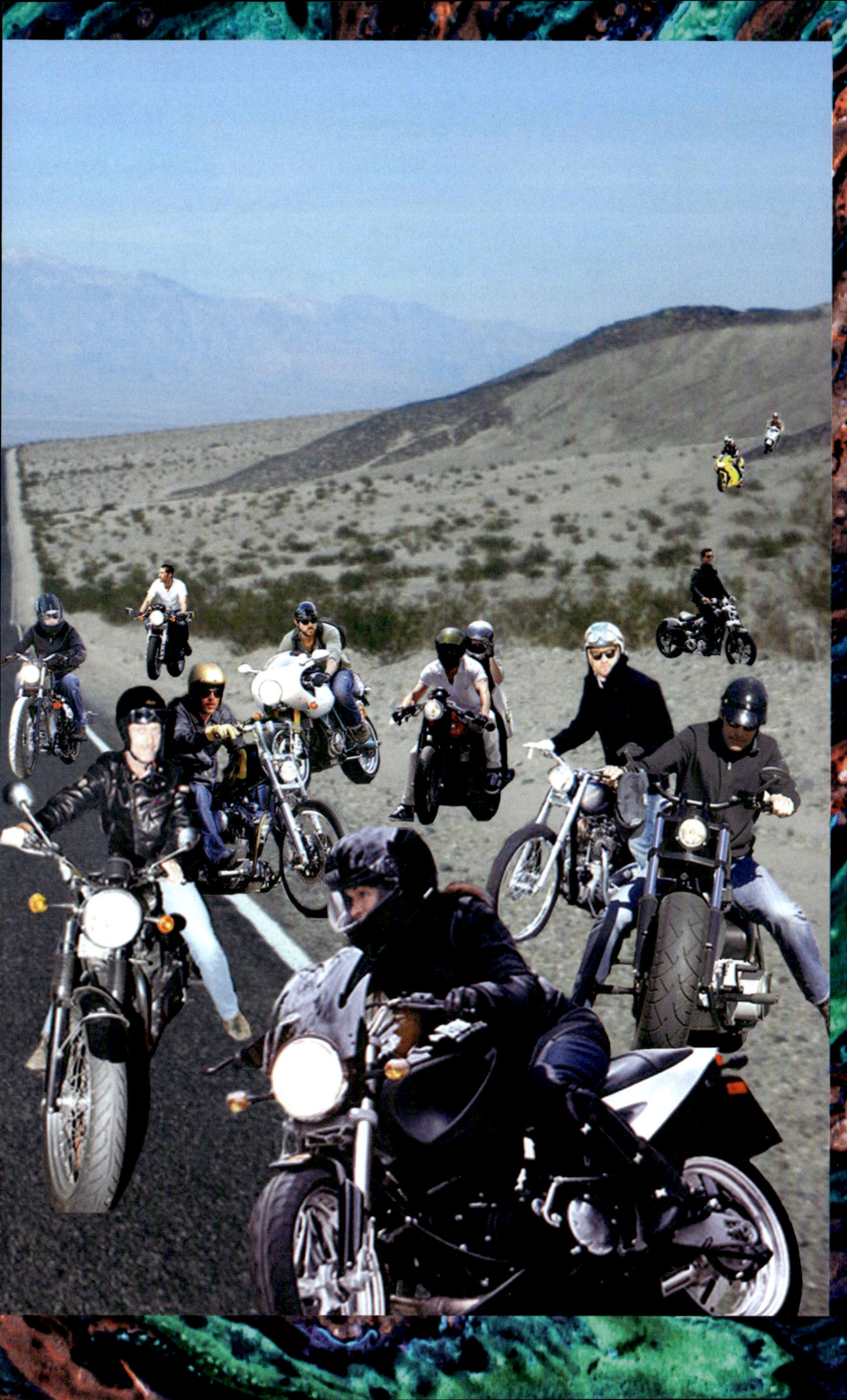

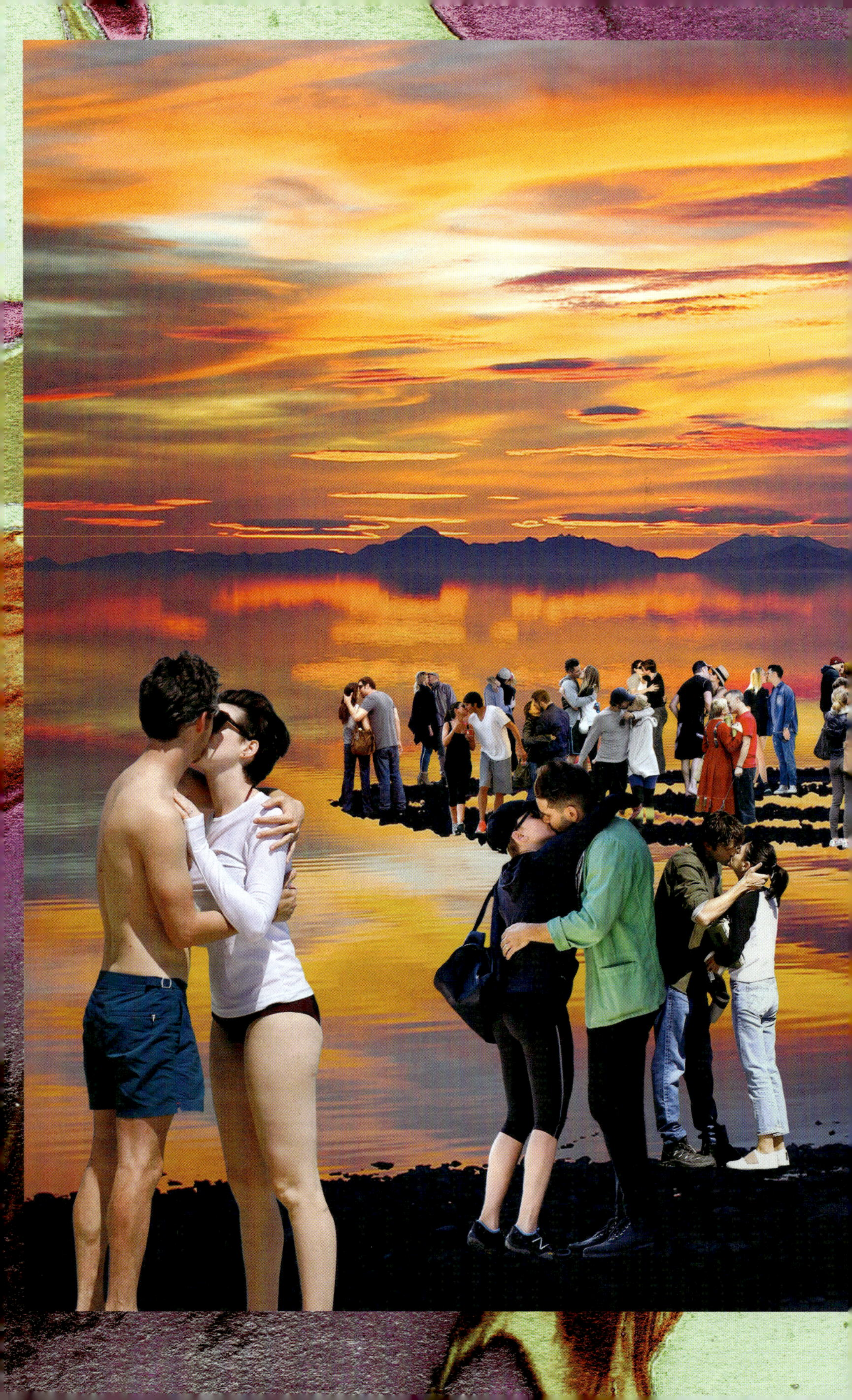

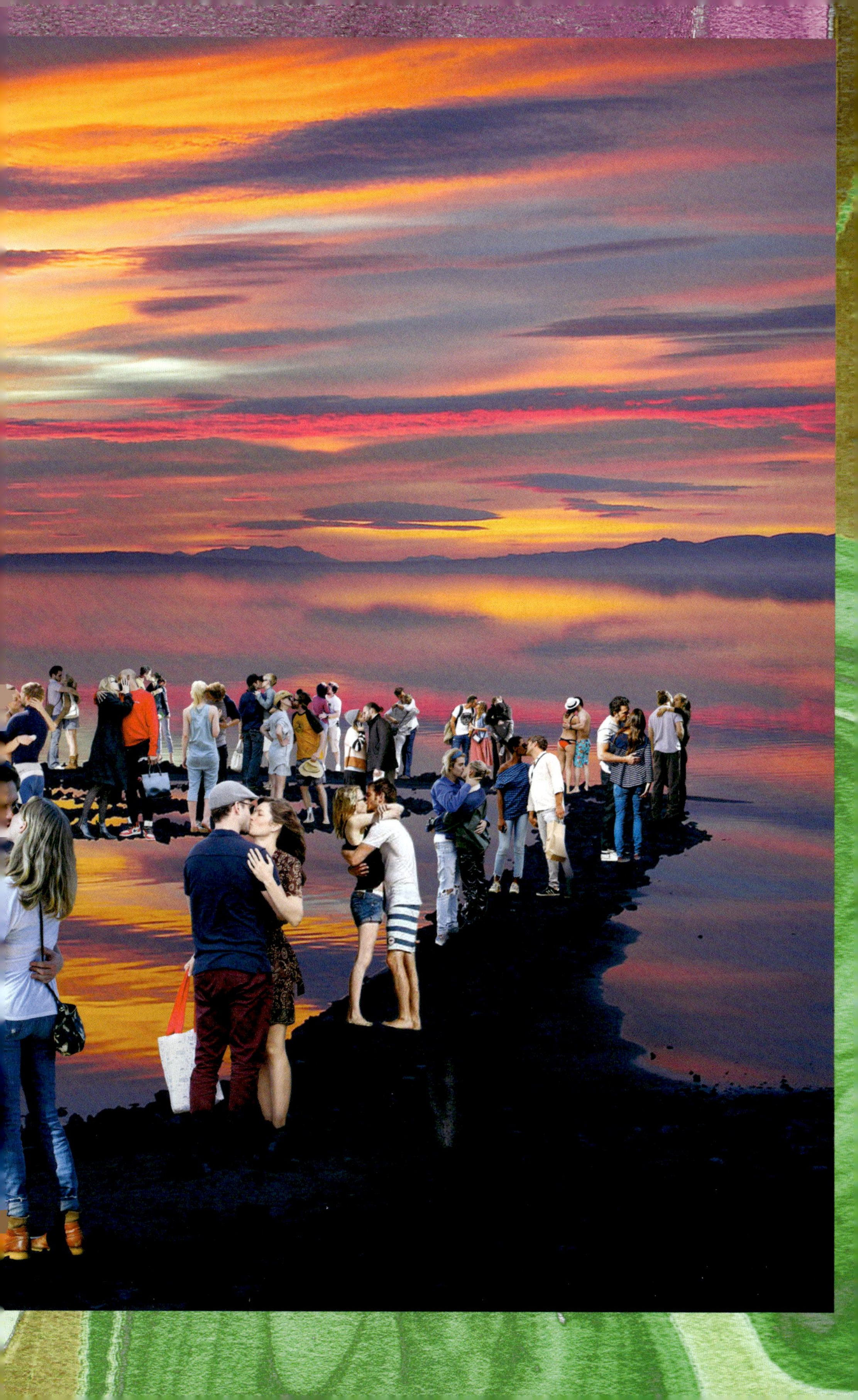

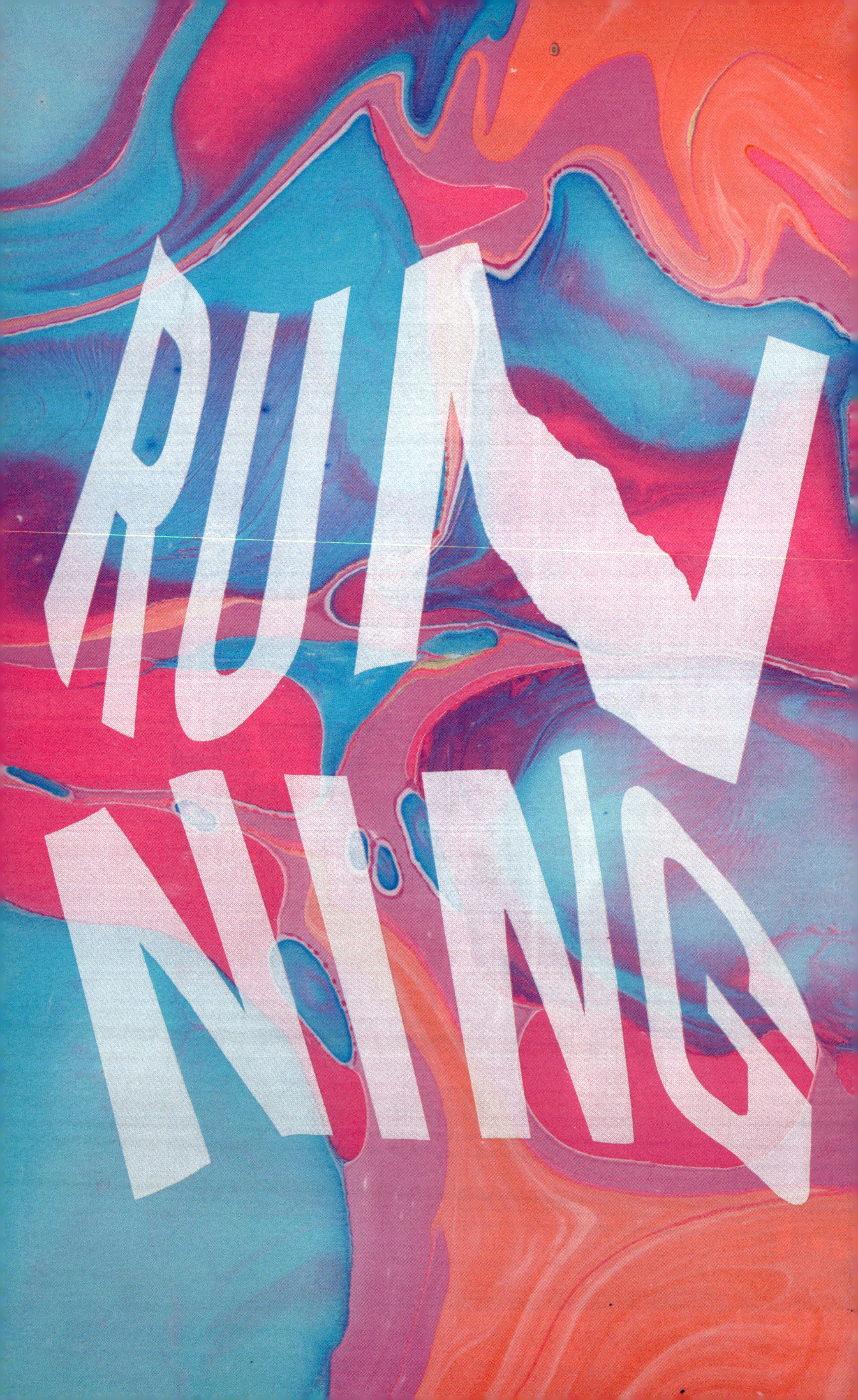
RUN
NING

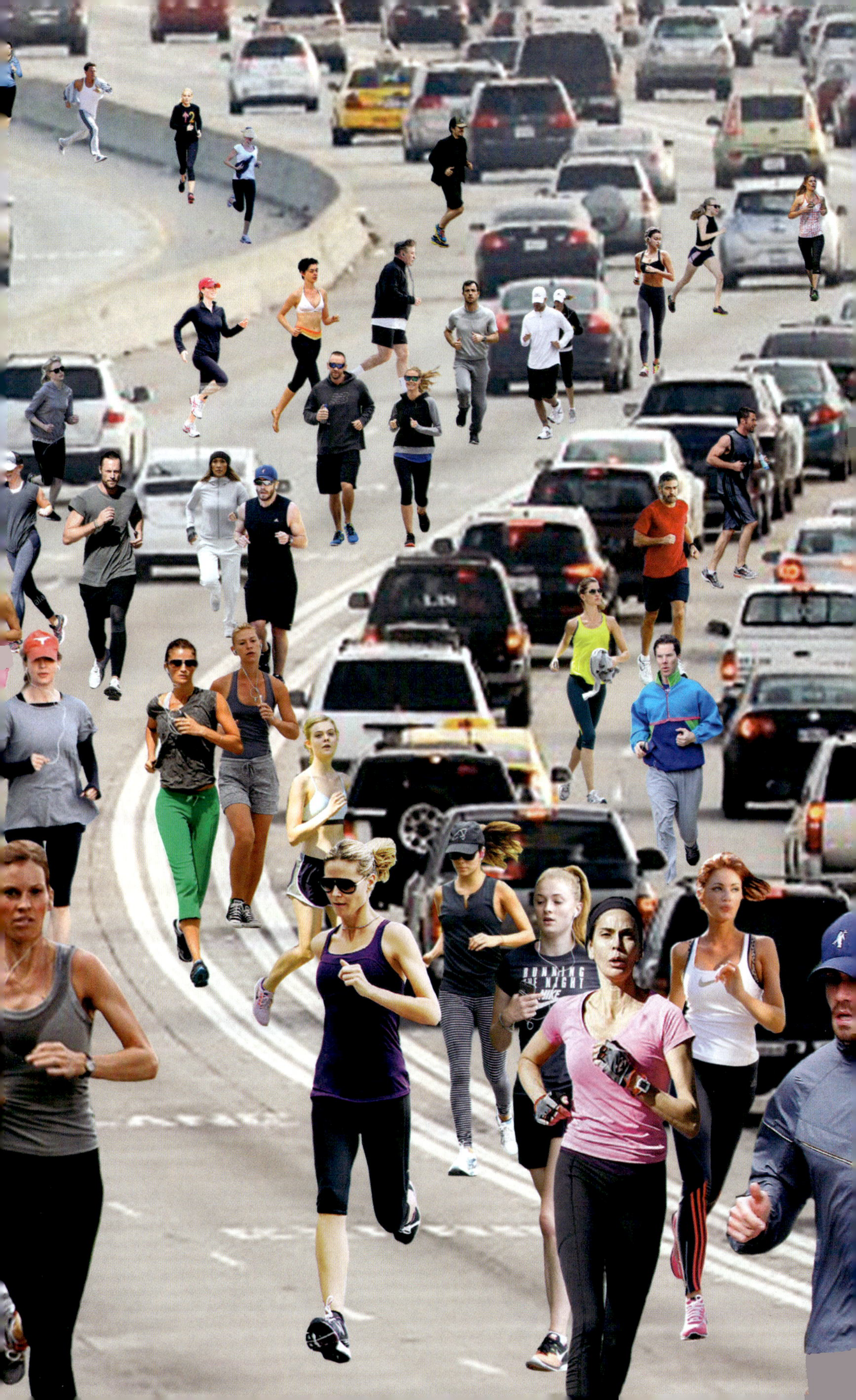

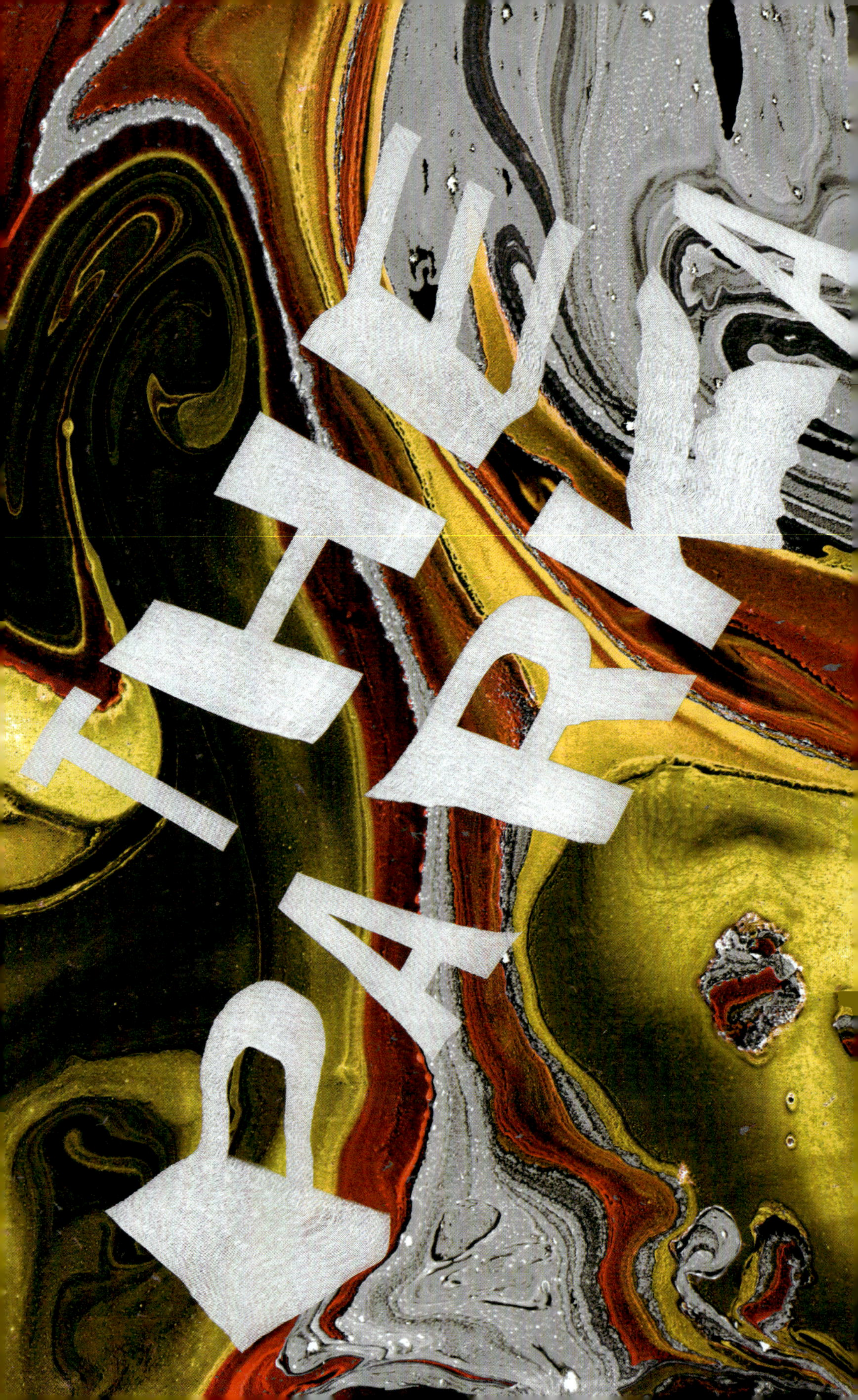
THE
PARK

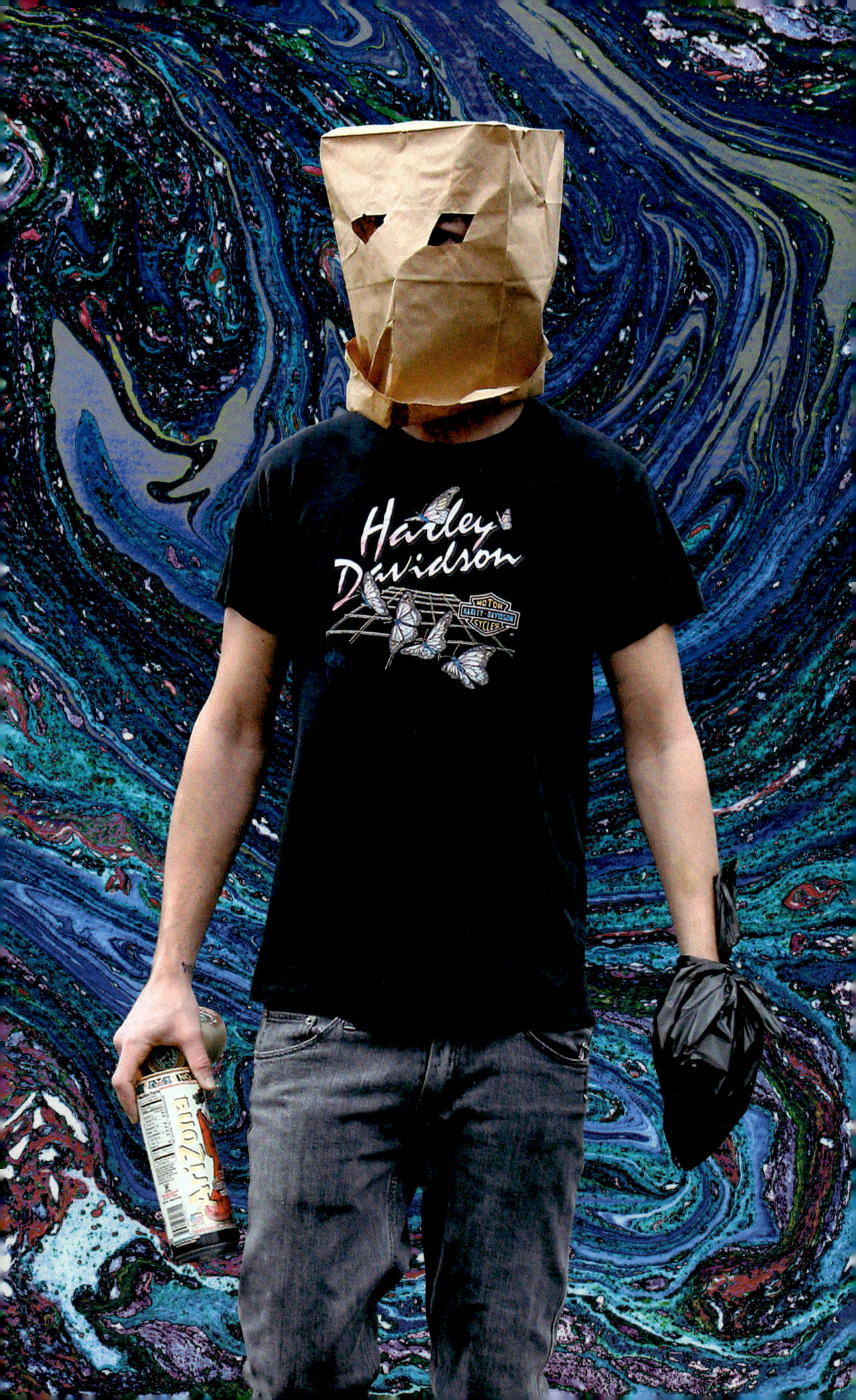
Harley Davidson
MOTOR
HARLEY-DAVIDSON
CYCLES
AriZona

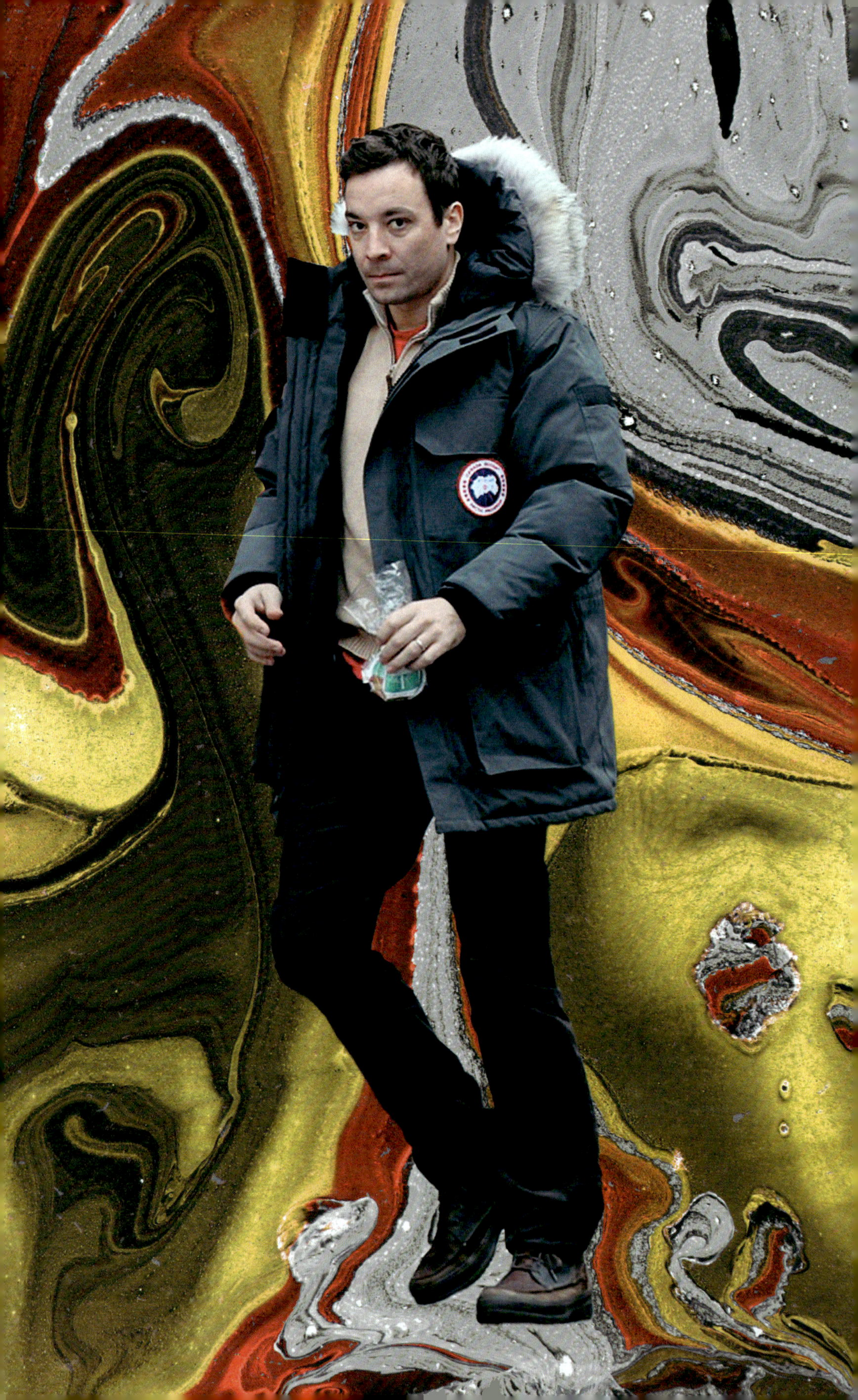

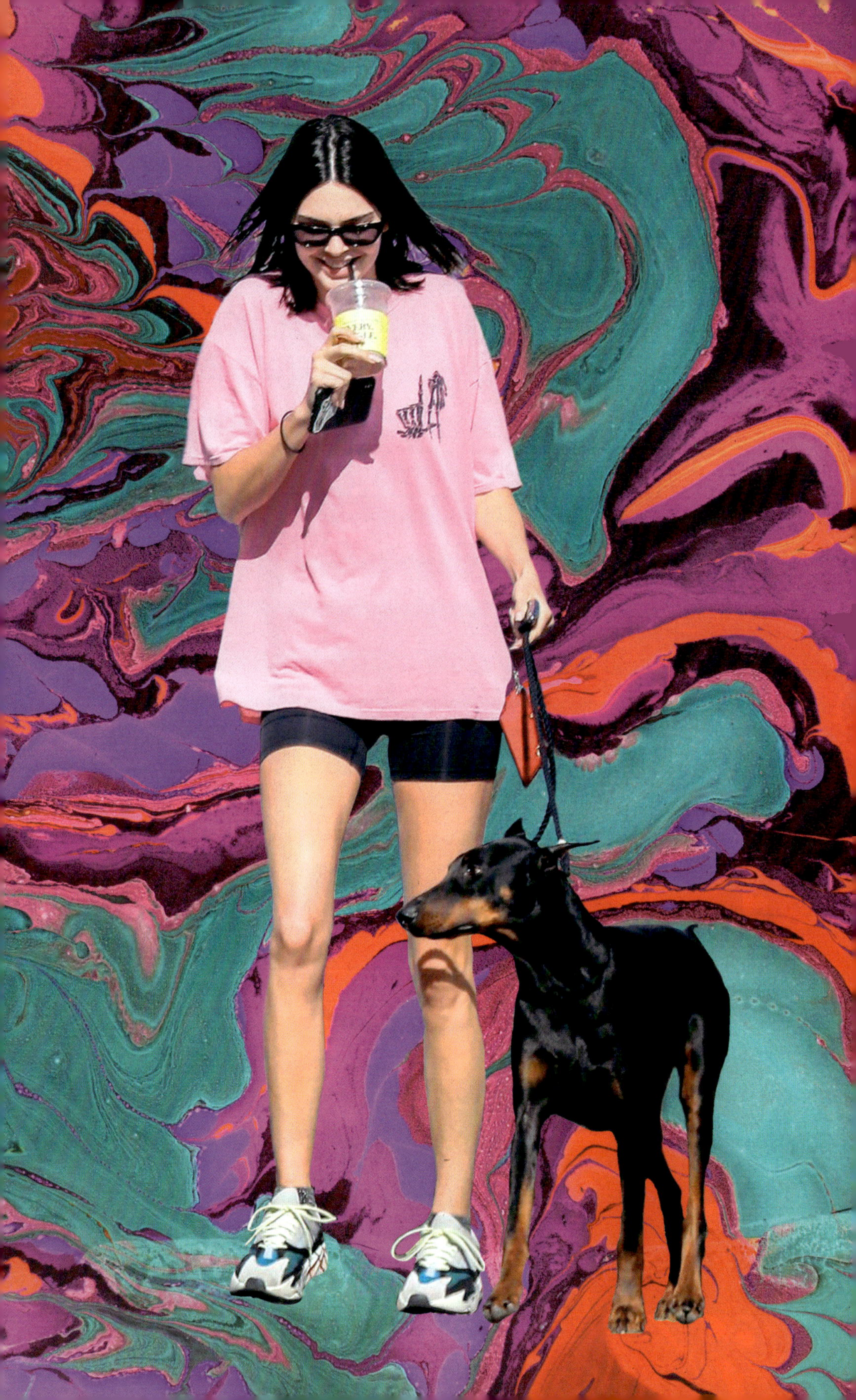

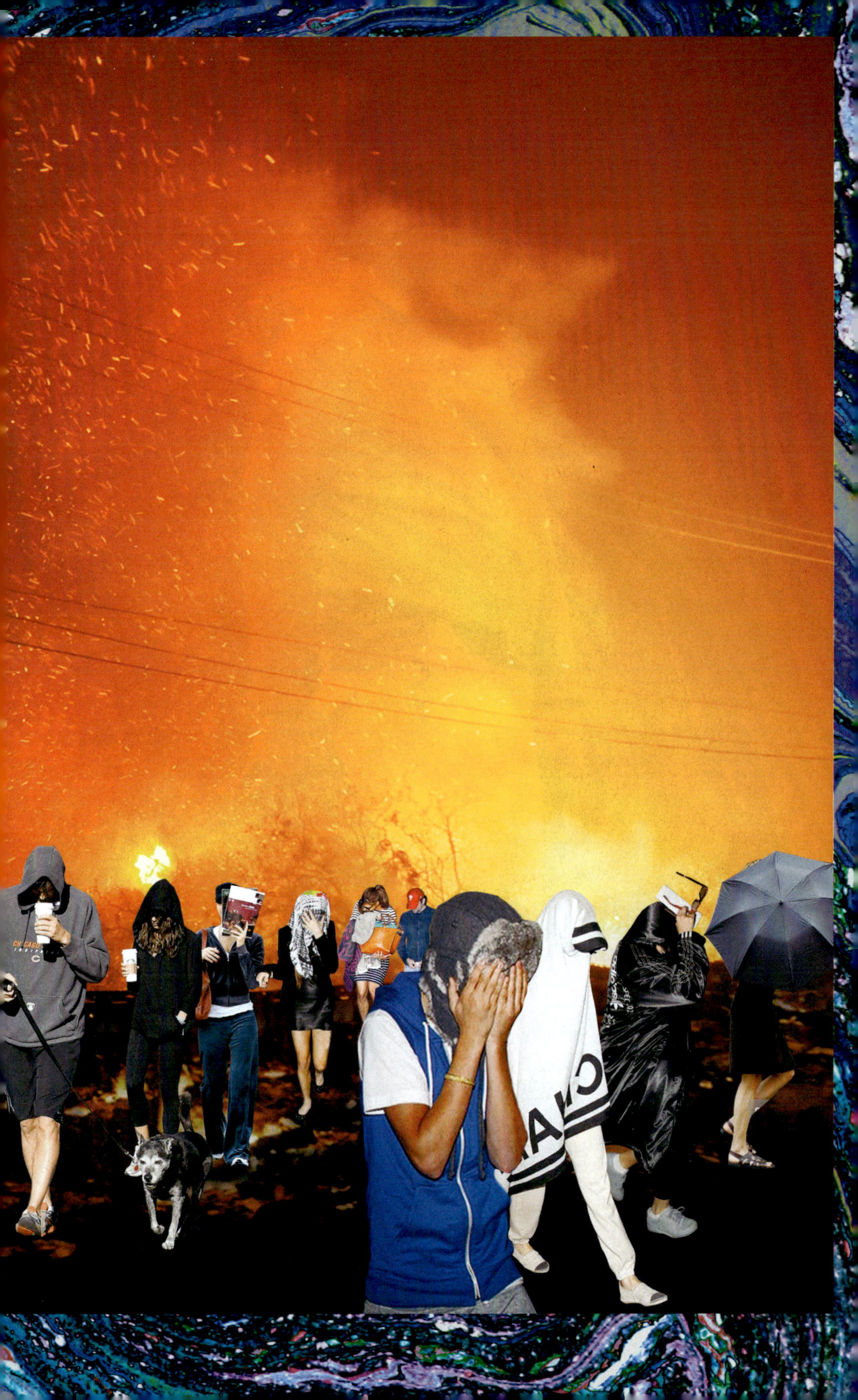

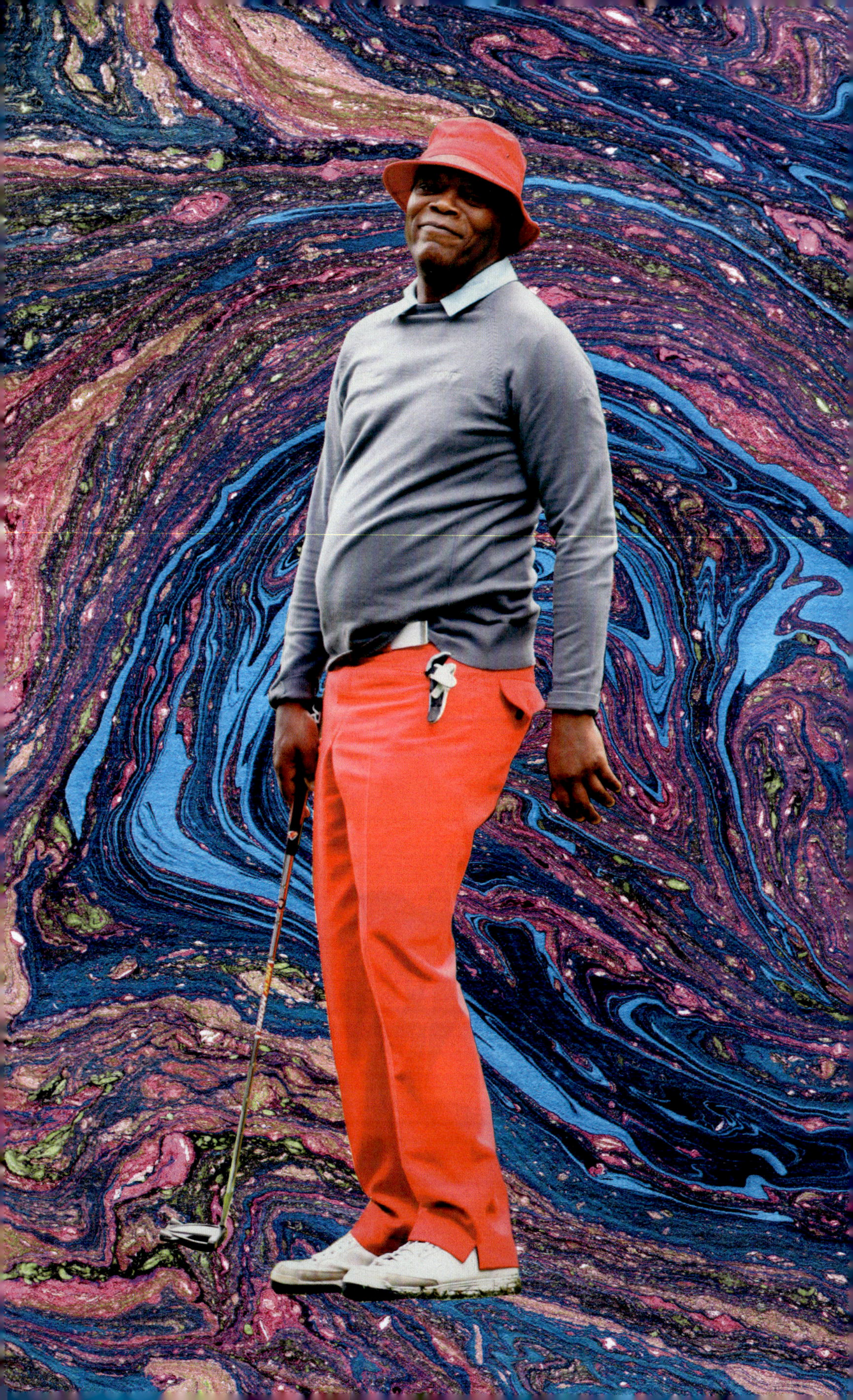

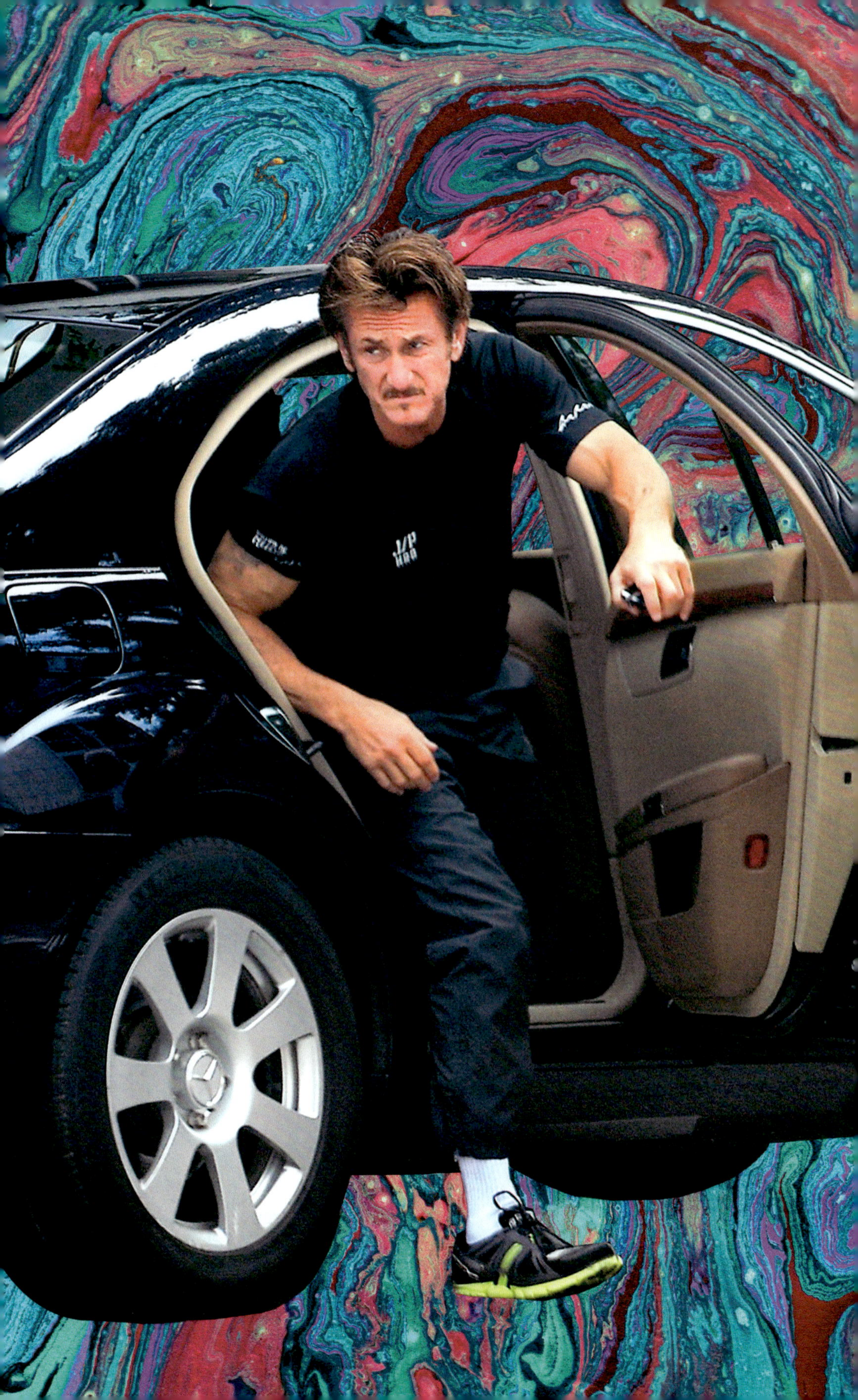
J/P

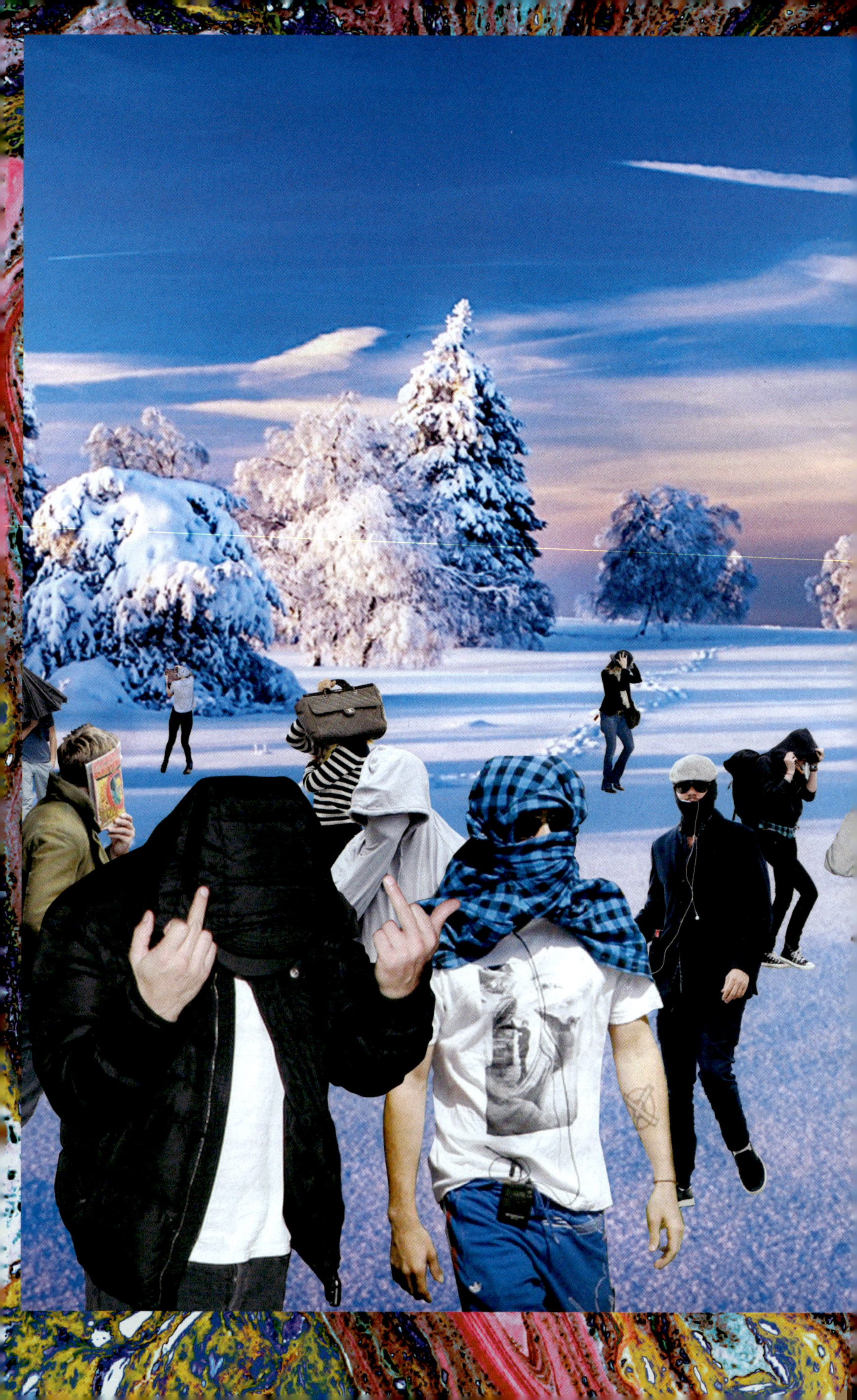

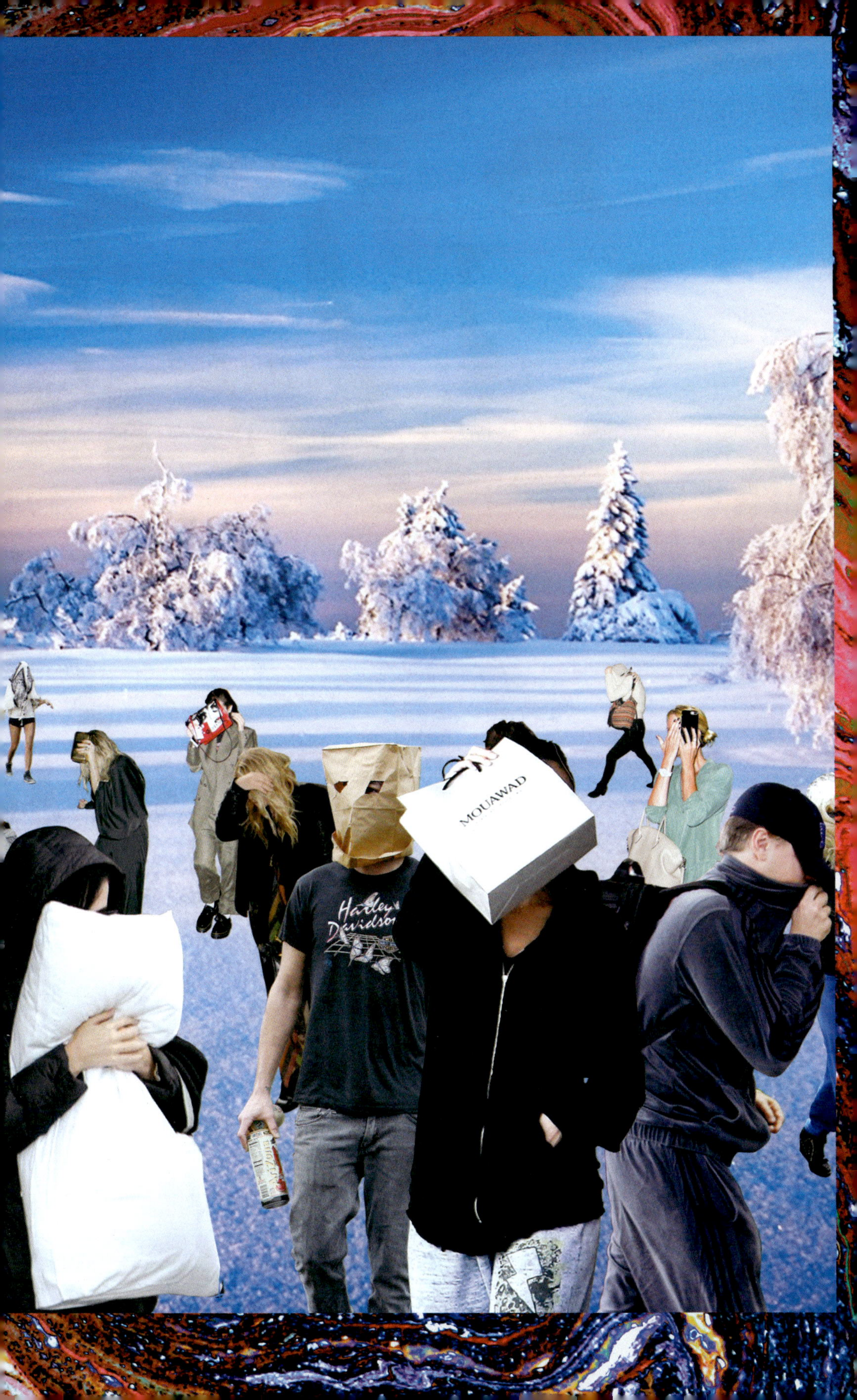
MOUAWAD

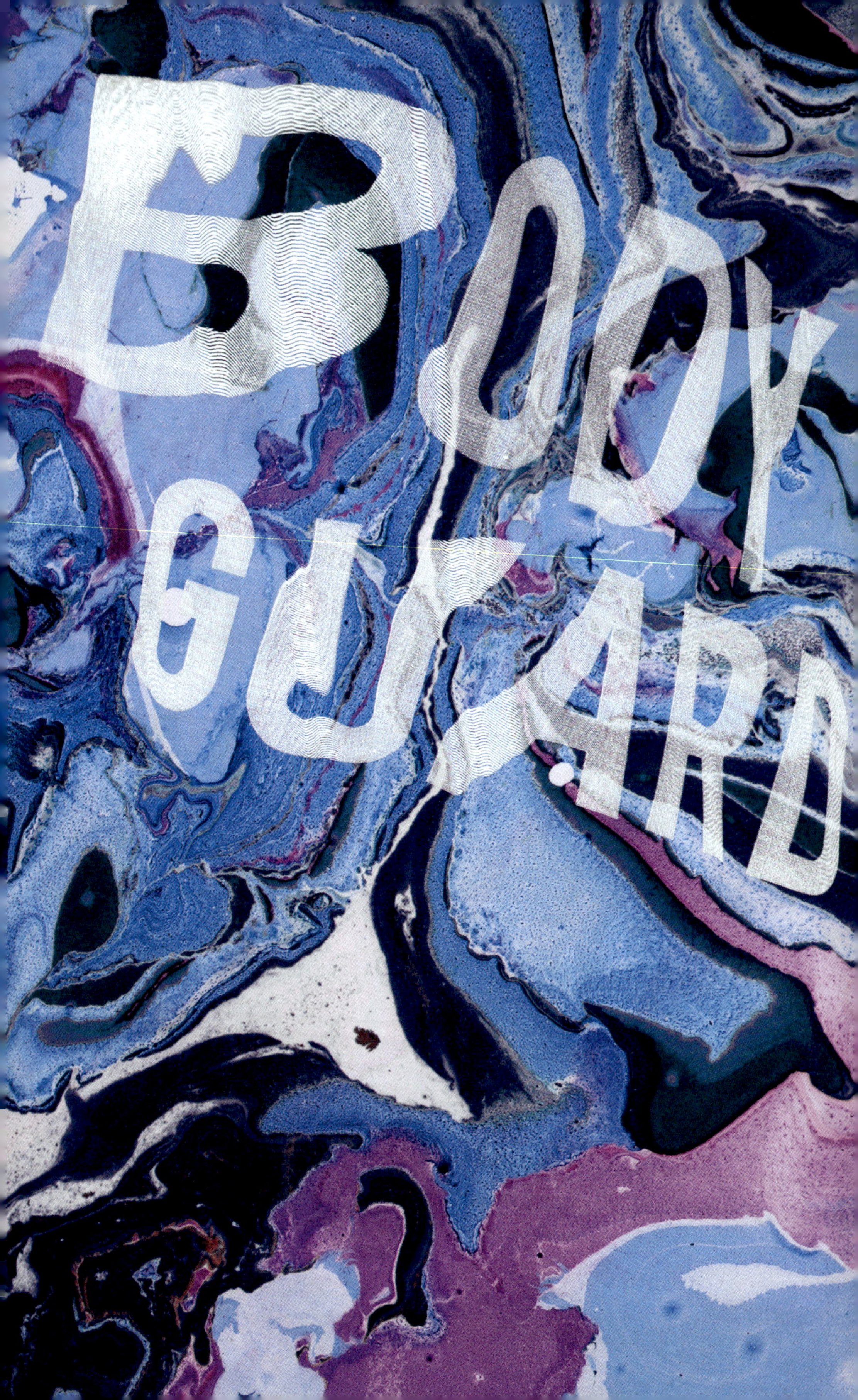
BODY
GUARD

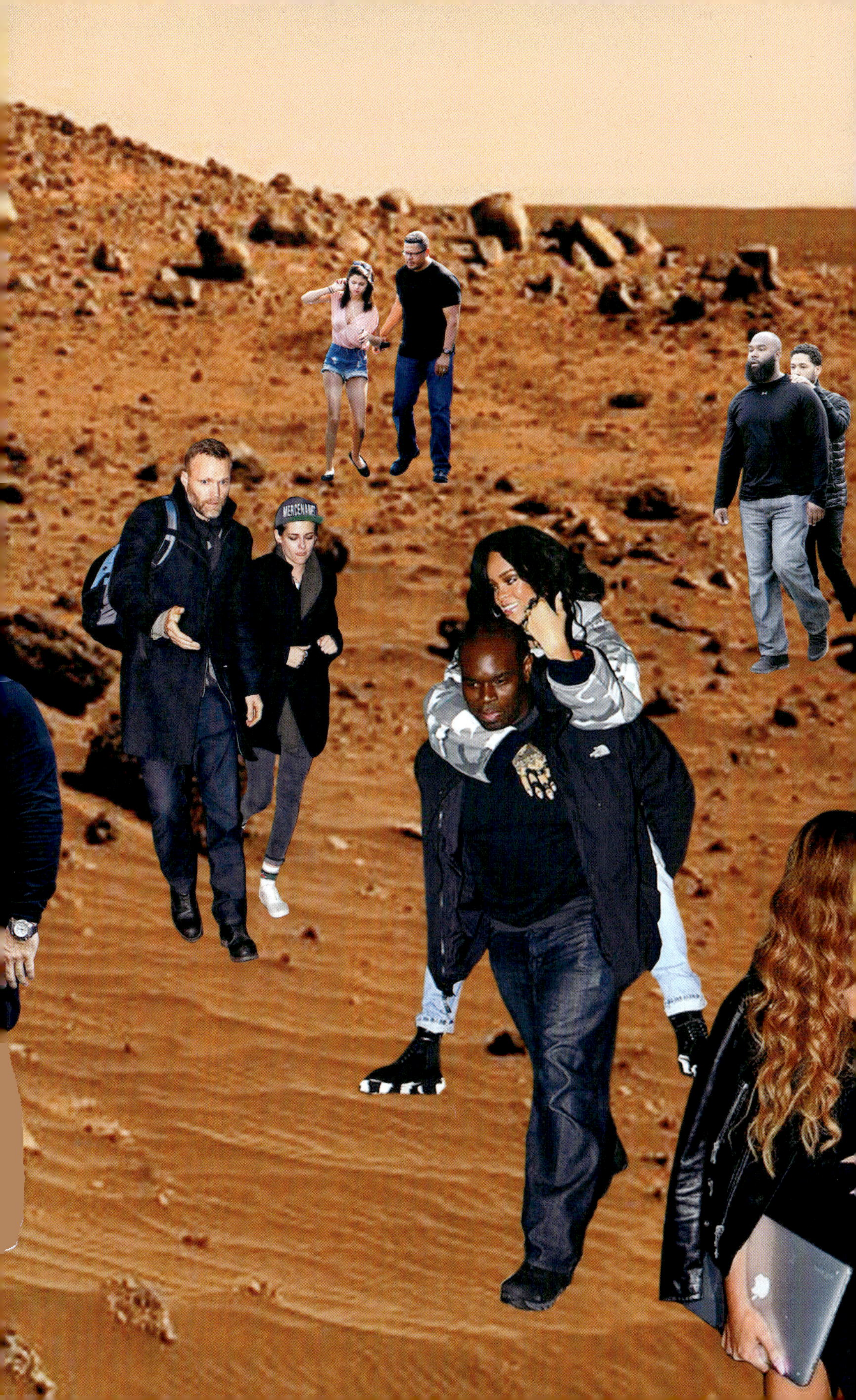

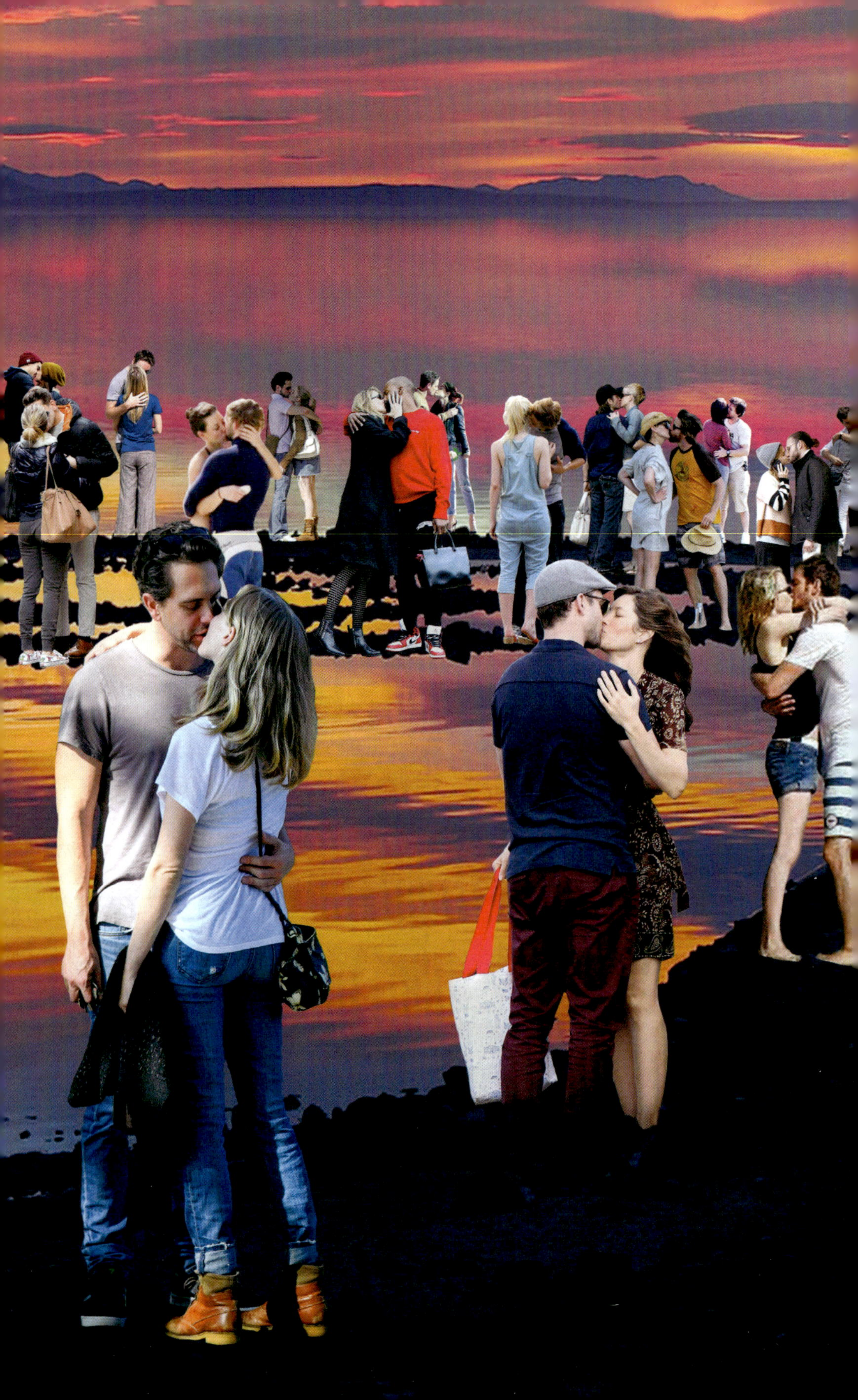

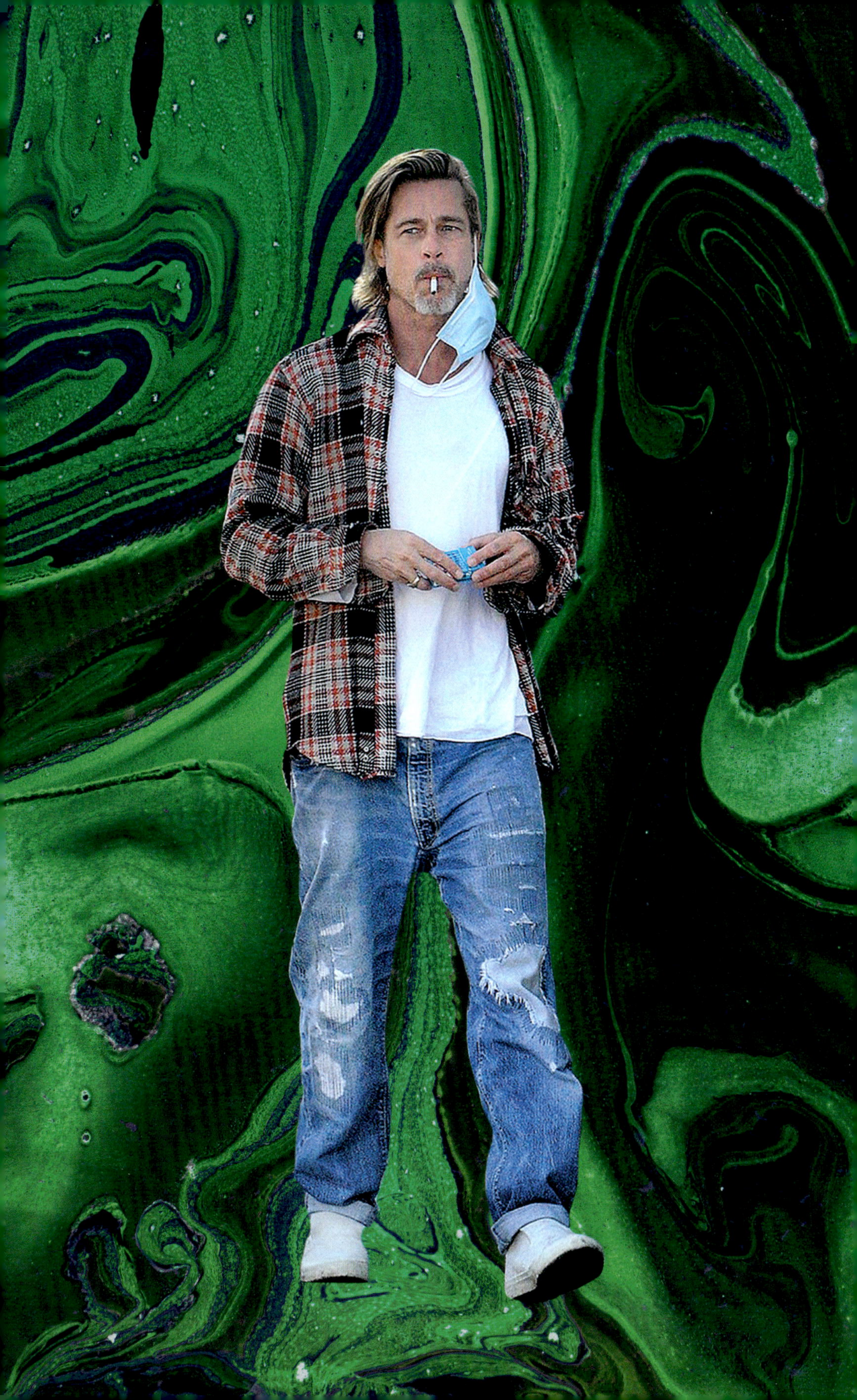

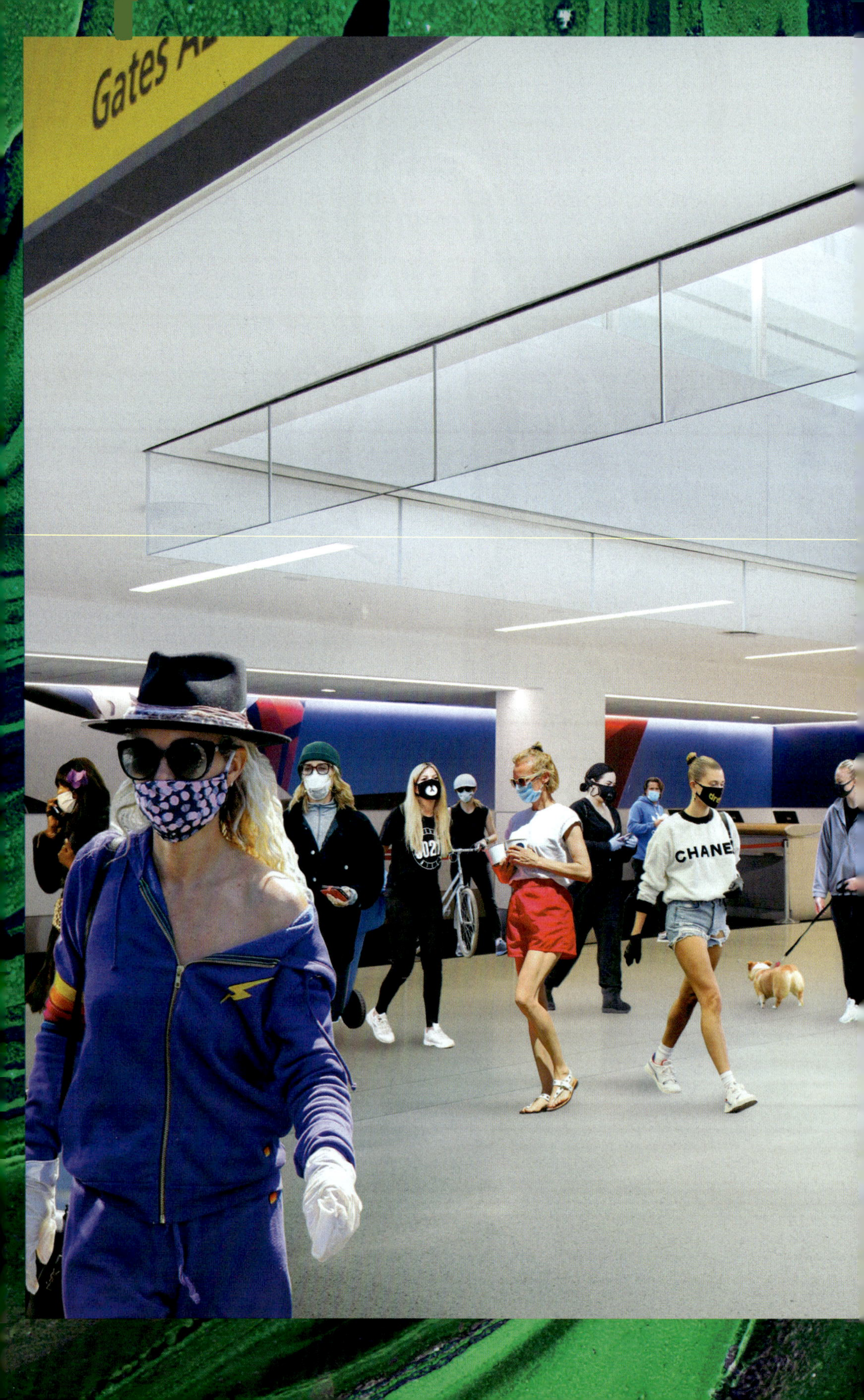

Gates
CHANE

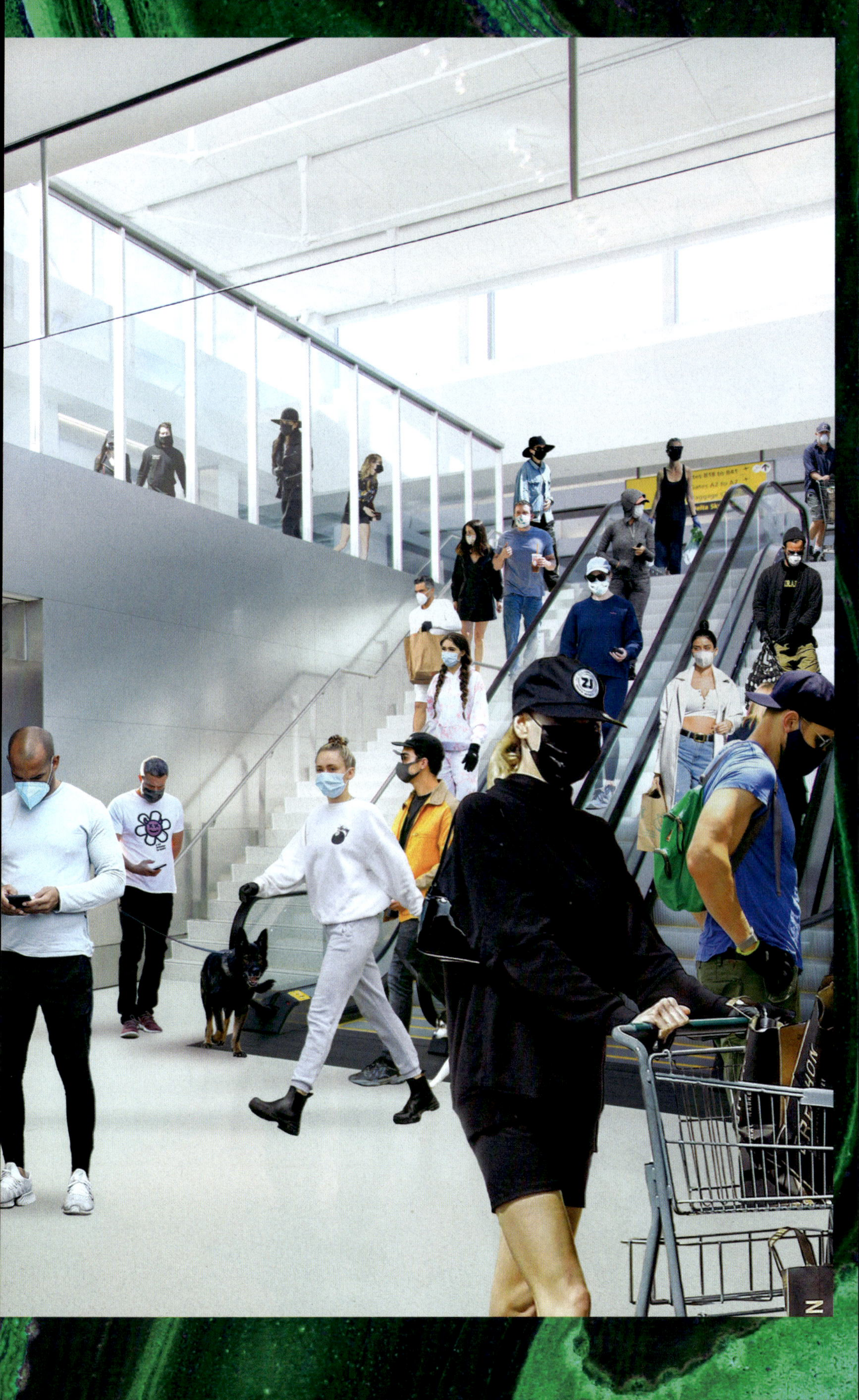

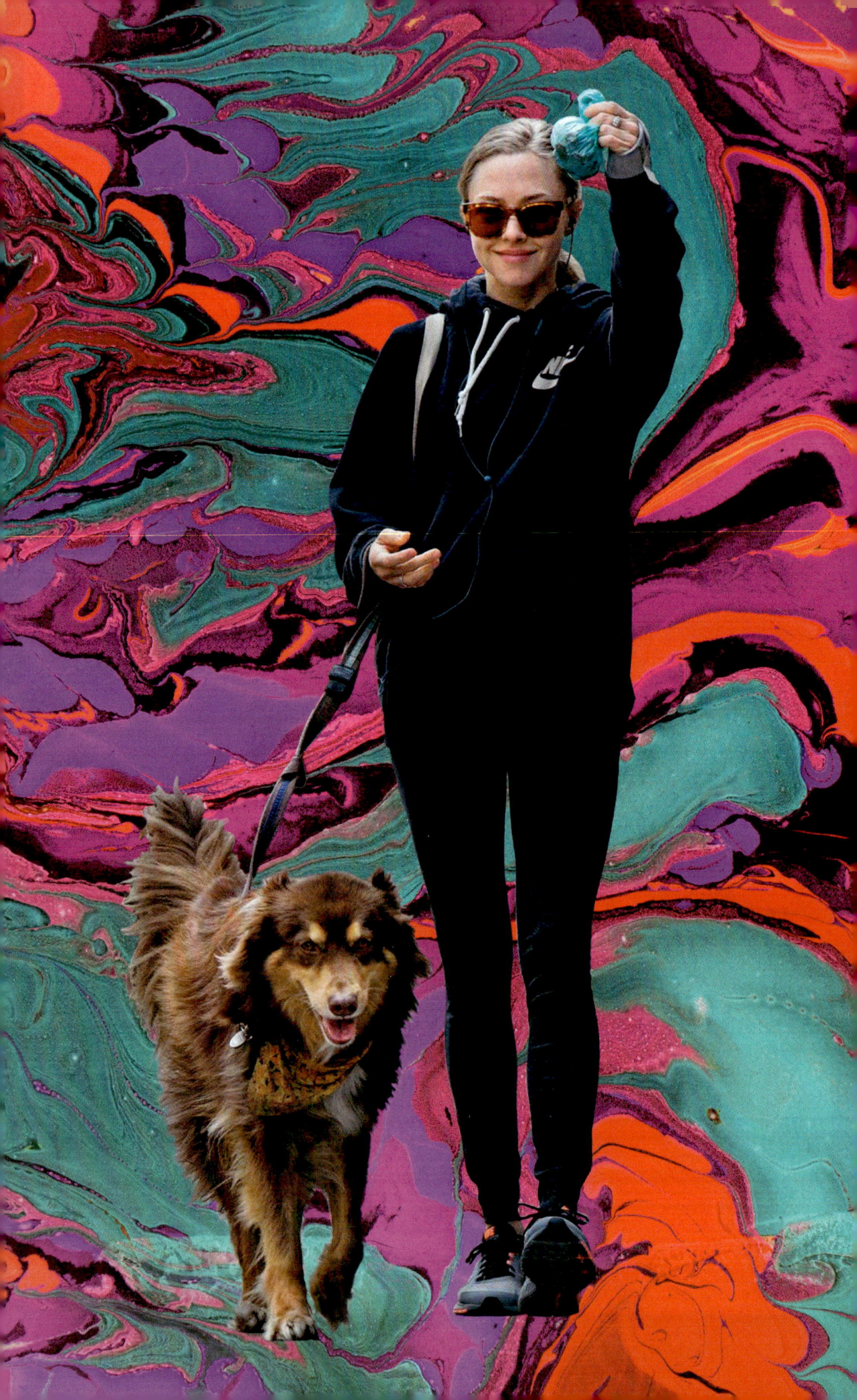

PAPARAZZI
MAZACCIO & DROWILAL

COLLAGES : MAZACCIO & DROWILAL
2012-2021
GRAPHIC DESIGN : MAZACCIO & DROWILAL,
ASSISTED BY ELIZABETH DELPHIN
PUBLISHER : RVB BOOKS,
MATTHIEU CHARON, REMI FAUCHEUX

ISBN 978-2-492175-05-3
ACHEVE D'IMPRIMER EN JUILLET 2021 EN ITALIE.
DEPOT LEGAL JUILLET 2021.

UMA VANESSA

ADRIEN ALEC ALESS

AMBER AMY

ANTONIO ARNOLD

BEN BENEDICT

BRAD BRADLEY

CAMERON

ALISTA CHRIS CHRIST

CHLOE COURTENEY

COLIN DITA

DIANE

ELLE ELLEN

FERGIE FREDD

HALLE HARRISON

HEIDI HILLARY

ATHER